For M[illegible]

from Tania

2007

Happy Birthday

P9-DXC-400

Celebrating Passion,
Pride & Achievement

Alberta
100 *journeys*

Written by Cheryl Mahaffy, Mary Oakwell and Faye Reineberg Holt
Edited by Wendy Campbell, The DAGNY Partnership

Published by the Alberta Motor Association in celebration of
Alberta's Centennial in 2005 and the AMA's 80th anniversary in 2006

The Alberta Motor Association requests that individuals restrict their travels to public areas marked for public use and refrain from trespassing on private property. Neither the Alberta Motor Association nor the organizations or individuals represented in this book accept any liability for property damage or personal injury of persons travelling to or visiting the locations described in the book.

Library and Archives Canada Cataloguing in Publication

Mahaffy, Cheryl, 1955-

Alberta, 100 journeys : celebrating passion, pride & achievement / written by Cheryl Mahaffy, Mary Oakwell and Faye Reineberg Holt ; edited by Wendy Campbell, The DAGNY Partnership.

"Published by the Alberta Motor Association in celebration of Alberta's centennial in 2005 and the AMA's 80th anniversary in 2006."

ISBN 978-0-9689594-1-1

1. Alberta—History. 2. Alberta—Biography. I. Oakwell, Mary, 1947- II. Reineberg Holt, Faye, 1948- III. Alberta Motor Association IV. Title.

FC3661M34 2006 971.23 C2006-906747-3

Design by Studio 3 Graphics

Cover design by Ronda Petersen, Imperial Printing

Excerpts of this publication may be used, provided credit is given to source.

The Alberta Motor Association
10310 G. A. MacDonald (39A) Avenue T6J 6R7
Mail: Box 8180, Station South
Edmonton, AB T6H 5X9

Telephone: (780) 430-5555

www.ama.ab.ca

Copyright © 2007 *The Alberta Motor Association*

Contents

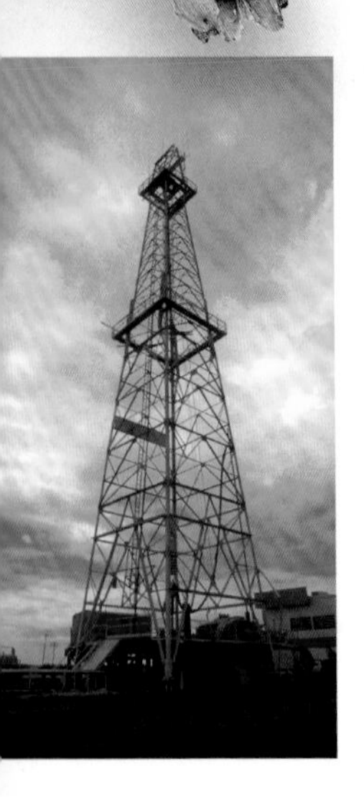

Alberta is an extraordinary province. Whether one measures its wealth by natural beauty, significance of achievement or the capacity to challenge adversity and come out the winner, our province is unique.

Alberta's splendid variety of natural wonders entices the modern explorer from prairie to foothills, into the mountains and to our beautiful north. All of these regions offer backdrops for tales of Alberta heroism, tragedy, triumph and endeavour.

The tales that spark our imaginations and make us proud to proclaim Alberta as our home are those of the people of the province. Albertans give our province its heart. From small-town skating rinks to big-time industry, Albertans have found their destinies from the foundations of Alberta life.

This book presents 100 stories – or journeys – that, together, paint a vibrant picture of our province. The word "journey" was chosen with care. *Alberta 100 Journeys* will become a favourite travel companion for Albertans eager to explore the places, events and delights highlighted in the book. For a day, a weekend or longer, these 100 journeys offer opportunity any time of the year.

Whether on the road or at home, readers will discover that these journeys offer gifts beyond their locations. They lead to explorations of our past, filled with challenge and hardship but also with courage and resourcefulness. They also offer a look beyond achievement to the values we treasure, and they invite every Albertan to sample our great province.

Accept the invitation. Enjoy the journey!

1 1988 Olympic Winter Games

Calgary had won its bid to host the 1988 Olympic Winter Games. The city and province buzzed with excitement. Staging the games brought together more than 900 volunteers, 500 staff members and thousands of fans. More than any other sporting event in Canada's history, the 1988 Olympic Winter Games meant huge financial commitments from the City of Calgary, then about 640,000 people, and the governments of Alberta and Canada, but it also meant that, through television coverage of the 16-day event, as many as two billion viewers worldwide were invited to Calgary.

At the opening ceremonies at McMahon Stadium, about 60,000 people thrilled at First Nations performances, RCMP riders, chuck wagon demonstrations and contemporary dance before the arrival of the Olympic Torch.

Throughout the games, Canadian fans everywhere were delighted when our athletes stood on the podium to receive their medals. That emotionally powerful moment was repeated five times for Canada's five medals. Two silvers were won by figure skating champions Brian Orser and Elizabeth Manley. Of the three bronze medals, two went to Karen Percy in alpine events and one to partners Tracy Wilson and Rob McCall in the figure skating ice dancing category.

Other Olympic legacies:

- The Saddledome (follow Olympic Way) in Stampede Park
- The University of Calgary campus (32 Avenue N.W. entrance) features a huge Olympic arch
- At the Olympic Oval, look for a sculpture of eight people holding up a steel arch
- An Olympic arch stands near the Eau Claire YMCA downtown

Many medal presentations were held in downtown Calgary's new Olympic Plaza, which became the ceremonial focal point of the 1988 Olympic Winter Games. Today, Olympic Plaza retains its power to draw visitors to appreciate the plaza's entertainments and to take in the impressive cityscape.

The games had many special moments. The world fell in love with little-known neophyte skier Eddie "the Eagle" Edwards and his spread-eagle jumps. From Britain, he was dead last in his competition but first in the headlines. The Jamaican bobsleigh team also earned top marks from fans as the team poured their hearts into the competition.

As well as warm memories, Calgary gained several world-class facilities from 1988. Thanks to the Olympics, top quality athletes have a range of superb training facilities around Calgary.

High performance athletes in ski jumping, freestyle skiing, bobsleigh, luge and Nordic events head to Canada Olympic Park to train.

Nakiska ski hill, on Mount Allan in Kananaskis Country, boasts 28 ski trails of which 14 per cent are black diamond expert trails. Nakiska's 735-metre drop guaranteed thrilling men's and women's downhill ski competition at the Olympic Winter Games – and a great training area now. Nakiska also boasted the most sophisticated snow-making equipment available in 1988.

The Nordic Centre in Canmore, which hosted the Olympic cross-country and biathlon competitions, continues to attract top athletes in training and recreational skiers.

The Olympic Oval at the University of Calgary was the only covered indoor oval in North America when it opened for competition in 1987. The Oval earned its reputation as the "fastest ice on earth" when seven world records were set during the 1988 Olympic Winter Games. By 2006, skaters on the Oval's speed-skating track had set 14 world records. Today, Calgary Speed Skating Association members train at the facility alongside skaters from around the globe.

TRAVEL TIPS

Visitors can tour Canada Olympic Park year-round with the Olympic Odyssey Audio Tour. It includes access to the Ski Jump Tower, the Olympic Bobsleigh Track, the Ice House, the ski chairlift and the Olympic Hall of Fame and Museum.

You can get in on the challenge and fun, too, on the bobsleigh runs, the luge, the ski hills and more.

Location: Canada Olympic Park is at the west edge of Calgary on Highway 1. Use the Bowford Road exit.

Phone: (403) 247-5452

E-mail: info@coda.ca

www.canadaolympicpark.ca

P

2 Alberta Legislature Building

This historic building makes an impressive sight on the bank of the North Saskatchewan River. Built adjacent to the Hudson's Bay Company's Fort Edmonton establishment, one can only imagine how it would have appeared to the Aboriginal fur traders and other locals in the area following the turn of the 20th century.

Construction began in 1907, just two years after Alberta became a province. The building was designed in the Beaux-Arts style, as were several other parliament buildings in Canada, and is known by its large central dome and glorious rotunda, the massive support columns for the portico and the T-shape of the rest of the building. Everything was done in magnificent style from the use of Vancouver Island granite and Glenbow quarry sandstone on the outside of the building to the lavish use of marble, mahogany, oak and brass on the inside.

The building was officially opened in 1912, but many changes have been made over the years, usually in celebration of important events. The impressive fountain in the rotunda celebrated the first visit of Queen Elizabeth II to Edmonton in 1959. Prior to the construction of this fountain, the central area of the rotunda was left open, allowing guests an unobstructed view through all five storeys of the building. Other changes include the addition of two bronze statues in the rotunda area, one of Princess Louise Caroline Alberta and the other of Chief Crowfoot. These statues were commissioned as part of the province's 75th anniversary and unveiled two years later in March 1982.

One of the great stories from the Legislature Building is that of the Assembly's first mace. This mace, which can still be found on display on the third floor of the Legislature Building, was something of a rush job. Rufus Butterworth made it out of readily available materials including plumbing pipe, a toilet tank float, shaving mug handles and bits of iron and wood for decoration. Gold paint helped its appearance considerably.

Mr. Butterworth must have been brought up on a farm with the inherent talent to make "something from nothing," but as odd as the finished product sounds, it was used for the next 50 years!

If you look closely, you can see many truly Albertan touches in the building. For example, while it draws upon European traditions, the Alberta crest includes representations of the Rocky Mountains, foothills, prairies and wheat fields, although St. George of England wasn't forgotten in the design. Again to celebrate the 75th anniversary of the province, other items were added to create the coat of arms, including a pronghorn antelope and the Alberta rose.

Another very important symbol of the legislative assembly, representing the authority of the assembly to make laws on behalf of the people, is the mace. It's a beautiful and ornate piece of artwork made of silver and gold that is carried into the legislature chamber each day. Its design features the beaver, a crown, the wild rose, sheaves of wheat, buffalo heads and both the royal and Canadian coats of arms. The crown is surrounded by gemstones whose first initials spell "A-L-B-E-R-T-A."

And nobody should miss standing on the "magic spot" located on the fifth floor. The interior layout of the building and the noise of the fountain combine to create an interesting acoustic effect. If you stand on "the spot" while the fountain is running, it sounds just as if you're in the shower and yet you don't get wet.

A truly amazing building!

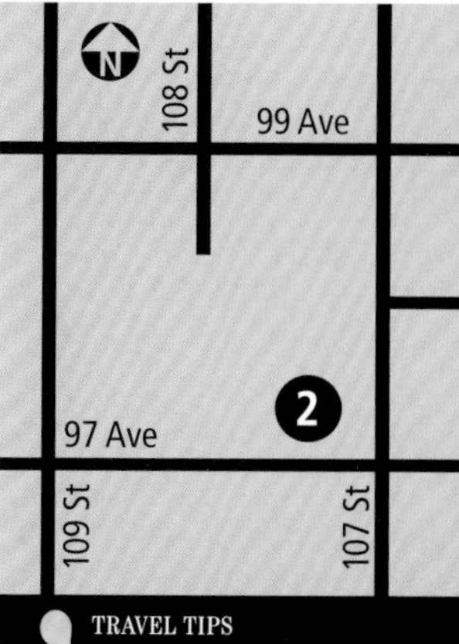

TRAVEL TIPS

Legislature Building tours are free and begin at the Interpretive Centre and Gift Shop located in the pedway.

Location: North of the North Saskatchewan River. Access parking off 98 Avenue on 107 Street or 108 Street. Parking has a two-hour limit.

Phone: (780) 427-7362

E-mail: visitorinfo@assembly.ab.ca

www.assembly.ab.ca

3 Alberta Prairie Railway Excursions

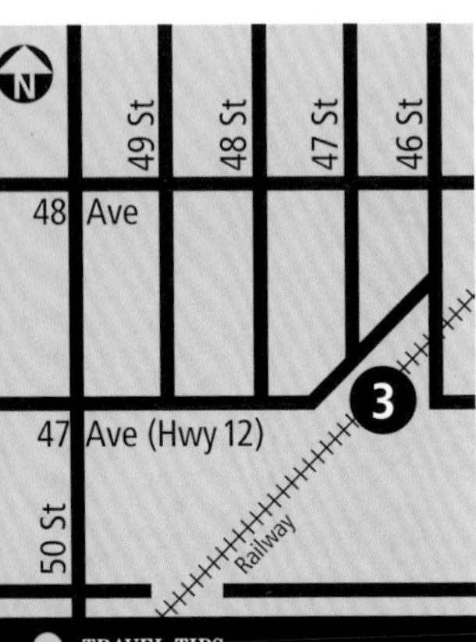

TRAVEL TIPS

The train travels 35 kilometres to Big Valley and returns to Stettler five to six hours later.

Summer excursions, May to mid-October, usually include a roast beef dinner in Big Valley. Winter runs, November through April, include onboard dining.

The railway offers numerous themed rides.

Fall is a great time to ride, when the days are cooler and the colours dramatic.

Location: 4611 47 Avenue, Stettler (70 kilometres east of Red Deer), across the tracks from a yellow grain elevator

Phone:
(403) 742-2811 in Stettler
(403) 290-0980 in Calgary

1-800-282-3994
(for reservations)

E-mail:
info@absteamtrain.com

www.absteamtrain.com

Smiles and waves greet locomotive No. 41 as she chugs to a stop in Big Valley, steam billowing from her stack. Hundreds of passengers step out of her coaches, anticipating a leisurely look at historic sites and perhaps a pleasantly fulsome roast beef dinner at the nearby community hall before re-boarding for the 90-minute return to Stettler. It's a trip back to the 1920s, when steam locomotion was young and rail first brought prosperity to the region.

The first leg of your journey offers plenty of variety in itself. Once the conductor punches your ticket, you can wander the train and catch it all. If you're of age, drop in for a pint 'round the tables in the saloon car, where period music invites impromptu sing-alongs. Catch the onboard cabaret, which visits each coach by the end of the trip. Stand at the rail of the open-air observation car to enjoy the gentle flow of prairie patchwork and perhaps spot a coyote or eagle.

And if that Bolton Gang shows up for a laid-back robbery, make sure you've got a window seat to watch Métis hero Gabriel Dumont dispatch the dastardly crew in equally laid-back style.

By then you'll be well acquainted with Mr. Dumont, who served as Louis Riel's military commander in the 1880s but is reincarnated here as the train's host and raconteur. Mr. Dumont will tell you, for example, why standard gauge track is exactly four feet, 8 1/2 inches wide; why the whistle sounds two longs, a short and a final long at signal four crossings; and how it happened that Big Valley grew like topsy thanks to mining, rail and ranching, then shrank just as fast.

The stop at Big Valley offers its own intrigue.

Hop on the people-mover for a free ride up the hill to St. Edmund's Church and discover why it gained that Maritime shade of blue.

Visit the restored 1912 railway station and duck into the nearby roundhouse, where trains were serviced by the dozens when Big Valley was a bustling node in the Canadian Northern Railway. Soak up some national rail history at the Canadian Railway Hall of Fame Pavilion.

Drop in at the old Alberta Wheat Pool elevator, where the floor grates and scrawled calculations remind us of how things used to be.

Stop in at the town museum, chock-a-block full of donations from local folk, and marvel at the volunteer energy behind all the heritage sites in town. Wander the shops of Jimmy Jock Boardwalk, where a doorway to nowhere recalls a house of ill repute set ablaze by angry wives.

Visit the oil pumper in Memorial Park, a salute to the 1950s oil boom that revived the valley's population for another decade or two.

Back on board, take it slow, take it slow. Let your pulse take a cue from the sway of the coach and settle into a rhythm of the time when the train was not just a mode of transportation, but a way of prairie life.

Alberta Prairie Railway excursions run on track that once belonged to the Canadian Northern Railway, incorporated in 1899 and built up over the next 20 years to become a transcontinental system. But the promoters depended heavily on government financing and ultimately had to give up all the shares of the troubled company, making it one of the first major components of what would become the Canadian National Railway (CNR).

In another CNR connection, some Alberta Prairie Railway excursions are powered by a vintage CNR steam engine built at Montreal in 1944. Designated locomotive 6060, it was retired from active service and placed on static display in Jasper National Park. The CNR later restored 6060 to operating condition to haul steam fan excursions. In 1980, to commemorate Alberta's 75th anniversary as a province, 6060 was presented as a gift to the people of Alberta and restored a second time. Now dubbed the Spirit of Alberta, 6060 is Canada's largest working steam locomotive.

4 Athabasca Oil Sands

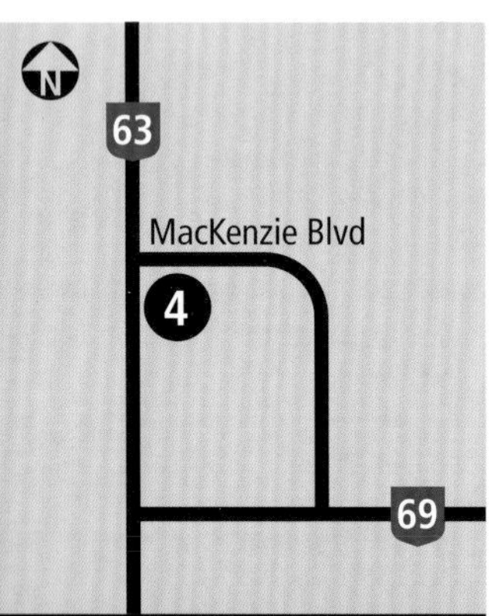

TRAVEL TIPS

Oil Sands Discovery Centre hours are 9 a.m. to 6 p.m. daily from mid-May to Labour Day and 10 a.m. to 4 p.m. daily except Mondays the rest of the year.

Behind the centre is a sample display of some equipment once used on the site, including Cyrus, one of Suncor's original bucketwheels.

Fort McMurray Tourism offers guided tours of the Suncor and Syncrude plant sites from May to September. Reservations are mandatory; some restrictions apply. Call 1-800-565-3947.

Location: Oil Sands Discovery Centre, 515 MacKenzie Blvd. and Highway 63, Fort McMurray

Phone: (780) 743-7167

E-mail: osdc@gov.ab.ca

www.oilsandsdiscovery.com

"Oil sands" is a very familiar term to 21st century Albertans; their central role in the province's booming economy has made the term almost a household word, but the raw material had actually been used for centuries to waterproof canoes. As early as 1719, a member of the Cree Nation had shown the "gum" or "pitch" to traders of the Hudson's Bay Company.

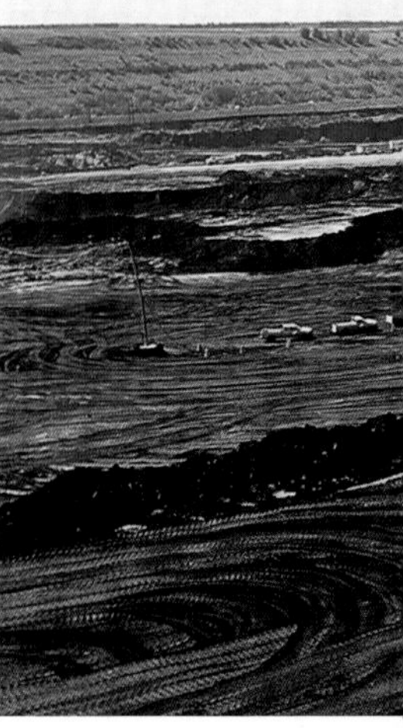

Fort McMurray was established in 1870. By 1912, enough drilling and researching had gone on to make it evident there was something important in the ground, whether it was salt or potential asphalt, and Fort McMurray's first boom was underway. Lots were selling for $200 or more.

Scientists were already developing means of separating the oil from the sand. Dr. Clark joined what is now the Alberta Research Council in 1920 and got to work on the problem. Clark and his assistant, Sidney Blair, built a small separation unit in the basement of the University of Alberta's power plant. For Clark, the goal always was to use the bitumen as a base for fuels and lubricants and, in 1928, he and Blair patented a hot water process for separating the oil from the sand.

More and more people and companies became involved as the stakes grew larger. New plants and refineries were

constructed throughout the 1930s and '40s, but technical difficulties and two major fires that destroyed the plants threw serious roadblocks in the way of progress. Also, the process was expensive and didn't seem to be financially feasible. The 1950s saw a lot of amalgamations and attempts to sell off unprofitable ventures.

In 1962, progress moved forward with the construction of a pilot plant. Between 1964 and 1967, the Great Canadian Oil Sands Group, now known as Suncor Energy Inc., completed a large-scale commercial project. Incorporated in 1964, Syncrude Canada Ltd., which became a joint public and private venture 10 years later, constructed a new plant north of Fort McMurray in 1973 and shipped the first barrel of oil Sept. 15, 1978.

The people who have chosen the beautiful, wooded region as home over the years value the quiet, traditional way of life in the area. They also understand that technology and the environment are often challenging each other. In one program to address this issue, Syncrude moved 29 bison onto an area of reclaimed land in the 1990s; the herd now numbers more than 200. Four kilometres of trails on the reclaimed land were also opened. Industry in the area works with the community on many different environmental programs.

And, in keeping with getting the most out of the product, another company is developing technology to try recovering metals and other materials from the sludge resulting from the oil sands process. Wonder if they can use any of it to waterproof canoes?

The area available for mining covers about 3,400 square kilometres and is north of the city of Fort McMurray. It is important to realize that the Athabasca oil sands are shallow enough to be accessible through surface mining. The area is covered first by up to 75 metres of clay and sand, topped by nearly three metres of muskeg. Underneath is flat limestone. The oil sands in the middle are up to 60 metres thick, meaning that the supply is extensive. Other oil sands in northern Alberta are in Peace River and Cold Lake, and, although these are not as close to the surface as those in Athabasca, at some point in the future, they too will be accessible. At present, Canada's oil reserves are second only to those in Saudi Arabia.

5 Atlas Coal Mine National Historic Site

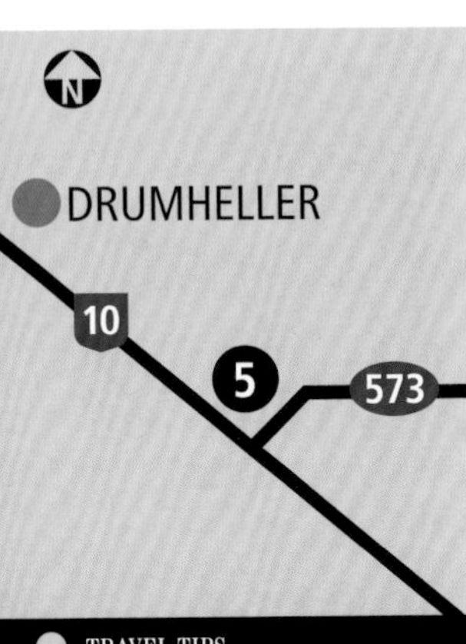

TRAVEL TIPS

Open May through Thanksgiving, with group tours all year.

Self-guided "Tipple Trail" and "Kids Discovery Trail" available all day during open hours.

Hourly guided tours, mantrap rides, demonstrations, storytelling and video showings all included in admission.

See the award-winning *Thunder in the Valley* video for helpful background.

No underground tours of the mines, which by law were sealed when abandoned.

Evening is a beautiful time to visit in the summer.

Location: On Highway 10 at the east end of the Hoodoo Trail, across from East Coulee. About 15 minutes east of Drumheller.

Phone: (403) 822-2220

E-mail: info@atlascoalmine.ab.ca

www.atlascoalmine.ab.ca

The eight-storey sorting tower, or tipple, that served the Atlas Coal Mine until its closure in 1979 invites a high-level scan across time and space. Below lies one of western Canada's best examples of the era when coal brought men and money to this valley of badlands and hoodoos, coulees and canyons. Standing here, you can imagine a miner emerging with a lunch bucket from the willowshack, collecting his pay at the mine office and entering the washhouse at shift's end to hose away the grime. Standing here, you also realize how swiftly an era can come and go.

There's no doubt coal shaped the history of this valley. It was a search for coal deposits along the river in 1884 that led Joseph Tyrrell to the dinosaur skull that kick-started the region's renown for fossils. The valley's largest town is named after Sam Drumheller, who was first to exploit the rich coal seams that attracted dozens of mines to the region in the early 1900s. With the advent of railways such as the Calgary-Drumheller, hunger for

coal mushroomed and business boomed. But within half a century, the demand for coal was replaced by the demand for oil and gas. Drumheller rode the next wave, thanks to oil and dinosaurs, but its coal mines were left behind.

Atlas Coal Co. Ltd. opened its first mine in 1917. This mine at East Coulee was closed in 1979 and became a National Historic Site in 2002. Left largely intact, its rusting rails and abandoned cars, furnished buildings and wealth of records invite your imagination to roam.

Take a guided tour to the top of Canada's last wooden tipple and drink in the view. Back on the ground, visit the mine office, miner's shack, washhouse and lamp house, keeping an eye out for historic characters and equipment demonstrations. Take a "mantrap" ride in a two-ton coal car pulled by an antique battery-operated mine locomotive. Walk the interpretive trails around the original mine site, poke around the antique equipment and hike up to the old mine head and dynamite shed.

As you roam, look ahead as well as behind, for this intriguing site was to its day what today's bustling energy extraction centres are to ours.

More than 2,000 mines have operated in Alberta, producing more than one billion tonnes of coal. At one time, 138 registered mines were operating in the Drumheller Valley. Now, the number of mines with current permits has dropped to 28, with only 11 producing coal.

The heyday for coal lasted about three decades. From 1928 to 1955, coal mines were working full blast to fuel Canada's expansion and particularly the railway's journey west.

Coal's strategic role was reflected in the work of Geological Survey of Canada explorers such as Joseph Tyrrell. Sent to the west for economic reasons, Tyrrell may be known today for finding dinosaurs, but what he really sought was coal.

Fossils proved the common factor between coal and dinosaurs, and the unique geology in the Red Deer River Valley laid the groundwork for the area's rich finds in both. While the world's major coal deposits resulted from materials laid hundreds of millions of years before the time of the dinosaurs, in the Carboniferous Period, the coal in the Red Deer River Valley is the same age as the dinosaurs, dating to the Cretaceous Period. That's why both coal and dinosaurs were found here in the same exposures of the river valley.

6 The Banff Centre

TRAVEL TIPS

There is visitor parking on site, but you can also walk up from town, either up Tunnel Mountain Drive or up the shortcut past the cemetery and through the woods.

Drop by the Banff Centre Box Office for a listing of current events and to pick up a Self-Guided Tour brochure.

Location: 107 Tunnel Mountain Dr., Banff

Phone: (403) 762-6100

E-mail: communications@banffcentre.ca

www.banffcentre.ca

The Banff Centre may have begun with a single course in drama, courtesy of the University of Alberta's department of extension, but more than 70 years later, it is an internationally renowned facility for the arts, business, the environment and, most recently, mountain culture.

Many thousands of artists of all kinds have participated in workshops, immersed themselves in one of the Leighton studios or just "retreated" into a wonderful space in which to create new compositions, literature or visual art. Others have performed their art on stage for festivals, competitions and pure entertainment.

The conference facilities at The Banff Centre have hosted groups interested in improving their leadership and management skills or learning more about how to live and work responsibly in our environment. The especially appropriate mountain culture program is one of the most recent initiatives offering everything from mountain photography and writing workshops to film and book festivals.

The Banff Centre has also hosted many internationally acclaimed figures in a variety of fields. Sir Edmund Hillary, the first to conquer Mount Everest, opened the Banff Mountain Summit in 2000 with a discussion on global mountain issues. Others, such as renowned environmentalist David Suzuki, author W.O. Mitchell, jazz piano legend Oscar Peterson and composer Aaron Copland have contributed to the goals of the centre and have spent time in this magnificent setting.

Growth and change have been constants in the centre's history. The most recent evolution is a revitalization plan that began in 2006 with a vision to build an environment for "creativity, innovation and leadership" where new

leaders and artists are inspired to push boundaries and pass on what they have learned to other generations.

In spite of all the famous people who have walked, talked and performed here, The Banff Centre is not locked away behind closed gates – it is accessible. The public is encouraged to take in the many concerts, art exhibitions and film festivals, and artists and business and community leaders can apply to study or take a workshop. The Sally Borden Fitness and Recreation Centre, featuring a 25-metre swimming pool, is open to the public.

The campus is a short walk or drive from the townsite. The road winds up Tunnel Mountain with a view of Banff's answer to a castle, the Fairmont Banff Springs Hotel, across the river. If you have some energy to spare, consider the short-cut trails that wend their way invitingly through the trees. Best of all, you can walk up the hill and stroll around the buildings to watch artists and students immersed in their chosen work, or you can just find a spot to sit and drink in the beauty of your surroundings.

The Banff Centre is governed by a board of governors that includes the president and chief executive officer of the centre and 15 other members, one of whom is appointed by the federal minister responsible for the National Parks Act.

Highlight events include the Banff Summer Arts Festival (May through August), Banff-Calgary Wordfest (October), Banff Mountain Festivals (early November), Playbill Series (throughout year) and Banff International String Quartet Competition (triennial August-September).

With more than 450 employees (66 per cent of them unionized), the centre is one of the largest employers in the Bow Valley.

7 Banff National Park

EDMONTON
16
JASPER
2
93
RED DEER
7
BANFF
1
CALGARY

TRAVEL TIPS

The park is open year round.

Banff National Park has many things to offer so stop by the information centre for help with maps, brochures, permits, backcountry reservations, up-to-date park information and weather, trail, avalanche and road reports.

Hours vary depending on the time of year, but core hours are 9 a.m. to 5 p.m., with hours extending in the summer to 8 a.m. to 8 p.m.

Location: Banff Information Centre : 224 Banff Ave., Banff

Phone (403) 762-1550

E-mail: banff.vrc@pc.gc.ca

www.pc.gc.ca/banff

Banff National Park was declared a UNESCO World Heritage Site in 1984 with good reason. The peaks, valleys, glaciers, waterfalls, caves and fossils – all found in the park – make it a place to be revered and preserved.

The Cave and Basin site commemorates the beginning of the park back in 1885, soon after the railway men's discovery of the sulphur hot springs. Before that discovery, the mountains and valleys had been home to the Stoney, Kootenay, Peigan, Siksika and others whose livelihood depended on buffalo hunts and the hunting and trapping of other game. Explorer David Thompson had travelled through the area in 1800.

Throughout the Cave and Basin National Historic Site, you can see (and smell!) the beautiful emerald-coloured water from the sulphur springs. There are also many displays of the early days, including a sad period during the First World War when Canadians of German, Ukrainian and other European descent were interned near the site. They built many of the roads in the area and their internment homes during the winter months were the buildings associated with development of the Cave and Basin.

Twenty-five kilometres from the Banff town centre, you can walk Johnston Canyon with its two beautiful waterfalls and the Ink Pots, fascinating cold-water springs that change from clear blue to almost black.

Preserving the park is a constant balancing act, certainly between people and nature, and also with nature itself. The stunning elk, or wapiti ("white rump" as the

Shawnee called them), which we all like to see along the side of the road, have created problems by eating too much. They are the main plant eaters in the park and their increasing numbers threatened to decimate the aspens and willows. With more and more people visiting the park, the natural enemies of the elk had moved away and the elk population was taking over. Wildlife predators had to be restored and a number of the lovely elk (particularly those who had decided they were 'townees') were relocated. The rest were gently persuaded to resume their migratory traditions.

The park has changed its boundaries several times in its history in order to satisfy different interest groups across the country. But with the sheltered valleys sporting their alders, willows and the popular elk, the lower slopes covered with Douglas firs and lodgepole pines, and the alpine zone boasting brief bursts of colour in the short growing season at that altitude, there is always something different to see and to ponder.

World Heritage designation is a two-edged sword. The United Nations Educational, Scientific and Cultural Organization (UNESCO) designates places that "exemplify an area's ancestry," attempting to ensure that those places will be preserved. While it is considered an honour to be selected, there is virtually no money attached to World Heritage status. The usual result of the lengthy process, taking nearly five years from the time a site is nominated, is that people become more aware of the site and are drawn to visit it. There are exceptions, however. Places like the Galapagos Islands with its delicately balanced eco-system, for example, do not benefit from increased tourism. Banff is currently one of 812 World Heritage Sites.

8 Bellevue Mine (Crowsnest)

Be sure to visit the Bellevue Mine for a fascinating, hands-on experience of the days of coal mining. The mine features underground mine tours and indoor and outdoor artifact exhibits that depict the rich mining heritage of the area.

Visitors don authentic mining lamps and hardhats and, with an interpretive guide, experience part of life as a miner while walking 300 metres through hundred-year-old tunnels of western Canada's only underground coal mine tour. Your lamp is the only light by which to see the artifacts and workings of the mine, which include two coal seams, a coal "room," loading chute and more.

Visitor safety and enjoyment rank number one at Bellevue – a museum, not a working mine. In 1990, the Crowsnest Pass Ecomuseum Trust Society opened and re-timbered 300 metres of the original haulage tunnel of the mine. Although the support systems are historically correct, the mine tour area is inspected

Also on the Highway 3 route and just three kilometres east of Bellevue is the Leitch Collieries Provincial Historic Site. You can visit and walk around this site at any time of the year. Static displays explain the mine operation. Between mid-May and Labour Day, trail interpreters are on the site from 9 a.m. to 5 p.m. and provide information and guided tours.

The Leitch Collieries was the first coal mine in the nation to be entirely Canadian owned. The mine was built in 1907, and its remains include coke ovens, power house and washery. Nearby is the mine manager's residence.

frequently and maintained by qualified mine engineers. Observe the large timbers keeping the roof and walls stable.

Historically, after prospectors discovered rich coal deposits in the area, Western Canadian Colleries Limited purchased a vast tract of land near Bellevue to meet the demand for coal from settlers and the Canadian Pacific Railway (CPR). Active development of the Bellevue Mine began in 1903, and by Dec. 2 of that year, the mine loaded its first CPR boxcar. The town of Bellevue grew as a bedroom community and supply centre for the miners, their families and Western Canadian Colleries.

Of the 11.8 million tonnes of coal extracted from the mine, about 90 per cent was sold to the CPR for its steam engines, making it the mine's number one customer. The influence of the CPR, both direct and indirect, was very strong and was felt right up to the day the mine closed.

The Bellevue Mine operated for seven years with a strong safety record. Then, on Dec. 9, 1910, a deadly underground explosion rocked the area. In all, 31 men were killed from a lack of oxygen and a high concentration of carbon monoxide and other deadly gases (afterdamp) in the aftermath of the explosion. The mine reopened a few weeks after the tragedy and reached its peak operation in the 1920s, when a workforce of 500 men produced 2,500 tons of coal each day.

Eventually, the railway's conversion to diesel engines in the '50s and dwindling coal markets led to the closure of Bellevue Mine in 1961.

Hearing coal miners' stories and entering the mine's dark tunnels is a moving, not-to-be-missed experience. Visit the historic mine and experience the past!

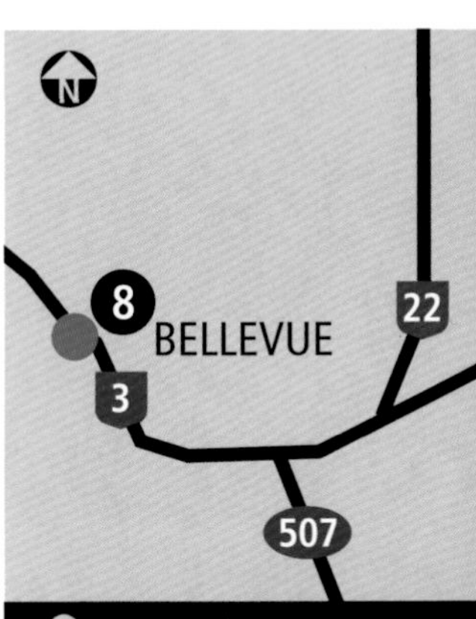

TRAVEL TIPS

The 30-minute mine tours are offered daily from mid-May to Labour Day in September, departing every 30 minutes beginning at 10 a.m. The last tour of the day leaves at 5:30 p.m.

The mine temperature is 3 to 7 C year round, so wear warm clothing and sturdy footwear.

The information centre offers displays, a DVD virtual tour, picnic area and gift shop.

Off-season pre-booked tours are also available.

Mine tours are not wheelchair accessible.

Location: Bellevue exit off Highway 3 in the Crowsnest Pass, Bellevue

Phone: (403) 564-4700 or (403) 563-3217 off season

E-mail: cpets@shaw.ca

www.bellevuemine.ca

9 Big Valley Jamboree

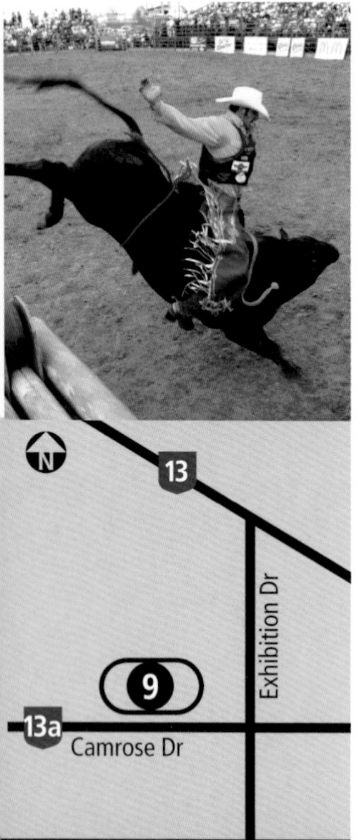

TRAVEL TIPS

Pets are allowed but they must remain on a leash and in your own campsite area.

You can take alcoholic beverages as long as you drink them in your own camping area only; glass bottles are not allowed.

Location: Off Highway 13 in Camrose

Phone: 1-888-404-1234 or (780) 672-0224

E-mail: bvj@bigvalleyjamboree.com

www.bigvalleyjamboree.com

Country music lovers from all over the country book four days in early August to be part of the Big Valley Jamboree in Camrose. Thousands of people pitch tents and park trailers on a 400-acre plot of land that creates a mini-village where neighbourliness is the order of the day.

The weekend starts the way every good summer event should – with a parade through the streets of town. Then you move over to a main stage that is on the go from morning 'til night. Some people purchase reserved seats for the shows, but most take along their lawn chairs and just find a good spot. If you are a bit late claiming that good spot, you can always see the show on the big screen and still be there to listen and absorb the wonderful sound through your pores. It's an amazingly good stage and sound system. High tech lighting and a 140,000-watt sound system guarantee a good experience even if you're mostly watching the big screen.

When you're not catching a show at the main stage, you can check out a workshop, perhaps the one for, and by, songwriters. You can watch the excitement of the team cattle penning event or wander over to the trade show and pick up a souvenir or two. Large breakfasts are available to start your day, and then you can move along to the "Bulls for Breakfast." You don't eat one, you watch people riding them or doing wild pony rides and trick riding. On Sunday morning you can calm down a bit, have the edible-type breakfast and take part in the music of a traditional gospel service.

The success of the Big Valley Jamboree is due largely to the hundreds of staff and service providers from Camrose and region who also book the four days to make the

events run smoothly. And since the Canadian Country Music Association voted the Jamboree its "Country Music Event of the Year" in 2001, 2004 and 2006, it can definitely be called a success!

While you're getting your fill of country music, you can take time to look at Camrose itself. It's a city of 16,000 people and includes Augustana College, now part of the University of Alberta. The Camrose Mainstreet Project, a provincial government initiative, has spurred renovation and restoration of many of the old main street buildings, the earliest one being Duncan Sampson's general store, built in 1904. Swans in Mirror Lake Park, right in the middle of the city, or a round of golf at the Camrose Golf Course are good, relaxing reasons to stay a little longer.

The jamboree attracts more than 80,000 attendees over four days. Imagine the organizational hurdles to hosting the party! Organizers provide banking machines on site, garbage bags and daily pick-up, message board and lost and found department, food concessions open from 3 p.m. to 3 a.m., medical assistance 24 hours a day, special services for people with disabilities (pick-up and drop off places), souvenirs, programs, assistance in locating lost children, an information booth, autograph tent, a shuttle service to and from downtown Camrose operating from 9 a.m. to 3 a.m., and fresh water and septic service for recreational vehicles.

It's a job well done. The jamboree was nominated as one of the American Bus Association's Top 100 Events in North America for 1997, 2001 and 2007.

10 Blackfoot Crossing Interpretive Centre

One hundred and twenty nine years after the signing of Treaty 7 between the Government of Canada and the Treaty 7 Nations, the Blackfoot Crossing Historical Park opened on the same spot. Chief Crowfoot had chosen the original location on the Siksika homeland as a place significant to the Blackfoot Confederacy, which included the Siksika Nation. The Blackfoot Crossing had for many years been a safe place for Chief Crowfoot's people to cross the Bow River and camp.

Today the stunning building that looks like a teepee spread out on the ground adds to the history and the beauty of the site overlooking the Bow River valley. Even the colours used to "paint" the teepee have been taken from the surrounding countryside. Seven teepee shapes adorn the roof and, of these, four extend down into the building and become galleries, each one representing a season.

The Blackfoot Crossing Interpretive Centre was a long time coming. A celebration of the 100th anniversary of the signing of Treaty 7 in 1977 attracted thousands of people including Prince Charles, the Prince of Wales. Since that historic celebration, interest built and a movement began to commemorate

TRAVEL TIPS

There is a cafeteria opening onto an outside patio with wonderful views of the river valley, a children's museum and a gift shop.

Location: 85 kilometres southeast of Calgary near Cluny, just south of Highway 1 accessed via Highway 842

Phone: 1-866-957-BCHP (2247) or (403) 734-5171

www.siksikanation.com

the Blackfoot Crossing historical site. Thirty years later, Blackfoot Crossing Historical Park opened its doors and the dream was realized because of the leadership shown 30 years ago.

The 1,550-hectare site includes the last teepee site of Chief Crowfoot as well as an ancient and sacred burial ground. One area yet to be developed is an earthlodge village believed to be from the 1700s and probably belonging to the Mandan tribe. In later years, the Siksika believed this village area had healing properties and the people would go there in times of sickness and during the devastating epidemics of the 1800s.

The stories of the Blackfoot Confederacy are told through music, dance, storytelling, demonstrations and exhibits at the interpretive centre. Artifacts that have been dispersed to other centres and museums over the years are now being repatriated since there is now a facility to house and preserve them properly.

One of the goals of the centre is to tell the Blackfoot interpretation of Treaty 7, which has been affirmed by the Supreme Court of Canada as a "sharing," not a giving up of their land and their way of life. The oral traditions, the handing down of stories, have been overshadowed by the written histories of the Europeans, and the remarkable Blackfoot Crossing Interpretive Centre is an opportunity to redress the balance.

11 Brooks Aqueduct

A technological wonder in its time, the Brooks Aqueduct is a National and Provincial Historic Site.

In 1903, a great tract of land within the Palliser Triangle, later Alberta and Saskatchewan, became the final Canadian government land grant to the Canadian Pacific Railway (CPR). But the railway company had a problem. What would convince settlers to come to a landscape where even trees lacked enough water to grow? Only one thing could transform the wasteland into productive fields: irrigation.

Near Brooks, 50,000 hectares were too dry to farm. The Bow River wound through the countryside, but the river was not enough. As part of its irrigation plan, the CPR created on-stream storage at the Bassano Dam. Completed in 1914, the new reservoir fed Lake Newel, the largest man-made lake in Alberta.

Often small canals were perfect conduits for irrigation streams, but in the CPR's eastern irrigation block, a wide, shallow valley separated the southeastern and eastern areas of the Brooks district. How would they carry irrigation water from one side of the valley to the other?

The CPR's assistant chief engineer for natural resources, Hugh B. Muckleston, had an innovative proposal: an elevated canal to carry precious water to the parched land. The concrete flume had to span a valley 3.2 kilometres wide while carrying the water beneath the CPR's mainline tracks and back up to grade, so design and construction know-how needed to be exceptional. Construction began

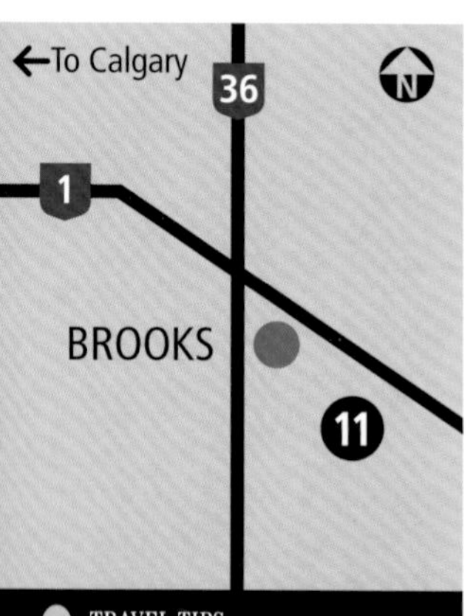

TRAVEL TIPS

At the shelters and visitors' kiosk, plaques and displays provide information on the aqueduct.

Tours are available from 10 a.m. to 5 p.m. daily from mid-May to Labour Day.

Picnic tables at the site encourage picnickers, or have lunch in Brooks.

The Brooks and District Museum at 568 Sutherland Dr. offers additional insights into local history.

Location: three kilometres south of Highway 1 east of Brooks

Phone: (403) 362-4451 (summer only) or (403) 653-5139

E-mail: aqueduct@eid.awinc.com

www.eidnet.org

in 1912 with steam-powered, horse-drawn equipment and the labour of some 300 men.

The design required that the barrel of the aqueduct be 6.4 metres wide and 2.4 metres deep. At its deepest point, the structure would tower 20 metres above the valley floor. In an era when reinforced concrete was still considered a new building material in Canada, 1,814 tonnes of rebar were needed. The trestle and barrel required 19,114 cubic metres of concrete and included an inverted siphon to carry the entire water course beneath the tracks and back to grade with the loss of no more than eight centimetres of "head."

The first irrigation water flowed through the continuous pour concrete flume in 1914. When completed, the Brooks Aqueduct was the largest in the world for this style of construction. The monumental concrete caterpillar made farming in the region possible, and settlers were drawn to the once-parched lands.

In 1935, at the height of the Depression, the CPR decided to quit the irrigation business and transferred ownership of the Brooks Aqueduct and the entire eastern block irrigation system to a local farmers' organization known as the Eastern Irrigation District (EID), along with a $300,000 grant to defray some of the district's immediate costs.

The EID used the Brooks Aqueduct until 1979. Cracks and leaks had always been problematic but studies revealed repairs were no longer realistic. The glory days of the aqueduct had passed. Given new technologies, an earthen canal had become a workable option, but the aqueduct structure remains a monument to ingenuity and the use of early technology.

Between 1857 and 1861, Captain John Palliser and his scientific expedition had already determined that about 1.2 million hectares of land in western Canada were too dry for agriculture. Named the Palliser Triangle, the tract was also known as the "Great American Desert."

Given the rivers running through Alberta and the CPR's determination to market land and transport passengers and freight, the company developed irrigation systems. Today, the Eastern Irrigation District, the largest in Alberta, provides water for 113,000 hectares of cropland, an area larger than Prince Edward Island. As well, it irrigates rangeland.

The province has 13 irrigations districts; some are very small. The second largest, the Western Irrigation District, includes Strathmore and area. Irrigation also serves farms near Magrath, Raymond, Lethbridge, Taber, Cardston, Vauxhall, Dunmore and Glenwood.

The Bow River is the source of water for the largest irrigation districts, but other rivers also provide water to parched fields.

12 Kurt Browning

Central Alberta is a rich, varied and inspiring part of our province. The area offers a wealth of stories about our heritage, awesome scenery and friendly, down-home people. But look past these delights to experience the land that nurtured our very own Kurt Browning, the "Kid from Caroline."

Kurt's magnificent rise to the pinnacle of world figure skating – coupled with his sparkling personality and winning smile – has thrilled Albertans and inspired young skaters who dream of someday earning similar accolades in the rinks of the world.

The world-famous figure skater was born at the nearby town of Rocky Mountain House in 1966, but soon the family moved to a ranch just west of Caroline, where Kurt's father still resides. Here, Kurt began a skating career that took him to the World Figure Skating Championships and the Olympics while it took Albertans' breath away.

To honour its favourite son, Caroline named its arena the Kurt Browning Arena. In the arena, stop by Kurt's Korner to marvel at the awards and memorabilia from the skater's career. You will be treated to displays ranging from Kurt's first skates to his photo with the Queen.

Like many Albertans who love the sensation of sailing across the ice, Kurt began skating at age three. At both outdoor and indoor rinks, he pursued his passion. He got his first figure skates when he was 10. By 1982, Kurt was competing in the Canadian Novice Championships and won his first Canadian Novice Championship in 1983.

As an amateur, the brilliant skater scored four world titles and four Canadian championships. Although he represented Canada in three winter Olympics, it was in 1988 that Kurt became the first man to land a quadruple jump at a world competition. With that achievement

To Rocky Mountain House
N
11
761
22
12
54
CAROLINE
22

TRAVEL TIPS

Kurt's Korner in the Kurt Browning Complex is open year-round from 10 a.m. to 3:30 p.m. Monday through Thursday.

While at Caroline, enjoy the Caroline Wheels of Time Museum where you will find a trapper's cabin, another restored log home and memories of the past.

Rocky Mountain House is 45 kilometres from Caroline – a pleasant detour while you're in the area.

Location: Kurt Browning Arena, 5103 48 Ave., Caroline

Phone: (403) 722-3022 or (403) 722-3781 for the village office

www.kurtfiles.com

acknowledged by the International Skating Union, the "Kid from Caroline" claimed a spot in the *Guinness Book of World Records.* Moving to the professional arena, Kurt won three World Professional Championships and four Canadian Professional Championships.

His skating success was rooted in more than awe-inspiring jumps. He became famous for his fast footwork, and his routines incorporated artistic themes as diverse as Casablanca and the cowboy heritage of Caroline.

Scoring countless wins in the regional, national and international championships, he instilled pride in the hearts of all Canadians. In 1989, 1990, 1991, 1993 and 1994, the Sports Federation of Canada named him Top Male Athlete. In 1990, with the Lou Marsh Award, he was recognized as Canada's Outstanding Athlete. Also that year, he was inducted into the Order of Canada. In 1991 and 1992, as the first figure skater to be awarded the Lionel Conacher Award, Kurt added the Canadian Press Male Athlete of the Year award to his list of achievements.

Kurt is honoured at the World Figure Skating Museum and the World Figure Skating Hall of Fame. It's no wonder some locals consider Caroline as Kurt Country.

If you're rarin' for information on other sports heroes, make a side trip to the Alberta Sports Hall of Fame near Red Deer. On Highway 2 just north of Red Deer, take the 32 Street exit.

Exhibits articulate the outstanding successes of the Edmonton Eskimos, Calgary Stampeders, Edmonton Oilers and Calgary Flames. Also well represented are baseball, soccer, curling, racket ball, volleyball and basketball.

While you're there, tip your hat to Alberta's great women athletes and teams. Check out the world-famous women's basketball team, the Edmonton Grads, as well as the 1990 and 1992 Canada West Ringette team.

Alberta's best individual athletes in skiing, skating, mountain climbing, wrestling, judo and more are also honoured.

If you want a high tech approach, the facility has a multi-sport interactive virtual system, which means having fun while you learn.

Check details at www.albertasportshalloffame.com or call (403) 341-8614.

13 Calgary Folk Music Festival

In 1987, after yet another rained-out weekend and a pretty serious financial loss, the Calgary Folk Music Festival almost folded. Seven out of its eight years had been plagued by wet weather, making it difficult to arouse the required level of enthusiasm for a fledgling festival. But those who did brave the weather *were* enthusiastic.

The festival began as a one-time event in 1980 to help celebrate Alberta's 75th anniversary. The provincial tour was organized by Mitch Podolak, founder of the Winnipeg Folk Festival, and Mansel Davies, founder of the Calgary Folk Club. The success of the anniversary celebration led to its inauguration as an annual event under Davies' leadership.

After the soggy ending of the 1987 event, there were still enough committed folk music enthusiasts who were anxious to keep the festival alive. New artistic director, Vic Bell, chose a permanent weekend that, besides having dibs on the best weather of the summer, placed the Calgary event between similar festivals in Vancouver, Winnipeg, Canmore and Edmonton. As part of a western Canadian circuit, the venue would be economically attractive to potential performers.

The Calgary event continued to grow with new producers and artistic directors. Current artistic director, Kerry Clarke, took over programming duties in 1994 and expanded the edgy and world music components of the festival. In 1996, Terry Wickham joined the team, bringing bigger names to headline the weekend. The festival is now on solid financial ground. In 2006, the festival expanded beyond the four-day Prince's Island event with the Boot Camp – intensive workshops in musical styles and songwriting.

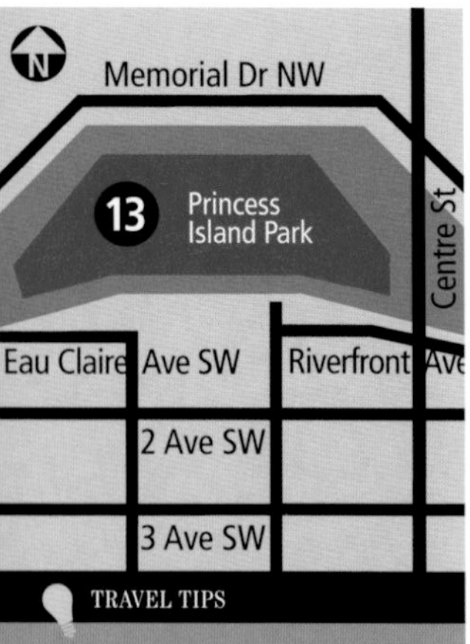

TRAVEL TIPS

There's lots of inexpensive parking around the Eau Claire district, and bus routes are handy.

There's secured bicycle parking and covered viewing areas for persons with disabilities.

Bring your own picnic.

Location: Prince's Island Park in downtown Calgary on the Bow River. The main gates are at the east side of the island, north of the Eau Claire Market.

Phone: (403) 233-0904

E-mail: info@calgaryfolkfest.com

www.calgaryfolkfest.com

With the support and commitment of more than 1,300 volunteers, the festival continues to grow and improve.

The four-day family-friendly cultural and musical jamboree features more than 60 artists from 15 countries on seven stages performing for daily audiences of 12,000. Artists perform in concert on the evening main stage or six more intimate stages, where sessions bring together musicians in unpredictable and magical collaborations that can become Celtic kitchen parties, country hoe-downs, Southern Baptist tent revivals, singer/songwriter song swaps, world music collaborations or all-out blues jams.

The festival is about great music and good spirits. Kids get in free, and they'll love the family area. The international craft market displays the work of independent vendors, artists' music is in the record tent and concessions have superb food from around the world.

You like blues? It's there. Prefer Celtic or traditional music? There's plenty of that, too, plus roots, world music, cutting-edge sounds, bluegrass, funk, country, hip-hop, dub, old-time and more.

Newcomers to the festival need to know that your first task, after you get your wrist band, is to stake out your spot with either your beach chair or your tarp. You will then move between six daytime stages, but people tend to leave their tarps and chairs (and cooler) parked in front of the main stage with a view to the evening performances. That cooler can hold food and drinks, but no liquor and no glass containers. If you don't want to be bothered with a cooler, there is a great selection of international food for sale on site.

14 Calgary Stampede

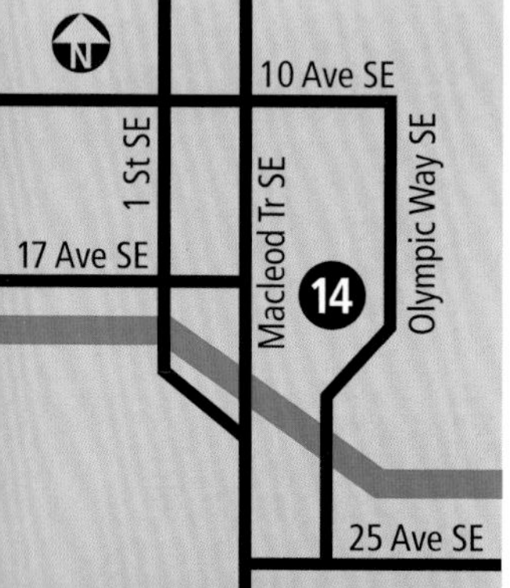

TRAVEL TIPS

Stampede dates are July 6-15, 2007; July 4-13, 2008; July 3-12, 2009; and July 9-18, 2010.

Check the website for special event days such as Sneak-A-Peek, Family Day, Western Heritage Day and BMO Kids' Day.

For your convenience, ride Calgary's Light Rail Transit system (LRT). Check www.calgarytransit.com for your Stampede time schedule.

Location:
1410 Olympic Way S. E., Calgary

Phone: 1-800-661-1260 (North America).
International toll free: Canada Country Code + 800-2610-1010

Email: reception3@calgarystampede.com

www.calgarystampede.com

To some, there is nothing in the world like the Calgary Stampede. From its humble beginnings as an agricultural fair, it has earned its reputation as "The Greatest Outdoor Show on Earth" through more than 100 years of celebrating the west – the old west, the wild west and, more recently, the new west. Stampede founder Guy Weadick's brilliant vision to create a frontier celebration in Calgary in 1912 set the stage. In 1923, the Stampede was blended with the original agricultural exhibition, resulting in a unique festival that has touched people in the 19th, 20th and 21st centuries.

The appeal of the Calgary Stampede stems from romantic imagery and tales of adventure and heroism, the mythology of cowboys and the settlement of the western half of North America.

But today's Stampede is built on much more than mythology. It's a festival of all things western.

The world-famous Calgary Stampede begins each year with a parade that winds through downtown streets past about 400,000 onlookers. Parade Day is an unofficial holiday for most downtown businesses. Free entertainment in Fluor Rope Square in the heart of the city gives a taste of what is to be experienced at the park itself.

Visitors come from across North America, around the world and from within Alberta to experience the heart-stopping action of one of the world's roughest and richest rodeos, the awesome power of the world's top chuckwagon races, the spectacular theatrical presentation of the evening grandstand shows, world-class agricultural

activities and adrenalin-pumping rides at North America's largest mobile midway.

A myriad of programs ensures everyone enjoys the Stampede. In the Indian Village, a cornerstone of the Stampede since 1912, visitors step back in time to share in authentic Plains Indians' cultural practices. The huge market and trade fair in the Roundup Centre offer hundreds of displays featuring everything from kitchen gadgets to western jewelry. Western Showcase embraces western culture through its world-class art displays. Just around the corner, singers, cowboy poets and musicians entertain visitors. And, of course, hundreds of food kiosks offer summer treats such as corn on the cob and miniature donuts.

First-time visitors from other places are amazed when they compare the Stampede to their fairs or festivals back home. While the midway and displays might be familiar, the scope, size and spirit of the Calgary Stampede make it a unique fair experience.

The party atmosphere that accompanies the Stampede is felt across Calgary during the 10-day festival. With free Stampede breakfasts all over the city, boisterous airport greeters, downtown activities and entertainment, Stampede parties and excitement every night in bars and clubs, there is absolutely no way to be in Calgary for those 10 days in July and not know the Stampede is in town!

Some visitors attend the Stampede for one reason only: to experience the GMC Rangeland Derby, the official name for the chuckwagon races, or "the chucks."

In 1923, Guy Weadick created "the Cowboy's Chuck-Wagon Race" to introduce a new competitive western sport. In the early days, ranchers brought their wagons and horses to town. Now, professional drivers, well-trained thoroughbred horses and four outriders for each wagon break out of a figure-8 start to race around the half-mile track in sunshine or in rain, to thunderous applause from tens of thousands of fans. In each heat, four wagons, 32 horses and 128 pounding hooves cross the finish line within fractions of a second.

In 1923, the prize purse totalled $275. Now, daily prize money and awards to the winners on the final night of competition total over $1 million.

15 Calgary Tower

For a bird's eye view of Calgary from the city's best-known and best-loved landmark, visit the Calgary Tower.

Over 190 metres high and located in the heart of downtown Calgary at Centre Street and 9th Avenue S.W., the Calgary Tower is the world's highest tourism tower – above sea level, that is. The Observation Deck itself stands at an amazing 1,240 metres above sea level.

The Calgary Tower is a symbol of civic pride, originally built in 1968 as a tribute to the citizens of Calgary. For the 1988 Olympic Winter Games, a natural gas-burning cauldron was installed at the peak of the tower. Lit for the Olympics and left burning continuously through the 16-day event, the ingenious invention created the world's largest Olympic torch. The flame is still lit today for special occasions, city and provincial events and in honour of great achievements.

Want to sample the heights near the giant torch? Step aboard! As the elevator doors open at the top, you will be greeted by an awe-inspiring 360 degree panoramic view from city streets to mountain peaks, from the Saddledome in the inner-city to Saddle Mountain, more than 150 kilometres away.

On the Observation Deck, just steps from the elevator doors, is the glass floor experience. The first of its kind

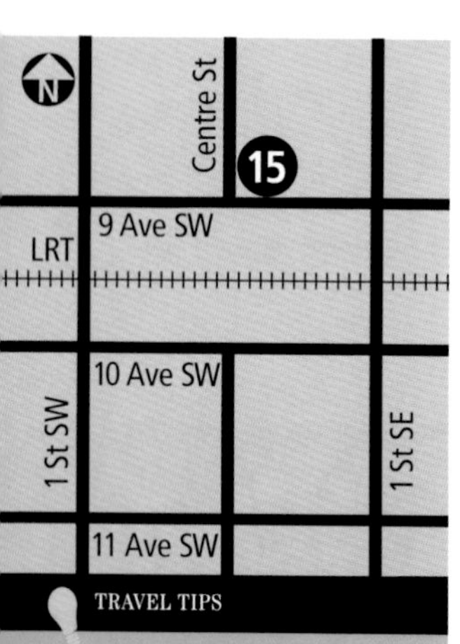

TRAVEL TIPS

Public parking is available at Tower Centre Parkade or ground level parking is located directly across 9th Avenue S.W.

Location: 101 9th Ave. S.W., Calgary

Phone: (403) 266-7171

E-mail: tourism@calgarytower.com

www.calgarytower.com

in the world, the glass-enclosed extension is 11 metres long and one metre wide. Get a whole new perspective on downtown Calgary as you are able to virtually step out into space above the bustling streets below. The glass panes in front leave an unobstructed view of the city, leaving each visitor feeling suspended in mid-air. Don't worry, though; each pane of glass can support the weight of two hippopotamuses.

After the thrill of the Observation Deck, head into Panorama Dining Room, located just steps below the Observation Deck, for an elegant meal in Calgary's most unique setting. Whether it's a special occasion, a light lunch or a one-of-a-kind dining experience, the motion of the revolving floor is barely perceptible as you enjoy world-class Canadian cuisine against a breath-taking backdrop.

After your meal, take your time browsing in the Spirit of Calgary Boutique.

Located at the base of the tower is the Tourism Calgary Retail and Information Super Centre. If you're looking for where to stay or what to do in Calgary, this centre has all the information and the knowledge to assist you in your next adventure.

After seeing the Calgary Tower, enjoy the city's downtown. Scotia Centre, Calgary Eaton Centre, Bankers Hall and other malls have a full range of boutiques, shops, services and restaurants. Linked by walkways, all you need is stamina to explore more than 200 shops and department stores.

If you love theatre and music, check out the downtown EPCOR Centre for the Performing Arts. The Calgary Philharmonic Orchestra, Theatre Calgary, Alberta Theatre Projects and One Yellow Rabbit Theatre Company present great performances year after year. For information and tickets, call (403) 777-000 or (403) 299-8888.

To escape the city centre hubbub, visit the indoor Devonian Gardens. Here, on the fourth level of the Toronto Dominion Square at 317 – 7th Ave. S.W., you can drink in the pleasures of subtropical plants, fountains and small waterfalls or occasionally enjoy the works of local artists. The gardens are an oasis to the travel worn so be sure to visit and renew your spirit.

16 Calgary Zoo

For an outstanding place to meet family and friends – human or animal – the Calgary Zoo should be at the top of your list. Home to more than 1,000 animals and one of the largest zoos in Canada, the Calgary Zoo is also one of the oldest. Dating back to 1929, its mandate is to conserve and educate. Not surprisingly, hours of pure amazement and fascination await visitors.

Much of the zoo is located on St. George's Island where the Bow River flows through the downtown vicinity. It has undergone many expansions, especially in recent years, with the modern mandate to place animals in large enclosures similar to their native habitat.

Although the Calgary Zoo is primarily about animals, it also provides the pleasures of a prehistoric park and a year-round botanical garden, the largest on the Prairies.

Even though their populations change constantly, the numbers of animals to see and learn about are astounding. The mammal population, representing 90 different species, exceeds 400. There are even more species of birds and almost as many specimens of reptiles. The Inland Bearded Dragon and the Australia Water Dragon will fire the imagination, but so will the boas, crocodiles and pythons. Nor will you want to miss the amphibians, arachnids, butterflies, fish and invertebrates.

Some animals are native to Canada. Others come from exotic places such as Ceylon, Chile, Madagascar and Australia. Popular highlights for your visit include the bears, cougars, lynx, mountain sheep, mountain goats, marmots, porcupines and snakes of North America. You may stand mesmerized by the large and small primates, especially the gorillas and Japanese macaques. Others focus on flying mammals, insects and birds, such as bats, Grecian shoemaker butterflies and flamingos. Still others

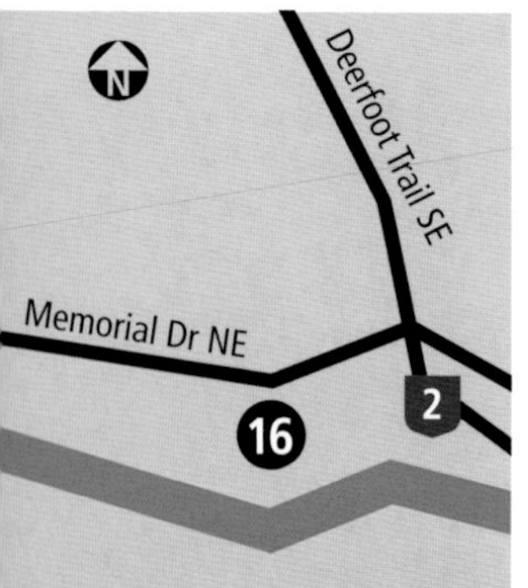

TRAVEL TIPS

The zoo is open throughout the year but exhibits are closed Christmas Day, during Zoolights evenings in December and early January, and for the annual fundraiser in September.

Plan to spend at least half a day, especially if you are bringing children.

Location: 1300 Zoo Rd. N.E., Calgary

Phone: 1-800-588-9993 or (403) 232-9300

E-mail: info@calgaryzoo.ab.ca

www.calgaryzoo.com

love the turtles, giraffes, lions, snow leopards, Siberian tigers and Asian elephants. The zoo also has tarantulas and a scorpion, and there are beautifully coloured fish and butterflies.

With some populations at risk of extinction, the Calgary Zoo participates in a species survival program and has had great success in its work with whooping cranes and Vancouver Island marmots. Other rescued animals or offspring born at the zoo have been released into the wild or loaned to other zoos for breeding purposes.

Live dinosaurs may not be an option, but the giant sculptures in the prehistoric park have always been popular with kids. Although not as anatomically accurate as later-day sculptures, Dinny, the Brontosaurus, has been a favourite of photo buffs for decades and has been declared an Alberta Historical Resource.

Current and planned theme areas of the zoo:

Arctic Shores & Antarctic Landing: This area will have indoor and outdoor exhibits, including king penguins in the Antarctic area.

Australia: Here you will find reptiles, birds and mammals of Oceania.

Botanical Gardens and Dorothy Harvie Gardens and Conservatory: The conservatory features an indoor butterfly garden, arid garden, rainforest and tropical garden. Outdoor gardens are sensational in spring and summer.

The Canadian Wilds: This large section focuses on the birds and mammals of North America.

Creatures of the Night: Nocturnal birds, small mammals and insects are displayed in spaces that resemble a forest at night.

Destination Africa: Indoor and outdoor exhibits recreate a rainforest and an African savannah. The lowland gorillas and lions are favourites.

Eurasia: Outdoor and indoor exhibit areas feature animals from Europe and Asia.

Prehistoric Park: Outdoor sculptures re-create the mighty dinosaurs of the Mesozoic era.

Primates: Monkeys, gibbons and prosimian species from South America, Asia and Africa are housed here.

17 Canadian Badlands Passion Play

The scene is set for the Canadian Badlands Passion Play just outside Drumheller under a big Alberta sky. Weather-blasted cliffs encircle the scene, creating a natural amphitheatre of surround sound. Uncannily similar to the Holy Land where Jesus Christ walked 2,000 years ago, this badlands setting is perfect for a gospel-inspired retelling of the Christian saviour's ministry, death and resurrection.

As hundreds of able actors in period costumes bring the drama alive, let yourself be transported back to a time and place that changed the course of history. Hear the call of the choir from a loft that truly is aloft. Enjoy the atmospheric instruments, whether from behind or onstage, integrated into the drama. Marvel at the way the high cliffs and weathered pyramids become part of the action – indeed, often star of the show.

Thousands experience this unique outdoor drama annually in July. They come from across Alberta and around the globe for a raft of reasons: spiritual pilgrimage, historical research, desire to see a spectacle, curiosity. Named Alberta's biggest cultural draw by Attractions Canada and listed among North America's top 100 events by the American Bus Association, the passion play is an unforgettable experience played on one of Canada's largest stages.

N
9
575
South Dinosaur Trail
17 St
17
9

TRAVEL TIPS

Remember it's an outdoor experience, so be ready for any weather.

The stage is huge so binoculars come in handy.

Parking is free, but a fair walk from the site. Wheelchair seating is available on request.

Dogs are not allowed in the audience area because of animals on stage.

Location: Enter Drumheller via Highway 9, follow South Dinosaur Trail (Highway 575) to 17 Street and look for the ski lift.

Phone: 1-888-823-2001 or (403) 823-2001

E-mail: pplay@telusplanet.net

www.canadianpassionplay.com

Nor does the story grow stale. Each year is unique, thanks to changes in script, music, actors and sets. Indeed, with weather cast as unpredictable scene-stealer in a show that goes rain or shine, each performance has its own stamp. The site also evolves each year, with the vision of becoming a year-round centre for biblically based arts. Ongoing projects include a lengthy Jerusalem Wall that adds to the authentic aura while providing working, living and public spaces. During intermission, check out the wall's Upper Room Interpretive Centre, where you can take a photo of your dramatically attired self in front of a passion play backdrop.

The passion play runs two weeks in mid-July, with several 3 p.m. and 6 p.m. showings. Behind the drama stands an expanding crew of thousands, mostly volunteers, whose passion matches the story. You'll see them directing traffic in the parking lot, selling beef on a bun at the refreshment counter, adding to the aura onstage. Among them are students, some drawn by a summer school that offers the potential of high school credit.

As the sun shifts and the audience departs after a cliff-top finale, snatches of conversation tell you that for many this show has lived up to its billing as "moving" and "world-class."

In summer, visitors can actually be on stage, explore the backstage area, find out how special effects are achieved and tour the interpretive centre. Off season, you must call ahead for this site tour.

The Calgary Philharmonic Orchestra has also graced the site with summer concerts called "Beethoven in the Badlands." The summer afternoon program has been presented only once each year, and it has been known to sell out.

If travel to the site is a problem for your group, there is a way to bring a passion play to you. Developed by Randall Wiebe, who has portrayed Jesus in the Drumheller production, "Thomas: Confessions of a Doubter" is a one-man, one-hour touring production that can be presented in any venue, indoor or out, with the only stage setting a bench. Details at www.sandalstrap.ca, (403) 820-1554, randall@sandalstrap.ca.

18 Canadian Finals Rodeo

Miss Rodeo Canada is crowned during the CFR. Young women from rodeo communities throughout Canada compete in various competitions, demonstrating great horsemanship and great modelling. Because the winner is an ambassador for the sport in the coming year, she needs to be a dynamic public speaker and comfortable with personal interviews. Judges are tough in their selection of the first lady of Canadian professional rodeo.

Throughout the year, Miss Rodeo Canada attends rodeos and is always a hit in parades. On tour, she represents the CFR at events across the country. As well, she is an official ambassador for the CPRA. In both capacities, she supports and promotes rodeo-related events and community concerns, including being a national spokesperson for the Canadian Breast Cancer Foundation.

Winners also give generously of their time and talents to countless charitable causes affecting the larger community well beyond the rodeo ring.

Where will you find the greatest Canadian rodeo champs and the wildest western social scene? Look for them at the Canadian Finals Rodeo (CFR) at Edmonton in early November. CFR is where the west turns wild, attracting about 95,000 people over five days of timed and rough stock or riding events. At each performance, you can thrill to the action as 102 finalists compete in bareback riding, steer wrestling, saddle bronc riding, tie-down roping, bull riding, team roping and ladies' barrel racing – the only professional rodeo event for women.

Qualifying doesn't come easy. The rodeo competitors pound the pavement to professional rodeos across Western Canada from spring to fall trying to finish the rodeo season at the top of the Canadian Professional Rodeo Association (CPRA) standings. The standings are determined by earnings at the various rodeos, and often only a few hundred dollars will make the difference between making the CFR and falling just short of grabbing one of only 12 positions up for grabs in each event.

CFR is more than just the sum of its rodeo events. With the world's best western-style feature performers, Canada's top country singers and unique theatrical opening ceremonies each night, it offers a complete entertainment package.

When first staged in 1974 at Northlands' former Edmonton Gardens arena, the CFR drew a total of 24,499 rodeo fans, and top competitors took home $29,478. In 1975, the finals were moved to Northlands Coliseum, now known as Rexall Place. After three decades of crowning Canada's best, today the CFR offers more than

$1 million in prize money, which means a paycheque of more than $9,000 for each night's event winners. The aggregate score for the week determines the champ and the ultimate size of his paycheque.

The CFR's Canadian Championship titles and rich paycheques are attracting world champions from around the globe. Top cowboys from the United States, Australia and New Zealand hit the Canadian rodeo trails to meet their minimum requirement of 17 Canadian pro rodeos through the year in their attempt to earn enough to qualify for CFR. This means a big boost to smaller Canadian rodeos and brings international stars to the CFR stage. These imports balance out the extensive list of Canada's top cowboys who are a big force at American rodeos and frequently rank in the world's top 10.

Which cowboy is the best of the best? Some rodeo fans have their stars, and some also follow entire rodeo families, applauding thunderously when they witness how the competitive skills and instincts have passed from grandfather to son to grandson. Some fans come to support hometown heroes. A few fans even root for the rodeo bucking stock.

And many people come for the casual, social atmosphere that only country hospitality can provide.

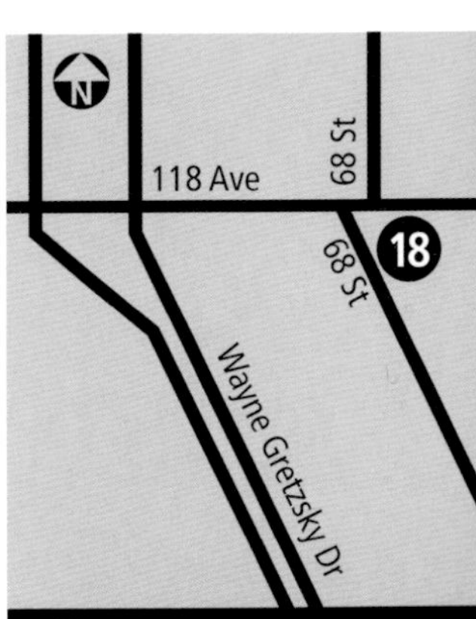

TRAVEL TIPS

Farmfair International begins the weekend before CFR and runs concurrently with the rodeo.

The Heritage Ranch Rodeo runs for three evenings just prior to CFR, showcasing teams of real ranch hands competing in events inspired by ranch chores.

At the CFR, the Country Vocal Spotlight gives Alberta's amateur performers a chance to compete and shine.

Location: Northlands AgriCom, Sportex and Rexall Place, 74 Street and 118 Avenue, Edmonton

Phone: 1-888-800-7210 or (780) 421-7210

E-mail: info@northlands.com

www.canadianfinalsrodeo.ca

19 Canadian Pacific Railway Reaches Calgary

Today, Calgary has more than a million people. No one could have dreamed of such massive expansion in 1875 when the North West Mounted Police joined Sam Livingston (who many say was Calgary's first resident), missionaries and a few others living in the vicinity of modern-day Calgary. Some years later, surveying began for a national railway, and with the government's recognition that American railways might garner business on Canada's southern Prairies, the Rogers Pass was chosen as the route through the mountains.

Speculators recognized that the railway would pass near the tiny village of Fort Calgary, and the community's very first boom period began. Exactly where the railway would be laid remained uncertain, even as surveyors, graders, tracklayers and front-trains laden with railway ties, spikes and rails made their way across the prairie landscape. Between Aug. 8 and 11, 1883, tracklayers and spike drivers began the bridgework near the Elbow River. On Aug.15, the bridge was finished. That day, a front-train steamed into what was to become downtown Calgary. Soon, trains steamed back and forth on the many crossings over the Bow River.

On Nov. 7, 1885, with the driving of the last spike at Cragellachie, B.C., Calgary was linked to the rest of Canada. The future of the community was assured.

Trains brought settlers and their effects, but freight became the real money maker. Grain, livestock, machinery and other goods could reach both eastern and western ports and markets. Situated on the plains but near the mountains, Calgary won a bid to provide a Canadian

N
3 St SW
9 Ave SW
LRT
19
10 Ave SW
4 St SW
2 St SW
11 Ave SW

TRAVEL TIPS

The CPR building is a business site and open only Monday through Friday. Ogden Shops is not open to the public.

Visitors can view locomotive No.29 or the Palliser Hotel (133 9th Ave., S.W.), but remember downtown is very busy during office hours on work days. The weekend is much less congested.

Location: CPR Building, Gulf Canada Square, 401 9th Ave. S.W., Calgary

Phone: (403) 319-7000

www.cpr.ca

Pacific Railway (CPR) maintenance and overhaul facility to prepare and repair trains for the arduous mountain route to and from Vancouver and for the long journey to Eastern Canada. Opened in 1912, the Ogden Shops became CPR's second largest facility of its type, expanding to cover 86 hectares. Today, at the gates to the shop, Oggie, an eight-metre man built of locomotive and freight car parts, greets arrivals.

Growth in the West and development of natural resources meant the route between Calgary and Vancouver became the busiest section of CPR line in the nation. In 1996, the company recognized that fact by relocating its head offices from Montreal to Calgary. Today, the CPR is among Calgary's top 10 private sector employers with more than 3,100 employees.

Outside its doors in the downtown, steam locomotive No. 29 proclaims the importance of the CPR to Calgary.

With Calgary increasingly important to tourists and business people, the CPR built the elegant Palliser Hotel, which opened in 1914. It was named for John Palliser who explored and studied the southern area of the Prairies as early as the 1850s.

Having the appearance of three adjacent towers, the hotel was designed in an Edwardian style of architecture, which was being heralded in Chicago at the time. Like other great CPR hotels of the time, its interior featured marble columns and floors, oak panelling and beautiful candelabras. Fitted with fine furnishings, rugs and art, it brought old world charm to the youthful Sandstone City. Fine dining as well as banquet facilities were available.

For years, some of Calgary's best known citizens, including former Canadian Prime Minister R.B. Bennett, made the Palliser their home.

Renovated and enlarged in 1929 and then again recently, the hotel continues to host countless visitors and is a gathering place for formal and informal events.

20 Canmore and Its Highland Games

Nestled below the Three Sisters Mountains, established in 1883 and steeped in mining history, Canmore's setting as the threshold to the Rockies inspires white water rafters, canoeists, kayakers, mountaineers, hikers, cyclists, heli-sightseers, photographers, golfers, travellers and locals.

It's great fun to wander around downtown to see how Canmore's businesses cater to the good life of outdoor pursuits and some serious pampering. Small strip malls enhance the shopping experience, but give yourself up to the magic of the mountain experience.

As well, the community hosts numerous festivals, including one that will attract the Scot in all of us – or anyone who wants a unique cultural and athletic event.

Annually on the Sunday of the September Labour Day weekend, the Three Sisters Scottish Society brings together outstanding athletes, pipers, drummers and dancers for its Highland Games.

Whether legend or history, many credit King Malcolm Canmore of 11th century Scotland for initiating the first Highland Games. As well as having the perfect name, the one-time mining town of Canmore can boast that its Highland Games are in very high country!

The games begin with an Alberta-style pancake breakfast before competitors and entertainers get serious. Spectators enjoy the performances of well-trained and talented dancers, but anyone in a highland outfit is welcome to participate. On stage, sword dances, lilts, jigs and flings have dancers and non-dancers focused on foot-work.

Music echoes through the valley and is a mainstay of the celebration. With performers dressed in their best kilts, everyone has a chance to root for a favourite soloist or band in the piping and drumming competitions.

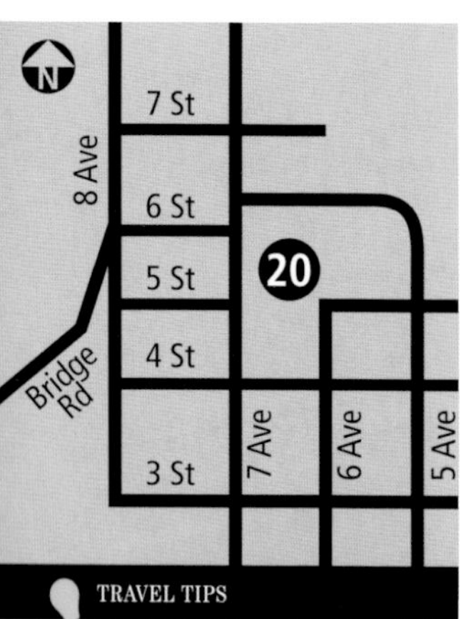

TRAVEL TIPS

Seating is limited for most events at Canmore's Centennial Park, so take a lawn chair.

Wear your kilt!

Book your accommodation early if you plan to stay in Canmore.

Location: 106 kilometres west of Calgary on Highway 1

Phone: (403) 678-9454

E-mail: canmorehighlandgames@telus.net

www.canmorehighlandgames.ca

Phone: 1-866-CANMORE

Email: info@tourismcamore.com

www.tourismcanmore.com

In the sports competitions, the "heavies" command special attention. Held at the ball diamond, the heavy sports such as stone puts, hammer throws and the caber toss attract outstanding Highland athletes and their fans. Once again, all competitors are required to wear kilts. Other rules are strictly enforced, too, and each event has up to a dozen specific rules.

Judges and athletes alike are intent as competitors in peak condition toss the caber, a giant log resembling a small telephone pole. Fans are keen to observe how the athletes throw their "hammers" – metal balls weighing more than seven kilograms and attached to a spring wire handle about 1.2 metres in length. "Putting the stone" bears close resemblance to shot put competitions. Other competitions are as intriguing as their names: throwing the weights for distance, tossing the sheaf and throwing the weights for height are part of the traditional and popular competitions.

Women are welcome to compete but must use the same implements as men.

Non-stop entertainment makes the festival tent a lively place particularly during the evening ceilidh that features top Celtic entertainers. Wander through the clan and vendor tents. Enjoy Scottish and Celtic displays and let yourself be tempted by the wares offered for sale. At the beer garden, the tired and thirsty can toast the famous Scottish poet Robbie Burns.

While you're in Canmore, take the five-minute drive up to the Canmore Nordic Centre. The centre and surrounding recreational lands form a beautiful provincial park. The area was an important venue for cross-country skiing and biathlon events during the 1988 Olympic Winter Games.

Today, the centre is the trailhead for 60 kilometres of skiing trails, used for hiking and mountain biking in summer. Traffic is often intended to be one way on the trails, so pick up maps and ask for information at the centre.

If you want more highland festivities, get a head start in late June at Red Deer, where the community and organizers proclaim *Ceud Mile Failte* or "A Hundred Thousand Welcomes." For mid-July, check out the Fort Edmonton Highland Games. In late August, High River sponsors its own games, and by early September, Calgary becomes host to highland competitors.

21 Chief Bobtail Smallboy

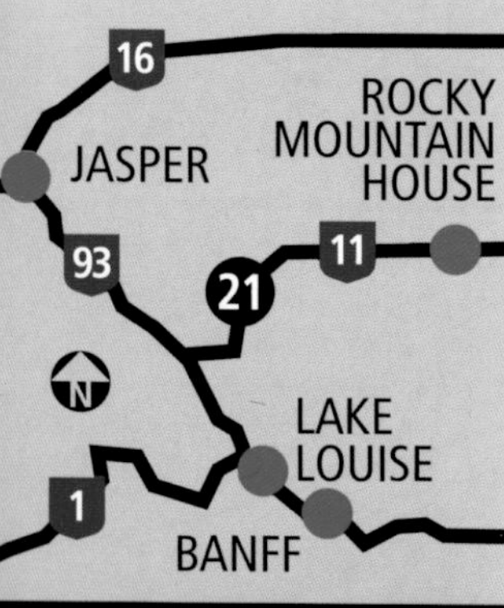

A Chief's Legacy

"Decision to Leave Hobbema," Smallboy's account of his 1968 exodus as translated by Eugene Steinhauer, appears in the *Western Canadian Journal of Anthropology (1969)*, Issue 1 p. 112.

Chief Smallboy: In Pursuit of Freedom, by Gary Botting (2005) puts the chief in historical context.

Location: Chief Smallboy's original camp was on the Kootenay Plains at the confluence of the North Saskatchewan River and Two Horse Creek, along what is now the David Thompson Highway. The band later moved north, close to Robb.

Phone: (250) 757-9916

E-mail: garybotting@shaw.ca

www.garybotting.com

Generations from now, First Nations children will know Bobtail Smallboy (Keskayo Apitchitchiw) not for his Order of Canada but for the fact that he led his people from toxic reserve life back to sacred land.

Elected chief of the Ermineskin Reserve south of Edmonton in 1959, Smallboy sorrowed over his people's poverty, unemployment, alcoholism, suicide and loss of traditional culture. Soon, he feared, Cree heritage would be lost while far too much young talent languished in jail.

Finding little support for creative solutions among fellow band leaders and none in Ottawa, Chief Smallboy invited anyone of Aboriginal heritage to join him in seeking another way. On June 25, 1968 – Pierre Trudeau's first day as Prime Minister of Canada – he led about 25 families to the Kootenay Plains to live in the wilderness, minus alcohol, drugs and TV.

Canada's first peoples have long held the Kootenay Plains and surrounding Rocky Mountains sacred. Treaty 6, which ceded vast expanses of Cree territory to Canada in the 1870s, specifically excluded the Rockies. But in Treaty 8, signed two decades later at Great Slave Lake a thousand kilometres away, Canada took possession of those sacred lands anyway – slyly and unjustly, Smallboy believed. Given that history, he felt justified in using the Kootenay Plains to alleviate overcrowding on reserves and create a haven from the temptations of white society.

The camp attracted controversy from many quarters and never received official government sanction. Perhaps most significantly, the Stoney Band resented Smallboy's intrusion on traditional Stoney territory, particularly since camp members took jobs harvesting trees to make way for the dam that would forever alter their landscape by creating Abraham Lake. Eventually heeding those concerns, the Smallboy camp moved further north, although its original site is still used for sacred ceremonies such as sun dances.

The Ermineskin Band elected a new chief in 1971. Yet Smallboy's camp became a magnet for those wishing to relearn Cree culture and rituals, and respect for his vision grew. His persistence helped quash the Trudeau government's ironically named 1971 White Paper, which pondered disbanding all reserves. Ten years later, when the prime minister sought to delay addressing Aboriginal issues until Canada's constitution arrived on Canada's shore, Smallboy and other chiefs helped ensure that Aboriginal and treaty rights were enshrined in the Constitution Act.

"Chief Smallboy was an ambassador for his people at a time when the entire First Nations could have been completely absorbed within this country, becoming second class citizens."

Gary Botting
Chief Smallboy:
In Pursuit of Freedom

A gentleman of innate dignity, Smallboy steadfastly refused to speak English. Yet even in translation, his eloquence attracted support from Pope John Paul II, the British House of Lords, Cree legal philosopher Harold Cardinal and Petro-Canada Chair Maurice Strong. It was Strong who nominated Smallboy for the Order of Canada, which he received in 1980.

Chief Smallboy died in 1984, a week after Trudeau left office. Although the Smallboy camp is but a shadow of its former self, the chief's spirit lives on each time Aboriginal peoples meet as "First Nations" – equal with the governments of this land.

Given his lineage, perhaps it's no surprise Bobtail Smallboy became one of Canada's most influential First Nations chiefs. Descended from Big Bear and Bobtail, the two chiefs who initially refused to sign Treaty 6, Smallboy was passionate about the culture they sought to preserve.

With the era of the buffalo behind them, Smallboy's family wandered Montana and Alberta until he was about 17, earning whatever living they could. Reluctantly leaving their nomadic way of life, in 1915 they accepted a parcel of land on the Ermineskin Reserve.

Smallboy's father spent much of his time in Montana, where he was in line to be chief, leaving his family to clear and tend the land. Smallboy excelled at that task and might have retired a rich farmer, particularly after oil revenues began flowing to the Ermineskin Band. Instead, he devoted his last 14 years to seeking justice for First Nations people.

22 Chinooks

Southern Alberta skies fill with drama. Within an hour, winter landscapes disappear. A chinook has descended from the eastern slopes of the Rockies and, for a few hours or days, dismal winter seems transformed into spring.

The fascinating natural phenomenon is both visible and invisible. In Alberta, chinooks can happen anywhere south of Red Deer and west of the Saskatchewan border. Travellers welcome the warm breeze that melts snow and ice, but motoring through slush and mud isn't always pretty. Yet, after frigid winter temperatures, Albertans breath a sigh of relief when they see the tell-tale arch over the mountains. With luck, there may be a heat wave!

The town of Chinook, Alberta seems a logical place to be warmed by the west wind, but Calgary is no stranger to chinooks. You are even more likely to experience the balmy winter weather in Waterton and the Crowsnest Pass. Also, chinook winds blow through Pincher Creek, Cowley, Lethbridge and Fort Macleod, a region that averages 30 to 35 days of chinook weather per year.

In 1992, Claresholm recorded the highest February temperature in Canada: 24 C! Thirty years earlier, in 1962, Pincher Creek claimed the most dramatic fluctuation. The temperature rose by 33 C in a single hour between midnight and 1 a.m. As well, Cardston residents have stories to tell. One year, townspeople and TV reporters claimed a chinook swept right down Main Street. On one side, the snow disappeared. On the other side, a bitterly cold Arctic mass kept snow and ice on the ground.

TRAVEL TIPS

Check road conditions in winter before you travel. When you're travelling in chinook country in winter, keep your windshield washer tank full. One day, the roads may be dry as a bone. The next day could bring significant snowfall, and a few days later, as a chinook blows through, there is so much slush and mud, you can't keep your windshield clean.

Phone: 1-888-298-5855

E-mail: info@pincher-creek.com

www.pincher-creek.com/windenergy

Derived from the Chinook language spoken by the First Nations tribe living along the Columbia River, the word *chinook* means *snow eater*. Soon fur traders were passing along true stories and tall tales about chinooks.

Facts confirmed by contemporary weather bureaus are almost as unbelievable as the tall tales. First, warm winds pick up moisture on the coast. Rain on the western slopes means dry winds reach Alberta. With every elevation drop of 100 metres, the temperature becomes 1 C warmer. A deep freeze might grip the plains. Then suddenly, warm west winds can boost temperatures by 30 C or more. The chinook could last less than a day or stay for a week before weather returns to seasonal norms.

People love the relief from winter, but the warm winds bring complications, too. Scientists have documented a relationship between chinooks and mood swings, migraines, sleeplessness and depression. Gardeners know that scant snow cover means losing plants to winter kill. Trees and flowers are tricked into believing spring has arrived. They bloom. Then the return of winter freezes delicate blossoms. Trains have been derailed by chinook winds and sudden temperature changes have cracked car windshields.

Yet when the sun sets behind a striking chinook arch and locals know the warm winds are approaching, most Albertans are happy to be just where they are – in chinook country.

Chinook Country Tourism serves large and small communities of southwest Alberta, and the vast area has something fascinating for most interest groups.

Some communities promote outdoor activities. At little expense in small communities, you can golf and meet the local people.

Boat tours are offered at Cardston and Waterton Lakes National Park.

Some communities adopt unique themes to attract tourists. Nanton, on Highway 2 south of Calgary, has its Nanton Lancaster Society Air Museum, but it also welcomes you to its antique and art walk in the downtown. There, you can see what earlier Albertans treasured and took for granted. Better yet, you can buy the antiques to add to your own treasure trove.

Pincher Creek has its rodeo in mid August, but in June, its Cowboy Poetry Gathering attracts cowboy word weavers from near and far to read and share their work.

Chinook country is a special place to live and visit – not simply because of the chinooks. Learn more at www.chinookcountry.com or www.albertasouthwest.com.

23 Citadel Theatre

Joseph Shoctor, a man of infinite talents and energy, grew up in the inner city. His interest in theatre was an early one. As a high school student, he created, produced and directed Victoria High School Varieties. He studied law at the University of Alberta, serving on the student council and taking part in a variety of clubs and organizations. Later on, he also became interested in football and was one of the original founders of the Edmonton Eskimo Football Club.

As a former "inner city kid," Mr. Shoctor was keenly interested in revitalizing the downtown area whether it was Jasper Ave. or the Old Towne Market Project.

Another passion was the United Way. After working with the organization for several years, he became its campaign chair and led a campaign that helped Edmonton surpass its goal for the first time in three years.

The building housing the Citadel Theatre is a work of art in itself. In the winter, its lush tropical gardens and indoor waterfall are especially inviting. But the theatre that began its life in the mind and heart of the late Joseph Shoctor actually started in an old Salvation Army Citadel building, thus its name. After extensive renovations and fundraising, that early building opened in 1965 with a performance of *Who's Afraid of Virginia Woolf?*.

Less than 10 years later, his vision still growing, Shoctor began fundraising again. The present Citadel Theatre opened in 1976 with a production of *Romeo and Juliet*. The first phase contained the large proscenium Shoctor Theatre for main stage productions and two smaller theatres, the Rice and the Zeidler, designed for more experimental theatre and films and lectures.

But the Citadel is much more than a theatre. Let yourself be embraced by the warmth and beauty of the Lee Pavilion with its indoor tropical garden, reflecting pond, winding paths, lush greenery and a truly impressive indoor waterfall. The Lee Pavilion, the Maclab Theatre and the Tucker Amphitheatre were added eight years after the construction of the Shoctor Theatre. Of interest, also, is the fact that the Maclab Theatre is the only thrust stage in Western Canada and one of five in Canada.

Want to know how your indoor tropical paradise looks from the heavens? Then take a wander upstairs, above the Lee Pavilion, to the Tucker Amphitheatre where you'll get a bird's eye view of the gardens.

Part of the Shoctor dream was to foster young talent in Edmonton and so the Foote Theatre School (FTS) was established. Thousands of young people continue to learn from and be motivated by the classes in the impressive classrooms within the Citadel Theatre building. Some classes are offered as summer and school-break camps, while others are longer fall and winter commitments. Scholarships are available and special discounts for FTS students allow them to see and experience Citadel mainstage performances as often as possible. With the firm belief that you're never too young to become passionate about theatre, the school offers classes for ages four and up.

There are also two performance companies for young people at the Citadel – the Young Musical Company for 13- to 17-year-olds, and an advanced performance company that expands on the work of the earlier FTS classes and for which the young people have to audition.

Joseph Shoctor has been described as a lawyer, civic booster, businessman and impresario. He knew his vision of Edmonton as an important theatre centre in Canada required a first-class facility, which he proceeded to establish. Others have built on that vision and the Citadel continues to be a destination for theatre fans from throughout Alberta. And while they wait for the curtain to go up, they can wander in a tropical garden and listen to the waterfall even when it's -30 C outside.

N
102 Ave
23
100 St
99 St
97 St
Jasper Ave

TRAVEL TIPS

The Citadel's East Bound Bistro and Bar offers an eclectic mix of cuisines before or after performances.

Please contact the Citadel Box Office for information about upcoming shows, facility information and Citadel hours.

Location: 101A Avenue (Shoctor Alley), across from Churchill Square, Edmonton

Phone: (780) 425-1820 or 1-888-425-1820

E-mail: boxoffice@citadeltheatre.com

www.citadeltheatre.com

24 CKUA Radio

Canada may have CBC, but Alberta has a public service broadcaster of its own: CKUA. Tootling down the highway, you feel at home anywhere in the province with CKUA on the radio dial and Lionel Rault, Monica Miller or some other virtual pal spinning tunes and dissecting ideas.

A bold experiment from the first, CKUA Radio Network launched November 21, 1927 from a tiny room on the University of Alberta campus with scavenged equipment, a minuscule grant, creative bookkeeping and 500 watts of power. The brainchild of an extension department intent on taking the university to the people, it was Canada's first public and first educational broadcaster. Chosen by CBC as its Edmonton outlet, CKUA shared a remarkable amount of programming with the fledgling network. In a time when radio *was* theatre, especially for rural areas, dramas produced in CKUA's tiny studio opened many ears to the work of Alberta artists – and to the world of make-believe.

> *"Just ask any reasonably successful Alberta recording artist where their record first got played, and the answer is CKUA, always, just always…. Most of them would lie down in front of a train for CKUA."*
>
> *Senator Tommy Banks*
> Edmonton in Our Own Words

In the decades since, CKUA has become a cultural icon. With a legendary library and the will to play the untried but true, the station has helped launch artists of all stripes, including k.d. lang, Jann Arden, Joni Mitchell and Bruce Cockburn. Household names have worked these boards, from Senator Tommy Banks to folk guru Holger Petersen. It's no accident that many go on to play key roles in cultural initiatives ranging from Edmonton's City Media Club to the 1988 Olympic Winter Games. The station, meanwhile, has outlived every other broadcaster in Canada – while surviving its own near-death experience.

That near death could be the scariest act in a drama whose intensity rivals the best CKUA productions. You can find the details in *Radio Worth Fighting For*, written by Marylu Walters to mark the station's 75th birthday in 2002. The condensed version goes like this: CKUA ownership shifted around over the years, to Alberta Government Telephones in 1945, and to ACCESS (a publicly supported educational broadcaster) in 1974. Then in 1994, amid deep budget cuts, CKUA was left dangling. "The government wants the station to survive, but it doesn't want to have to pay for it," news supervisor Ken Regan told a national arts magazine at the time. The station's following was small then, but loyal. One Lloydminster man had donated a transmitter worth $50,000 so his corner of the province could hear the station's eclectic programming. Another benefactor earmarked a six-figure donation to create the survival plan that saved the day.

CKUA survived another wallop in 1997 when funding meant to help the station privatize ran out amid poor management and political squabbling. For five agonizing weeks, the station shut down. Again listeners rallied around, forming a foundation that assumed control from government-appointed directors.

Now independent and fiercely supported, CKUA can be heard across the province on AM and FM via strategically located transmitters – and worldwide on the Internet. As usual, the station was ahead of the pack in going online. Now you can have a taste of home no matter where you roam by clicking ckua.com on your digital dial.

N
102 Ave
Jasper Ave
24
100 Ave
106 St
105 St

CKUA Nuggets

You can tune into CKUA anywhere in Alberta at 580 AM.

For FM frequencies: Edmonton, 94.9; Red Deer, 101.3; Calgary, 93.7.

CKUA has 175,000 Alberta listeners weekly through its network of 17 transmitters and is heard via the Internet in 60 countries.

CKUA was the first broadcaster in the world to provide coverage of a legislative assembly's question period.

For more CKUA, visit Alberta's Arts Heritage (http://www.abheritage.ca/abarts/index.htm) and the CKUA Sound Archives (http://66.244.199.219/CKUA_Archives/eng/index.aspx)

Location: Edmonton: 4th Floor, 10526 Jasper Ave.; Calgary: EPCOR Centre for the Performing Arts, 205 8th Ave. S.E.

Phone: 1-800-494-2582

E-mail: www.ckua.com

www.ckua.com

25 Dr. Karl Clark

In our fast-paced 21st century, almost every Canadian is aware of the boom that has taken place in Alberta because of the development of the Athabasca oil sands. Yet, Dr. Karl Clark, the Canadian who invented the process for separating the oil from the sand, was born in the 19th century, in 1888.

Dr. Clark did not herald great academic or scientific achievements in his early school days in Toronto; at one point, he actually had to be persuaded by his father not to quit school. By the time he was 27, however, he had obtained his PhD in chemistry from the University of Illinois, in the United States.

After working for the Canadian Geological Survey and Mines Branch in Ottawa for a number of years, Dr. Clark moved to the University of Alberta in Edmonton and, in 1921, was appointed the first full-time employee of what is now the Alberta Research Council Inc. (ARC).

At that time, serious research had begun on the Athabasca oil sands, or tar sands as they were known back then, and Dr. Clark was charged with finding a way to use them for the benefit of the province. In the early 1920s, it was generally believed that the tar sands would be used to surface roads. Even then, however, Dr. Clark envisioned that when refining techniques were sufficiently advanced, the greatest potential of the sands would be as a source of crude oil.

The process Dr. Clark developed was based on a simple hot water washing procedure, patented by the Government of Alberta in 1929. However, it was not until after the Second World War, some 20 years later, that its technical viability was proven at a pilot plant the government built on the banks of the Athabasca River. It is this process, scaled up to commercial requirements, that is used in the three big plants operating today.

Between 1950 and until he retired from ARC in 1964, many companies consulted with Dr. Clark about the oil sands, but his longest association was with Great Canadian Oil Sands. This company, which eventually became Suncor Energy Inc., built the first large-scale operation to succeed in the commercial extraction of oil.

IN HIS NAME

Dr. Karl Clark's work and his commitment to it have been recognized in many ways.

Today, the Dr. K. A Clark School opens its doors to elementary school-aged children in Fort McMurray and the Alberta Research Council in Edmonton is on Karl Clark Road.

For more on Dr. Clark, check out *Oil Sands Scientist: The Letters of Karl A. Clark, 1920-1949*, edited by Dr. Clark's daughter, Mary Clark Sheppard, and published by the University of Alberta Press, or the Alberta Heritage Foundation's Alberta Online Encyclopedia at www.abheritage.ca.

Despite his dedication to research, Dr. Clark wasn't only a scientist. He was a professor in the University of Alberta's department of mining and metallurgy and became its head in 1945. He played the clarinet in two orchestras and was also a good carpenter. He particularly loved his family's summer cottage and built two boats for use there. He was married with four children and always stayed in good physical shape, enjoying a variety of outdoor activities.

Dr. Clark died at the age of 78, nine months before industrial production of oil from the Athabasca oil sands of Alberta began in 1967.

The Alberta Research Council Inc. (ARC) is a key instrument for achieving the province's strategic priorities in the area of unleashing innovation. The Government of Alberta invests in ARC to advance the Alberta economy by creating sustainable prosperity – jobs, wealth and well being.

ARC delivers innovative science and technology solutions to meet the priorities of industry and government in Alberta and beyond. ARC accelerates the development and commercialization of products, processes and services in the energy, life sciences, agriculture, environment, forestry and manufacturing sectors. Visit ARC at www.arc.ab.ca.

26 Columbia Icefield

More than 100 icefields line the scenic Icefields Parkway, a 237-kilometre drive between the town sites of Jasper and Lake Louise that's among the world's most spectacular.

The parkway's story began more than 125 million years ago, when a seafloor that covered much of Canada rose and crumbled, forming dramatic mountains around a V-shaped valley. Over time, glaciers gouged that valley into the enormous "U" that now cradles the communities of Jasper, Lake Louise and Banff.

Unlike many mountain roads, the parkway is an easy drive, with numerous pullouts and stopping points. Highlights:

- Athabasca and North Saskatchewan rivers
- Athabasca Falls
- Goat Lick near Mt. Kerkeslin
- Sunwapta Falls
- Columbia Icefield, Athabasca Glacier and Icefield Centre
- Sunwapta Pass, the boundary between Jasper and Banff national parks
- Weeping Wall
- Saskatchewan River Crossing
- Mistaya Canyon trailhead
- Bow Summit and Peyto Lake viewpoint

The mammoth Columbia Icefield in Jasper National Park invites sheer awe in anyone standing small beneath it. This 325-square-kilometre mantle of pale blue ice is the Canadian Rockies' largest icefield, a living endowment from the Ice Age long past. Adding to the intrigue, it's written like a riddle: advancing yet retreating; ages old yet newly formed; unimaginably huge yet a shadow of its former self.

It's a riddle worth investigating, and the green-roofed Icefield Centre across the road from the icefield is a wise place to begin. There, interactive displays and models bring home the icefield's breadth and stunning placement amid many of Jasper National Park's highest peaks. Blanketing a high-level plateau, the icefield is just a remnant of the thick ice mass that mantled most of western Canada's mountains during the last Ice Age. Yet it remains as big as Canada's capital city and deep enough to easily cover Toronto's CN Tower. Straddling the Great Divide, ideally placed to catch much of the moisture carried across British Columbia by Pacific winds, it is nourished by seven or more metres of snow a year.

What defines an icefield? The ability to move. Over time, snow compacted into ice until the entire mass was thick enough to creep downhill under its own weight. Flowing at a snail's pace through gaps in surrounding mountains, it created the great tongues of ice we call glaciers, which continue to creep downhill even as they shrink due to a warming climate.

"The highway to Jasper from Banff, without question the most heavenly road in the world, mountains blue and purple to either side, every bend a breathtaking vista."

Aritha van Herk
Mavericks, An Incorrigible History of Alberta

Most of the Columbia Icefield remains hidden beyond mountains, visible only to climbers, skiers and those flying above, but six glaciers spill out like arms of an octopus. Three of those, the Dome, Stutfield and Athabasca glaciers, can be seen from the aptly named Icefields Parkway.

The Athabasca Glacier, its tongue visible from the Icefield Centre, is the most accessible. In fact, it is our continent's most visited, most studied glacier. Even though the glacier is advancing several centimetres a day, its reach has receded more than 1.5 kilometres in 125 years. That retreat is accelerating, as shown by date markers marching across the moonscape of ground bedrock left behind. The glacier has already lost half its volume, a significant concern since this one body holds the Rocky Mountains' largest reservoir of ice and snow. Major river systems flowing into the Atlantic, Pacific and Arctic oceans depend on the Athabasca for their supply.

One has only to step foot on the glacier to realize how huge the glacier remains. But beware – glaciers hold hidden dangers. Deep cracks called crevasses have caught people unawares, pulling them to their death. Never venture onto the glacier alone and never cross barriers without a guide.

Excellent options for exploring this glacier include guided hikes, guided ski tours, helicopters and giant all-terrain "Ice Explorers." Whichever route you choose, expect to be further awed as you feel and see the power of sun on ice.

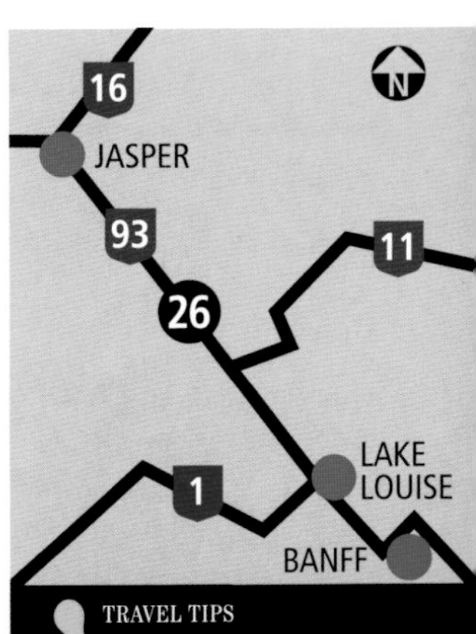

TRAVEL TIPS

Icefields Centre is open May 1 to Oct. 15, weather permitting.

On the glacier, wear warm layers, non-skid footwear and sunglasses.

Book mobile glacier tours while at the Icefield Centre or at 1-877-423-7433. Book guided ice walks at 1-800-565-7547.

Hikes along the parkway with panoramic icefield views include Wilcox Pass and Parkers Ridge. Map and hiking guides are available at www.maptown.com, 1-877-921-6277.

Location: Highway 93 between Jasper and Banff

Phone: (780) 852-6288

E-mail: pnj.jnp@pc.gc.ca

www.pc.gc.ca/jasper

www.icefieldsparkway.ca or www.columbiaicefield.com

27 Cowboy Trail (Highway 22)

If you're talking about the character – and characters – of Alberta, tales of cowboys will mosey into the conversation pretty quickly. Ranching and farming were two of the early occupations in southern Alberta, and the wide open ranges attracted many settlers. Unfortunately, the land wasn't suited to farming, but cattle and horses thrived on the grasslands, and the cowboys were on hand to manage the numerous ranches that began to appear on the prairies and in the foothills.

The intriguing life of the cowboy is the stuff of legend, and this kind of heritage makes Alberta's Cowboy Trail a remarkable route to travel. The trail winds its way past the eastern slopes of the Rocky Mountains from Cardston to Mayerthorpe along Highways 5, 6 and 22.

Over the years, Hollywood has romanticized the cowboy genre. Often, movies have depicted young men on their horses, striding along under the wide blue sky without a care in the world. Of course, the reality of a cowboy's life was very different from the movie version. Early cowboys and ranch hands worked long, hard days on the trails rounding up cattle for branding, dipping, winter feeding or simply to prepare them for shipping to market.

Fortunately, the 700-kilometre Cowboy Trail manages to represent the mythical and the real cowboy equally well through numerous attractions and historic sites. In addition, the trail offers amazing accommodations, authentic western cuisine with Alberta beef well represented and plenty of activities to keep a modern cowboy busy.

Start at the north end of the trail, in Mayerthorpe, and head south along the foothills to Rocky Mountain House, established originally as a fur trade post in the 19th century. You can learn the rich history at the National Historic Site.

Further south on Highway 22, check out Sundre and then the excitement of Calgary. Make sure you take in the picturesque village of Bragg Creek before heading south again to Diamond Valley, which includes the towns of Millarville (and its 110-year-old historic Anglican log church) and Black Diamond/ Turner Valley, where Canada's first crude oil discovery was made. Just south of the Village of Longview is the National Historic Site of the Bar U Ranch where the ranching history of Alberta is celebrated through authentic presentations. Don't miss Pincher Creek and Fort Macleod before heading to Head-Smashed-In Buffalo Jump.

You're getting close to the unspoiled environment in Waterton Lakes National Park where you can take tea at the Prince of Wales Hotel. Then travel over to Cardston, home of the Remington Carriage Museum and a magnificent Mormon Temple, as the last stop on your tour.

Take in a local rodeo and witness the struggle between man and animal. Attend a cowboy poetry festival and listen to poets celebrating the western way of life. Give yourself a genuine cowboy experience by hiring a professional outfitter or guide to take you into the back country where you'll discover some of Alberta's prettiest country. Spend a day shopping for local crafts or western antiques.

Aboriginal suppliers along the Cowboy Trail add their special touch to the experience. There's something for everyone, whether it's a headstall, a saddle or traditional moccasins.

If you're just looking to relax, then check into your choice of accommodation and unwind in a hot tub or treat yourself at a spa.

Whatever you choose to do or see along the trail, you'll discover communities and places that share a rich western and native legacy. You'll see cowboys out herding cattle, families on horseback, or men and women working on the ranch like they have for generations.

Travelling the Cowboy Trail is stepping back in time to a simpler era that symbolized the western way of life.

TRAVEL TIPS

To find out more about the Cowboy Trail, its activities and accommodations, get in touch with the Cowboy Trail Tourism Association, P.O. Box 5245, High River, AB T1V 1M4.

Cattle drive etiquette: don't panic! Slow down, watch and listen for directions, and get the camera ready. The cattle drive, a tradition that's rapidly disappearing, is used to move cattle to and from various grazing locations.

Phone: 1-866-627-3051
or (403) 652-7010

E-mail:
cowboytrail@telus.net

www.thecowboytrail.com

28 Crowsnest Pass

Golfers, prepare for a swing through the Crowsnest Pass Golf Course.

Located in Blairmore, this Les Fuber designed course is both challenging and magnificent. With its men's rating of 73 and its women's rating of 74.6, the challenge is the slope – dictated by rolling terrain and huge elevation changes. This mountain course requires careful club selection and imaginative shot making.

The difficulty of the course, however, is tempered with some of the most scenic views in Alberta. For golfers, it is a hidden gem, and the view from the highway only hints of the grandeur that lies beyond.

The quaint clubhouse has an outdoor patio and lounge facilities, which afford patrons spectacular views of the heart of the Crowsnest Pass.

Enter the Crowsnest Pass, and walk in the footprints of our past among mountain scenery that seems to take eloquently silent pride in presenting a character quite different from its mountain neighbours.

The mountains are neither as high nor as rugged as those near Banff and other mountain areas; indeed, the area offers a natural pass through the mountains. The Crowsnest River is neither as wide nor as raging as some. The less-forbidding landscape meant First Nations had good camping in the wide valleys, and livestock from British Columbia and the western states could be herded through the pass to Alberta ranches.

Today's travellers consider the Crowsnest Pass an easy route to many adventures. In winter, countless skiers and snowmobilers journey along the winding highway to reach the powder skiing at Castle Mountain and Fernie, B.C. and cross country trails at Allison. With more than 1,200 kilometres of groomed snowmobile trails, the Crowsnest Pass is one of the best snowmobile areas in Canada.

Geography dictated the area's history. One day, a mountain tumbled. Another day, an explosion at Hillcrest Coal Mine left disaster in its wake. Fires such as the 2003 Lost Creek wildfire have raged.

In the heyday of coal, work in the coal mines attracted many immigrants from Italy, Poland and Ukraine, as well as some from Britain and the United States. Jobs in lumbering and with railways lured others. The need for services brought more hardworking people, all of whom gained a reputation for resilience.

More recently, fine artists, artisans and outdoor enthusiasts have opted for life at its best in "the Pass."

The small communities of Bellevue, Hillcrest, Frank, Blairmore and Coleman make up the Municipality of Crowsnest Pass and run from east to west along Highway 3. Each has its own dramatic story, so stop often.

Today, recreation properties in the Pass are hot commodities, but locals have always taken pride in the area's fishing, hiking, scenery, wildlife and good times.

Residents have even been known to celebrate their link to the wild side. During Prohibition, imbibing and rum running were rampant. From the teens to the '30s, the Crowsnest Pass had a reputation for lawlessness. Why? Well, the most famous rum runner in Alberta's history, Emilio Picariello, was in his hey-day. Booze flowed. "Emperor Pic" made money, but he also looked after his own – the people of the Pass. A love story gone wrong led to his execution.

Still, the folk hero claims a place of honour during Rum Runners Days in mid-July. After the parade, each town hosts festivities. Finally, the dancing, singing, sports, special tours, midway fun and other entertainments culminate with *Thunder in the Valley*™ Fireworks to celebrate our Alberta heritage.

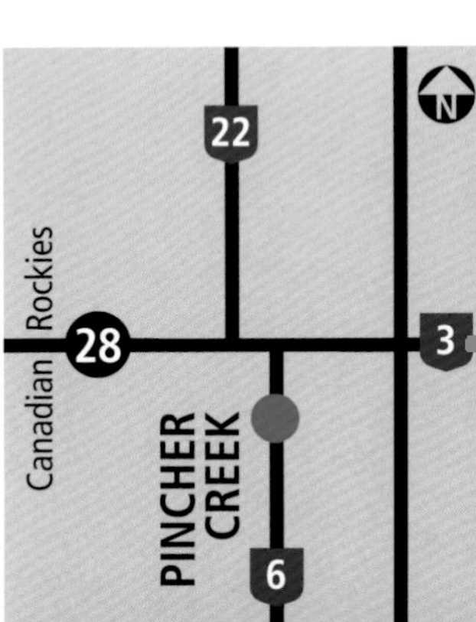

TRAVEL TIPS

The 300-hectare Allison-Chinook Recreation Area and other locations offer year-round recreational opportunities.

Other area visits:

- Crowsnest Museum in Coleman
- the unique shops in historic Downtown Coleman, which is in a National Historic Site
- the Rotational Public Art Gallery and gift shop in Blairmore for local art
- the Allied Arts Public Art Gallery and gift shop on Highway 3 in Frank for local art
- Bellevue's mine tour, and notice the drive-in chapel.

Location: Highway 3, 50 kilometres west of Pincher Creek

Phone: (403) 562-8857

E-mail: edo@crowsnestpass.com

www.crowsnestpass.com

29 Cypress Hills Interprovincial Park

After miles of open prairie on Highway 41 south of Medicine Hat, travellers come upon a unique and special landscape. The Cypress Hills form their own island in the midst of the prairie and have been an escape from summer's baking heat for centuries.

In 1989, the Cypress Hills became Canada's first interprovincial park. The entire park encompasses 39,000 hectares of land, 20,000 of which are in Alberta. On the Saskatchewan side is the famous National Historic Site of Fort Walsh; on both sides of the border, trails allow you to explore a natural world where events in human history helped shaped the West.

Much of the terrain holds surprises. For example, the cottage community at Elkwater is 1,234 metres above sea level. Although nearly the elevation of Banff, it is not surrounded by towering mountains, so few visitors feel they are in high country. The best viewpoint, Horseshoe Canyon, has an elevation of 1,450 metres. The peak elevation at Head of the Mountain is 1,466 metres, making it the highest point between Labrador and the Rockies.

Given the park's name, visitors expect cypress trees, but they won't find any here. Métis called the area "montagne aux cypres," but to them, "cypres" referred to lodgepole and jack pine. Here, even lodgepole pines are a surprise. Native to the mountains, their presence on the plains is unusual.

MEDICINE HAT
N
1
29
ALTA./SASK. BORDER
41
601
13

TRAVEL TIPS

The Elkwater Lake Visitor Centre is open year round, with interpretive programs and events scheduled throughout the year.

The Elkwater Lake Lodge and Resort offers the only accommodation in the park. Call 1-888-893-3811 for reservations.

Campsites are available on the Alberta side of the park.

Winter fun for all skill levels is easy to find in the Cypress Hills.

Location: TransCanada Highway 1 to Highway 41, then 32 kilometres south

Phone: (403) 893-3833

E-mail: cypress.hills@gov.ab.ca

www.cypresshills.com

Learn more about the unusual, and the area's unique geology and climate, human history and, of course, the fauna and flora of the area at the new visitor centre. The hills support many kinds of orchids. The fescue grass, native to the prairie and once grazed by bison, is also carefully safeguarded since the aggressive lodgepole, white spruce and aspen endanger the park's grasslands.

Summer temperatures rise above 30 C and winter days can drop to -45 C. Spring run-off travels in two directions: to the South Saskatchewan River and into Hudson Bay, or to the Milk River, which feeds the Missouri River and flows south.

If you're wondering which creatures drink from these waters, the Cypress Hills are home to cougars and coyotes. After disappearing from the area, elk had to be re-introduced in 1938. Don't be surprised if you see a wild turkey. Not native to the region, they found a home here through an exchange program with an American park.

At the Cypress Hills, you are in a dark sky preserve, so the night skies above you are as important as the land beneath your feet. Achieving the designation required approval from two provincial governments, National Historic Sites of Canada and the Royal Astronomical Society of Canada – no small feat!

Special programs help you learn more about counting stars and identifying astronomical bodies or constellations. As a dark sky preserve, the park and cottage community avoid development that might bring light pollution. What a fantastic place to glimpse a falling star and make a wish!

Camping has a long history in the Cypress Hills. Eight-thousand-year-old campsites have been discovered near the lake, and human presence likely preceded the campsites.

Captain John Palliser and fellow explorers camped here in July 1850, and he described it as a "perfect oasis in the desert we have travelled."

By the 1870s, Métis regularly wintered in the Cypress Hills and, at one site, artifacts from 19 cabins all from prior to 1885 have been found.

The lawlessness of the Cypress Hills, as illustrated by the Cypress Hills Massacre, prompted the government to send the North West Mounted Police (NWMP) west. The NWMP were thankful for the Cypress Hills to escape the hardships of their 1874 march.

Later in the hills, Canadian cowboys camped near grazing cattle herds. Today, modern-day campers enjoy the wide-ranging recreations in the park.

30 Dinosaur Provincial Park

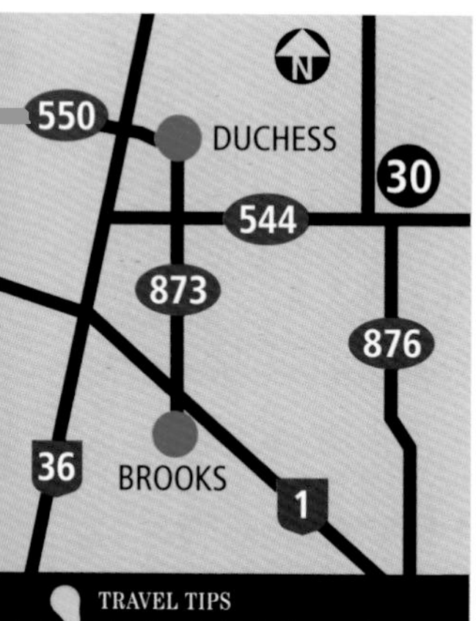

TRAVEL TIPS

Visitor centre hours are 8:30 a.m. to 9 p.m. daily from late May to early September. Hours are 9 a.m. to 4 p.m. the remainder of the year. Closed weekends and holidays.

The park has 126 campsites. Make reservations for summer weekends.

Enjoy bus tours and guided hikes available in summer. Tour reservations are strongly recommended. See phone numbers on the website.

A service centre has washrooms, showers, laundromat and convenience store.

Location: Highway 36 to Highway 544 to Dinosaur Park Road

Phone: (403) 378-4342

E-mail: comdev.communications@gov.ab.ca

www.dinosaurpark.ca.

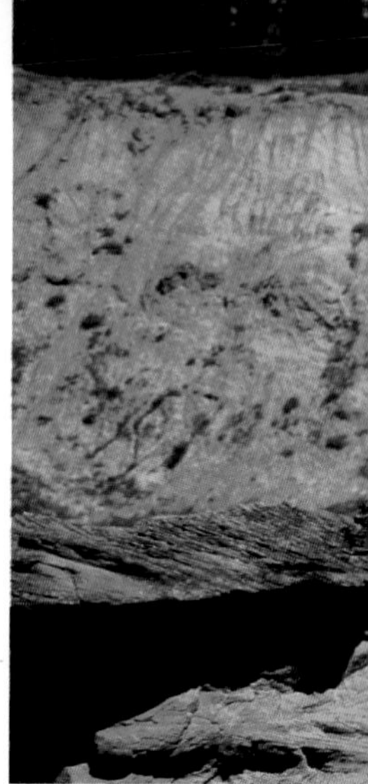

The badlands near Brooks attract everyone serious about bones – ancient dinosaur bones, that is. Tucked away in southeastern Alberta, Dinosaur Provincial Park is less well known than Drumheller's Royal Tyrrell Museum, but the journey to this field station reaps rewards. Here, many of Alberta's greatest, earliest and most diverse species of dinosaur fossils were found.

The site, situated near the banks of the Red Deer River and once known as Steveville, intrigued the world. In 1955, the 73-square-kilometre area became Dinosaur Provincial Park. In 1979, because of the number and diversity of vertebrate species and fossils found here, and because the park is home to endangered habitat, the park was designated a UNESCO World Heritage Site. Today, the park remains the largest and most spectacular fossil bed in Canada.

When you near the park, stop at the viewpoint overlooking the valley. A family once erected its teepee here, perhaps for the magnificent view of hoodoos. With the campsite exposed to the wind, camping in protective woods or near the life-giving river likely seemed more comfortable. The family moved, but their teepee ring still remains hidden in the grass.

From the viewpoint, journey down to the valley of the Red Deer River. As you drive the winding road, you travel to earlier times, evident for those who can read the stories

in the exposed bedrock. Prairie becomes the Bearpaw Formation of about 74.5 million years ago when the Bearpaw Sea covered the area. Then you descend to the Dinosaur Park Formation created two million years earlier. Beneath that is the oldest bedrock in the park, the Oldman Formations dating back 77 million years.

Nestled in the dramatic landscape, the Dinosaur Park Field Station and Visitor Centre await. Nearby are the river and trails where you can explore ancient history. Whether you take a self-guided tour, hike with an interpreter or tour the badlands by bus, you will marvel at the history. In fact, it's an opportunity to see real dinosaur bones still embedded at the sites where they were found but protected from the elements by shelters.

Compared to Drumheller and the Royal Tyrrell Museum, your visit to Dinosaur Provincial Park will be intimate and quiet. Although small, the visitor centre has excellent exhibits, including touchable displays where adults and children feel the texture of geological materials. Your kids will enjoy the wall panel displays – and so will you. Turn one of the photos to find additional photos and information related to birds at home in the sky above the park. Other panels reveal flora and fauna flourishing near the top of the hoodoos or in the grass and soil.

As well, the day-to-day lifestyle of early dinosaur hunter Charles H. Sternberg comes to life at the 1914 replica tent. Through the audiotapes, eavesdrop on conversations he and others might have had about those phenomenal bones!

The first fossils of the Albertosaurus were discovered in Dinosaur Provincial Park, but the most common family of dinosaurs found here are the Hadrosaurs, duck-billed dinosaurs assumed to be strong swimmers.

Many ceratopsian fossils have been unearthed, too. Most similar to modern rhinoceros, they have a bone "frill" like a large protruding collar at the back of the skull.

Another interesting inhabitant was the plant-eater Ankylosaurs. Although slow moving, these animals were well protected from meat-eating predators by their tough skins and protective bone plates. Some of the species had spiky protrusions along each side of their backs.

The bird-like dinosaur Dromaeosaurus had large eyes and a brain proportionately larger than most of its contemporaries. It was the speediest and most agile of the early park residents.

The dinosaurs may be gone, but geology in the badlands remains diverse and captivating, with hoodoos, rills, pipes and tunnels all providing great photo opportunities.

31 Dreamspeakers Film Festival

For four days each June, Edmonton becomes the host of an international gathering of filmmakers, performers and other artists involved in the film making industry. The Dreamspeakers Film Festival gathers these people together to show the rest of the world what aboriginal people can do, and have done, in the field of filmmaking and to celebrate their achievements. The Dreamspeakers Society supports and markets these achievements and provides training for aboriginal people in the arts and culture fields.

The festival started in the early 1990s with a dream of broader screening of Aboriginal films. After trying a few different personas – an attachment to the Global Visions Festival was one and a showcase for a variety of Aboriginal music and crafts was another – Dreamspeakers has evolved into a celebration and showcase specifically for Aboriginal film. It has grown as well as changed over the years and new features have been added. In 1996, the Dreamspeakers Film Industry Awards were launched, paying tribute to the work of all those involved in the making of films, from the writers to the film technicians.

The emphasis of the Dreamspeakers festival is the screening of Aboriginal movies. There are many to see each year. In past years, featured films have included *Legends of the Fall*, *Dances with Wolves*, *Moccasin Flats* and *North of 60*, to name just a few. The year 2006 saw the introduction of the first golf tournament, a fundraising venture with proceeds going to the promotion of Aboriginal arts, culture and heritage. A one-day Film Trade and Career Fair was added to the roster of events in 2006, giving both professional and beginning film makers an opportunity to meet representatives from industry, government and trade guilds to ask questions and make presentations.

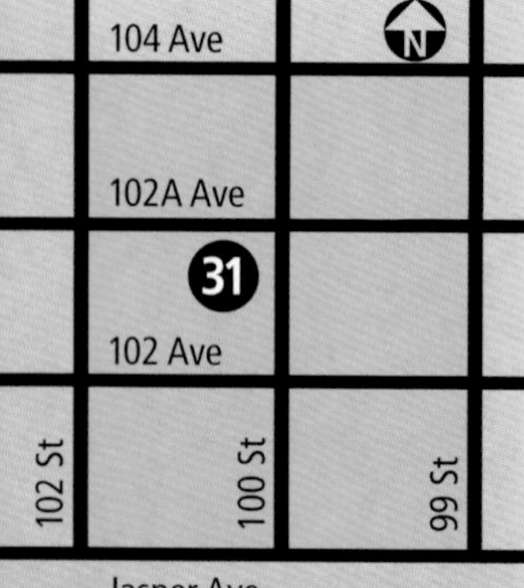

TRAVEL TIPS

From its inception until 2006, the festival has been held at various locations in the arts district of downtown Edmonton, but festival organizers are looking for a more permanent site for the event.

Phone: (780) 378-9609

E-mail: info@dreamspeakers.org

www.dreamspeakers.org

The four-day festival begins with an opening night gala. In 2006, for example, it was held at the Citadel and featured Gil Cardinal's film, *Indian Summer: The Oka Crisis.*

Youth Day is another popular event, this time for the 15- to 20-year-olds, and it involves workshops, guest speakers and more films to study. There is also an opportunity to showcase what young people can do with a two-minute video contest offering cash prizes.

In 2005, the Walk of Honour was created, paying tribute to the aboriginal artists who have pioneered in the film industry. Both nationally and internationally recognized artists attend and the evening finishes with the new inductees making their handprints in concrete near City Hall. The location is a temporary one and festival organizers are working to find a permanent, but visible, location for the future.

One of the inductees for the Walk of Honour in 2006 was Tantoo Cardinal, an actress widely recognized in North America.

Ms. Cardinal was born in Fort McMurray in July 1950. Always a strong advocate for realistic portrayals of aboriginal people in films, she has been working in the film industry since the early 1970s and has more than 50 films to her credit.

She has won many awards including being named the Best Actress of the Year by Maclean's magazine in 1991. In 1993, she won the Best Actress Award at the American Indian Film Festival. In 2006, she was awarded the Sun Hill Award for Excellence in Native American Film Making by the Harvard Film Archive.

32 Drumheller

Some 70 million years ago, the Drumheller area was flat, tropical and crisscrossed by rivers – a perfect spot for dinosaurs. The Ice Age came and went, leaving behind a valley marked by hoodoos, canyons and coulees. Around 11,000 years ago, this valley with its majestic river attracted animals, plants and people. Over time, all that life resulted in layers of fossils. White explorers entered the scene in the 1880s; Joseph Tyrrell sparked the search for Alberta dinosaurs when he discovered a dinosaur skull while prospecting for coal deposits along the river's eroded banks.

Drumheller is still very much in the spotlight. Famous feet have walked Drumheller streets: Clint Eastwood and Gene Hackman (Unforgiven), Brad Pitt and Anthony Hopkins (Legends of the Fall), Jackie Chan (Shanghai Noon) and hundreds more. Filmmakers love this valley's twisted rock formations and almost desert-like landscape.

If Alberta had its own alphabet book, Drumheller would be a shoo-in for "D." D for Drumheller and its dinosaurs, not to mention its dramatic, desert-like badlands. What's more, dinosaurs and badlands go together like desert and dry, for the same wind, water and ice that carve Drumheller's badlands also turn up dinosaurs by the dozens.

The Red Deer River valley plays a distinctive role in the drama that is Drumheller, cradling the town deep below the prairie skyline. As a result, approaching Drumheller is an experience in itself. Suddenly, the road curves downward and rolling fields give way to coulees ridged with eroded rock.

Arriving downtown, recover some of that elevation by climbing the world's largest dinosaur, a 26-metre T-Rex. Stand in the dinosaur's mouth, if you dare, for a spectacular panorama of the town and surrounding valley. Visit the information centre, and you'll walk out with a week's worth of explorations.

Expect to spend a day or more along the Dinosaur Trail, a 48-kilometre loop stretching northwest from Drumheller. It includes the world-class Royal Tyrrell Museum of Palaeontology, as well as such sites and sights as the Homestead Antique Museum, Funland Amusement Park, the Canadian Badlands Passion Play site, the six-seater Little Church, the Badlands Go Kart Park and a ride on the Bleriot Ferry, one of Alberta's few remaining cable ferries. Besides badlands and dinosaurs, the journey dips into such aspects of the region's past as coal (at Midland Provincial Park) and ranching (at Horsethief Canyon).

You'll also want to visit the expansive Horseshoe Canyon, southwest of Drumheller via Highway 9. Considered haunted by aboriginal peoples, this U-shaped canyon offers some of the area's most spectacular scenery and hiking. Be aware, though, that the clay underfoot becomes extremely slippery when wet. Along this road you'll also find the turnoff to Rosebud, a scenic village that owes its revival to a popular dinner theatre.

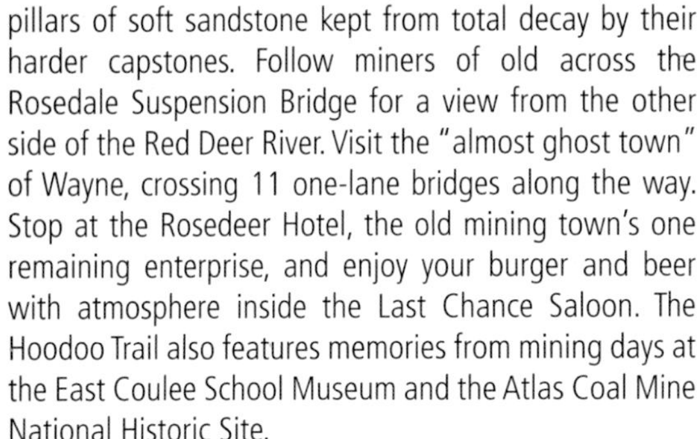

Another day, enjoy the Hoodoo Trail heading southeast from Drumheller. Here you'll see the best of the badlands' hoodoos, pillars of soft sandstone kept from total decay by their harder capstones. Follow miners of old across the Rosedale Suspension Bridge for a view from the other side of the Red Deer River. Visit the "almost ghost town" of Wayne, crossing 11 one-lane bridges along the way. Stop at the Rosedeer Hotel, the old mining town's one remaining enterprise, and enjoy your burger and beer with atmosphere inside the Last Chance Saloon. The Hoodoo Trail also features memories from mining days at the East Coulee School Museum and the Atlas Coal Mine National Historic Site.

Downtown Drumheller deserves attention as well. Walk through time at the Badlands Historical Centre, the region's first fossil museum, whose founder spent a lifetime unearthing finds from the Red Deer River valley. Walk through space along the 15-kilometre riverside system running from town to the Royal Tyrrell Museum. Enjoy the historic buildings dotted around town, count the dinosaur sculptures on many street corners – and take this thought home: "D is for Drumheller."

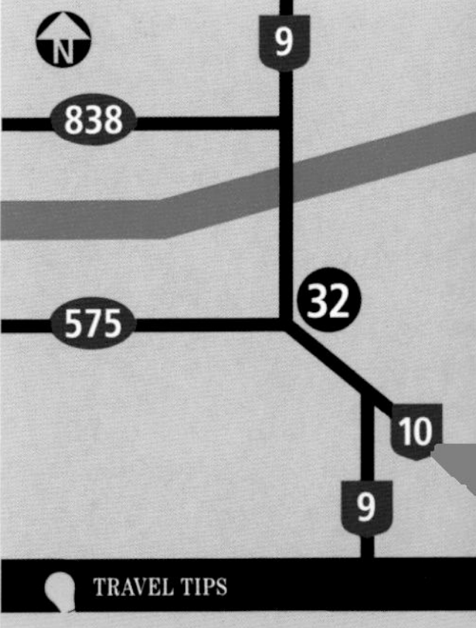

TRAVEL TIPS

Do not climb the hoodoos! Minus their capstones, they erode rapidly.

If you like Drumheller, ask about Alberta's 770-kilometre Canadian Badlands Trail.

Location: 138 kilometres northeast of Calgary.

Phone: 1-866-823-8100

E-mail: info@drumhellerchamber.com

www.traveldrumheller.com

www.canadianbadlands.com

www.dinosaurvalley.com

33 Dry Island Buffalo Jump Provincial Park

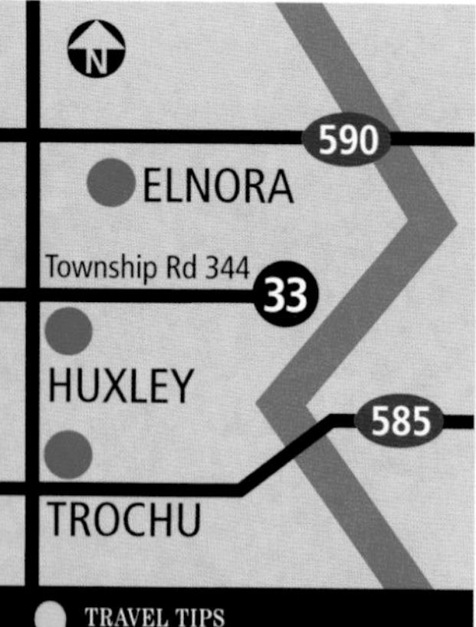

TRAVEL TIPS

The park is open 8:15 a.m. to 12 noon and 1 p.m. to 4:30 p.m. Monday through Friday year round; closed weekends and holidays.

If you visit at dusk in late July or early August, shine your light on the water and watch the annual spectacle of goldeye surfacing to feed on clouds of newly hatched mayflies.

Location: Near Huxley, 15 kilometres east of Highway 21 on Township Road 344

Phone: 1-866-427-3582

E-mail through "Contact Us" on the website.

www.albertaparks.ca

Crunching along Township Road 344 somewhere between Trochu and Big Valley, it seems the rolling ranch land will never end. Then the route curves left and your startled eyes sweep across a sunken moonscape of sculpted cliffs. This is Dry Island Buffalo Jump, the lesser known but steepest, most northerly and arguably most dramatic of Alberta's known buffalo jumps.

The road calls you down into the canyon, but stop at the trailer drop-off first to browse the interpretive signs and soak up the stunning panorama. To your left, set apart from the Red Deer River, the flat-topped 200-metre high dry island for which this park is named seems a sleeping giant, dusky green in early morning light. Far below, the placid river glints in the sun, barely hinting at the power that continues to carve this evolving, yet somehow timeless, scene. At right, prairie sod stops short, like frosting cut by a knife, revealing a giant cake of layered clay.

Along these cliffs, aboriginal hunters once herded bison to certain death. In silence cut only by the clicking of crickets, imagine the din as a river of panicked beasts rolled ever nearer the 45-metre plunge. The thundering hooves, the choking dust, the yells from fur-clad decoys. The fiery heat and bloody stench as women turned a mountain of death into food, hides, shelter and fuel.

Not that we need to rely on imagination alone to piece together the history of this awesome site. Archeologists have found ample evidence of aboriginal life, including bone and pottery fragments, graves and fire pits. The park also contains a significant dinosaur bone bed that is helping paleontologists understand life millions of years ago, when the Albertosaurus roamed. Some of Alberta's best freshwater fish fossils have been found near here as well.

The days of the buffalo jump are gone, but Dry Island Buffalo Jump remains a testimony to the circle of life and death. Standing here, it's easy to see why this canyon inspires repeat pilgrimages by those in the know. Truly stunning, it is a sight to behold.

Suitable buffalo jumps were surprisingly rare for aboriginal peoples centuries ago. Each jump, therefore, saw repeated use. Dry Island Buffalo Jump was likely used sporadically until about 500 years ago. For this reason and more, residents of nearby Huxley made it their goal to protect this dramatic canyon, and in 1970 it became a provincial park.

If weather permits, take the steep gravel road down into the canyon. Unpack a picnic, launch a canoe or sample the maze of paths for a closer look at the sculpted clay and rock-capped hoodoos.

Keep an eye out for the rich variety of animals, birds and plants that thrive in this park, an amazing rendezvous of prairie, aspen parkland and a hint of boreal forest where prickly pear cactus and white spruce exist side by side.

Interpretive signs purposely do not pinpoint the buffalo jump and dinosaur beds. If you come across those sites, please leave them intact as they are protected by law.

34 Dunvegan

If someone is keeping a list of places where the past and the present are beautifully melded together, Dunvegan will be on it.

The Peace, like other rivers, was a major transportation route in northern Alberta 200 years ago, and Dunvegan, on its banks, became the site of a North West Company Post and later a Hudson's Bay Company (HBC) fur trading post and two missions. The river takes its name from the peace that was made between the Cree and the Beaver First Nations in the 1780s and would have seen everything from spruce or birch bark canoes to rafts, York boats and stern-wheeler steam ships sail upon it.

At Historic Dunvegan, the HBC Chief Factor's House, built in 1878, has been meticulously restored, preserving as much of the original building as possible. The Manitoba maples grown from seeds brought by an Anglican missionary in the next decade still grow close by. That same Anglican missionary and his wife also left behind the gravesite of one of their little daughters.

The Oblate fathers established the Roman Catholic St. Charles Mission in 1867 and built its church and rectory in the late 1880s. The outsides of the buildings are tidy and utilitarian and when you step inside the church you are happily surprised by the beautiful paintings and bright colours. Father Emile Grouard (later Bishop Grouard) used one of his many talents to decorate the walls and the altar area – a touch of beauty in a time and place where survival was all that most people could think about.

Before the arrival of the fur traders and missionaries, the First Nations peoples had lived in the area, using local plants for a variety of purposes. Saskatoon berries were an important food in the summer and nettles were worked into fishing lines. Fireweed was used for stomach ailments and meadow rue for perfume.

While the Europeans relied heavily on the Indians for their superior knowledge of survival in Rupert's Land, they often learned through trial and error that could cost them their lives. In the days of the North West Company, before it amalgamated with the Hudson's Bay Company in 1821, several men ate poison water hemlock thinking it was rat root, a harmless plant. One of them died, but the rest recovered after an anxious time.

This beautiful spot was bypassed for development when the railway route was established elsewhere, at a time when transportation was moving away from the water and onto the rails. Eventually, by 1909, Dunvegan had become more of a crossing than a landing point. It depended on a ferry until 1960 when the airy suspension bridge was flung across the river, enabling those in a hurry to fly over this little vignette of Alberta's history.

Today, Dunvegan Provincial Park invites visitors to step off the highway and take a detour through a slower and yet much harsher time. The step back in time is guided by knowledgeable interpreters as well as an audio visual presentation and a number of displays.

If you don't have time to stop, the drive and the lovely views of the river from the road and the bridge are still worth a look.

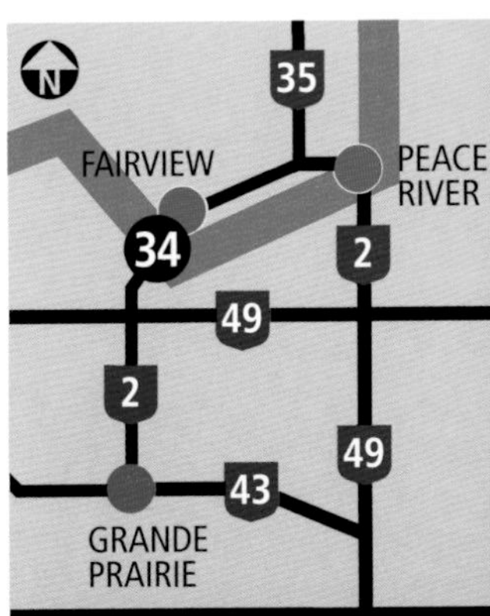

TRAVEL TIPS

Hours of operation: 10 a.m. to 6 p.m. May 15 through Labour Day. Guided tours are available.

Dunvegan Provincial Park includes campsites and a large picnic area for day use.

Just down the road from the park are market gardens where you can buy fruit and vegetables grown just as they were a hundred years ago.

Top off your picnic with an ice cream cone from the Dunvegan General Store.

Location: 90 kilometres north of Grande Prairie just off Highway 2

Phone:
(780) 835-7150 in season
(780) 431-2321 off season

E-mail: hd@gov.ab.ca

www.cd.gov.ab.ca and click on "Enjoying Alberta"

35 Edmonton Eskimos

"Ole Spaghetti Legs," "Gluey Hughie" and "Gizmo." Ninety, 115, 591-417-18. Blue and white, green and gold. In sports, it's all about names, numbers and colours. (Check the sidebar for details!)

These particular ones relate to a storied Canadian Football League (CFL) franchise.

The Edmonton "Esquimaux," later Eskimos, first took to the field in 1892 and won their first of six provincial championships (rugby at the time) before the 20th century had even begun. These gridiron heroes later became the first western team to play in the national football championship Grey Cup (1921), the first to score a touchdown by forward pass (1928) and the first to host a playoff game under the lights (1950). Unfortunately, they also surrendered the first interception return for a touchdown in that 1928 tilt, and lost the night playoff game. That's sports.

The Eskimos found their first glory in the mid-'50s. They were best in the west from 1953 to 1957 and swept the Montreal Alouettes in three consecutive Grey Cup match-ups in '54, '55 and '56.

The next winning streak was bigger and better in every way. Moving next door to the newly constructed Commonwealth Stadium in 1978 greatly increased seating capacity and eventually led to CFL records for attendance at both a regular season and a Grey Cup game. On the field, consecutive championships reached five (1978-82), a CFL record.

These dynasties were built on the principle of "once an Eskimo, always an Eskimo," more than just a motto displayed in the team's dressing room. Many stalwarts have been distinguished with appointments to Halls of

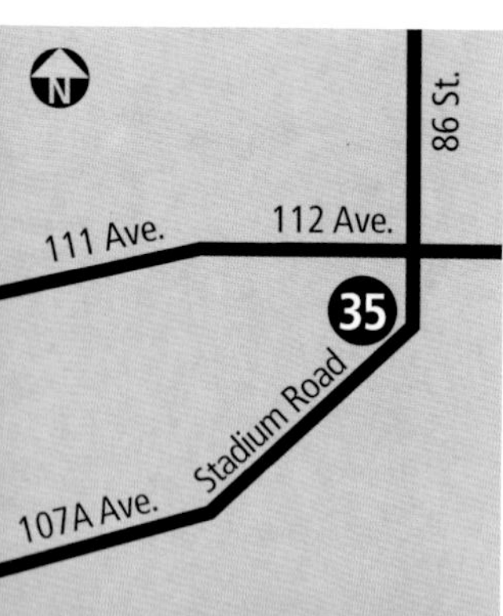

TRAVEL TIPS

Commonwealth Stadium, home of the Eskimos, also boasts a first-class sports and fitness centre.

Sports and fitness centre hours: Monday-Friday, 6 a.m. to 11 p.m. Saturday and Sunday: 8 a.m. to 10 p.m.

Location: Commonwealth Stadium:11000 Stadium Rd., Edmonton (corner of 112 Avenue and Stadium Road, or 86 Street)

Phone: (780) 944-7561

E-mail: comments@esks.com

www.esks.com

Fame and Walls of Honour, including a couple of dozen in the Eskimos' own shrine at Commonwealth Stadium (plus another set of builders in a "contributors" category). The Eskimos count among their alumni a big-city mayor, a provincial premier and a lieutenant governor.

Another guiding principle for what many consider the CFL's flagship franchise has been community ownership. In 1948, 20,000 shares were sold to local residents for $1 each. Noted businessmen took leadership roles and their successors direct the club today. It's an ownership structure found only in the CFL.

Also unique in football: *Ole Spaghetti Legs*, Jackie Parker, a nine-year Eskimo star in a 15-year playing career, won three consecutive Grey Cups as an Eskimo and later coached the team. *Gluey Hughie*, Hugh Campbell, a 30-year CFL veteran, has been outstanding as a player, coach, general manager and President & CEO. Named Esks head coach in 1977, his teams produced six straight first place finishes, six straight Grey Cup appearances and five consecutive wins. *Gizmo*, Henry Williams, arguably the best kick returner in pro football, played 14 record-setting seasons.

Interested in numbers? Read on! Ninety, the number of yards Jackie Parker ran in 1954 for a Grey Cup touchdown and a CFL record for longest fumble return. One hundred fifteen, the number of yards Gizmo Williams ran in 1987 for a Grey Cup touchdown and a CFL record for longest missed-field goal return. And 591-417-18, the Eskimo's won-lost-tied record 1911-2005. Blue and white, the Esquimaux original team colours, changed to green and gold in 1949.

If you want more statistics, the Edmonton Eskimos had 24 Grey Cup appearances up to 2005, winning 13.

The capacity of Commonwealth Stadium is 60,081, and the largest crowd for a CFL regular season game was 62,444 on Sept. 5, 2003 for a Labour Day Classic shutout of the Calgary Stampeders. The largest Grey Cup crowd hosted in the stadium was 62,531 on Nov. 24, 2002 when the Montreal Alouettes took home the cup.

Commonwealth Stadium is the only all-natural grass field in the CFL.

36 Edmonton Folk Music Festival

For the thousands who religiously reserve the second weekend in August for the Edmonton Folk Music Festival, it's an overdose not to be missed. An overdose of music, yes. Boundary-defying music, with moments of bliss. But equally anticipated is the overdose of sights, sun, tastes and smells.

A starring role in this sensual experience is played by the site, Gallagher Park. Nestled in Edmonton's river valley, it's a natural amphitheatre that takes easily to its annual transformation from ski hill to host for 85,000 mellow music fans. Hours before the gates open each day, the periphery jams with action as folkies intent on staking out a spot within spitting distance of main stage try to outwit the latest lottery system. Gradually the patchwork begun by those eager beavers extends up the hill, dominated by the blue and orange of your standard tarps. A time-lapse photo would see bodies flowing on, off and over that green-edged quilt as main stage performances tag team with a dizzying array of workshops. As midday heat gives way to evening cool (or, in the mucky years, a deluge of rain), the hill twinkles with candles and glow sticks. The music just keeps getting better, elegantly backdropped by a downtown skyline that's putting on its best face.

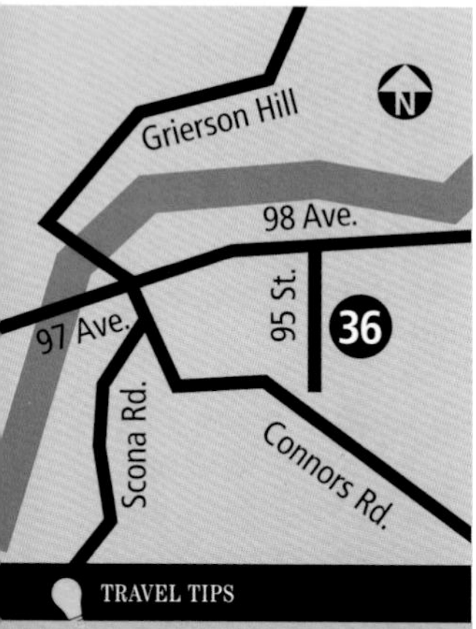

TRAVEL TIPS

Takes place Thursday through Sunday following the August long weekend.

Tickets go on sale June 1, and weekend passes sell fast.

Children, seniors and residents living near the park get in free.

No parking on or around the site. Take Park & Ride or bike and use the free lockup just outside the lower gate.

Great-to-have items include low chairs (less than six inches off the ground), water bottles, rain gear, sun screen, insect repellent and toonies to rent reusable plates.

All tarps and gear must be taken home each night.

Location: Gallagher Park, Edmonton river valley

Phone: (780) 429-1999

E-mail: tickets@efmf.ab.ca

www.edmontonfolkfest.org

Add to that the taste bud-tantalizing elephant ears and kettle popcorn. The beer garden. The chance meetings with friends you haven't seen for exactly a year. The kids' performers and crafts. No wonder weekend passes now sell out more often than not.

One of several events launched in 1980 to mark Alberta's 75th anniversary, the Edmonton Folk Music Festival has earned a spot among the world's elite. It really hit the jackpot in 1994 when Joni Mitchell agreed to give Edmonton her first concert in five years. That coup attracted Elvis Costello in '95 – and Edmonton became the first Canadian folk music festival in 25 years to sell out.

"A festival is always a leap of faith, but if you build it they will come. It sounds corny, I know, but that's my attitude."

Terry Wickham, Festival Producer

Ask organizers to name a secret ingredient and you'll soon hear this word: accessibility. A broad and deep spectrum of world-class music playing at a huge site run mainly by sweat equity adds up to great value, and everything from reasonable concession prices to loose rules about bring-your-own food reinforces that fact.

On the final night, it all culminates in a hug-fest to the tune of that Ian Tyson favourite, *Four Strong Winds*. It's a song whose opening chords bring memories flooding back to a growing throng of folkies.

The Edmonton Folk Music Festival is a bright star in a galaxy of music galas around Alberta. Outside the province's urban centres, for instance, there's the Shady Grove Bluegrass and Old Time Music Festival at Nanton, the intimate Waynefest (attendance limited to 500) at Wayne and the North Country Fair and Solstice Celebration near Joussard. Take in the Big Valley Jamboree at Camrose and the Magnificent River Rats Festival in Athabasca for more of the finest folk sounds around.

A sampling of Calgary's numerous musical attractions includes the Jazz Festival and the Folk Music Festival, plus the nearby Canmore Folk Music Festival.

Check each event's website to confirm dates, locations and details or visit the Alberta festivals page on the Alberta Community Development website through www.gov.ab.ca.

37 Edmonton Heritage Festival

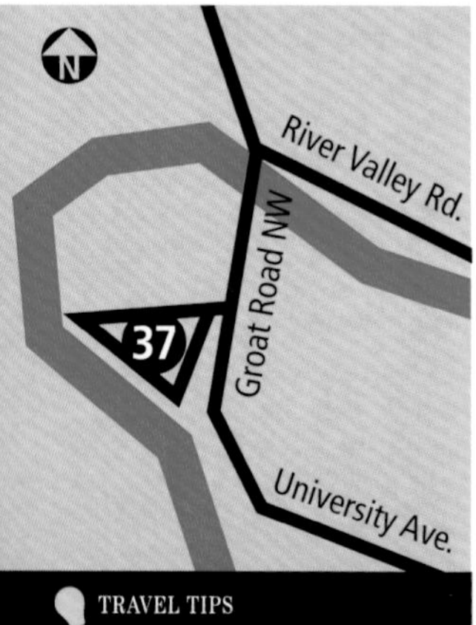

TRAVEL TIPS

You will likely spend a whole day at the festival, so don't forget to take your chair or blanket, water bottles, rain gear, sun screen and insect repellent.

Check the website for a listing of ETS Park & Ride locations as well as ETS bus routes to the park.

Download the festival map and menu in advance.

Location: Hawrelak Park, Edmonton

Phone: (780) 488-3378

E-mail: info@heritage-festival.com

www.heritage-festival.com

The August long weekend has long been a time to recognize the wonderful and varied cultural heritage of the province. Beginning more than 30 years ago, Heritage Day was celebrated in Edmonton with a multicultural concert at Fort Edmonton Park. The venue was moved to Hawrelak Park in 1976 and has been growing ever since. Close to 400,000 people come out over the weekend to see more than 55 different countries demonstrating their particular culture through music, dance, theatre, sport or what have you. It's a remarkably colourful sight, but it's perhaps the aromas that keep people coming back – the aromas of all that ethnic cooking.

You buy food tickets in advance or at numerous food ticket booths, a system the organizers have found considerably speeds up the process of serving the multitudes. Then wander around 'til you find a meal that appeals, or check out your favourite pavilion. Then find a nice patch of sun or shade, depending on your preference, and eat and drink in the midst of all the sights and sounds. It is a very inexpensive weekend of fun, as there is no entry fee to the park. There is no parking at the site, so you are invited to walk in, ride your bicycle or take the Park & Ride service from depots throughout the city. People are requested to bring a donation for the Edmonton Food Bank as their price of admission, something that has made the Heritage Festival the food bank's single largest annual food drive. Everyone wins.

There's a main stage with a number of events, but each pavilion performs its own show, either on the hour or on the half hour, so you can see many of them over the three days. The roaming performers are great fun, too, as they will keep you amused if you have to line up for food tickets or are waiting for a bus to take you home.

Attending Heritage Days is a great way to spend the day or even the whole weekend, watching performances from all over the world, eating new and different foods (or sticking to your old favourites), and enjoying the outdoors with friends and family. It's a non-alcoholic event, so a great place to take the kids. And a great place to be reminded of all the cultures that comprise and enhance Alberta.

The Edmonton Heritage Festival takes place at William Hawrelak Park on the North Saskatchewan River. The park is named after one of Edmonton's most controversial mayors who, during his three periods of office in the 1950s, '60s and '70s, did not complete any one of his terms.

Despite this dubious distinction, his legacy to Edmonton includes what is now the Stanley Milner Library, a new city hall (built in 1956 and replaced with the current city hall in 1992), a number of beautiful parks (including the one now named after him), the Valley Zoo and the Yellowhead Trail through Edmonton. Edmonton's first mayor of Canadian Ukrainian descent, he died during his third term in office.

38 Edmonton International Fringe Theatre Festival

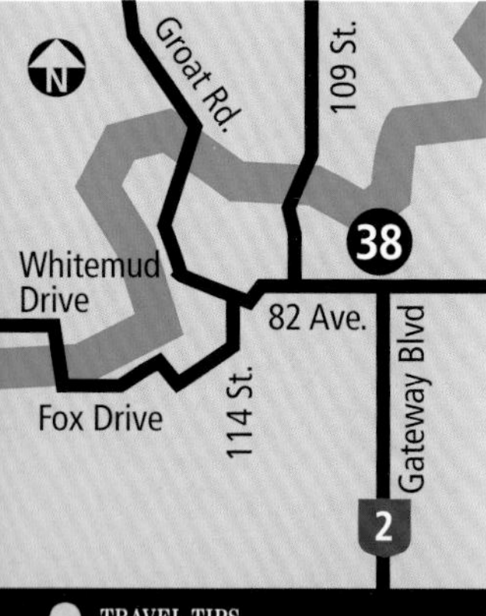

TRAVEL TIPS

Buy an official Fringe program! With almost 150 plays on offer, your program becomes your best friend.

The Fringe is a busy place so it's best to take advantage of ETS Park & Ride and bus services to Old Strathcona.

Scan the theatre critic reviews and talk to people in line about plays they've seen to get an idea of what will appeal to you.

Location: TransAlta Arts Barns, 10330 84 Ave., Edmonton

Phone: (780) 448-9000

E-mail: fta.fringetheatreadventures.ca

www.fringetheatreadventures.ca

For 11 craze-filled days in August, life is truly a stage in Edmonton's historical Old Strathcona neighbourhood as the Edmonton International Fringe Theatre Festival unfolds its multi-coloured curtain. The largest and oldest Fringe festival on the continent features more than 140 unjuried and uncensored shows from around the world, an entertaining street scene and a plethora of food vendors and craftwork by local artisans.

Within a five-block radius you'll find the Fringe's 13 indoor theatres, two outdoor stages, 14 BYOVs (Bring Your Own Venue) and a gaggle of busking circles. When one show ends in a venue, another begins an hour (or less) later; more than 1,000 performances delight throngs on the indoor and outdoor stages from noon to midnight. That definitely gives you a lot of choice!

Check out the Fringe program to see what appeals to you and buy your tickets in advance. Or wait to see what friends and critics have to say, talk to people in the line-ups or beer tents or just take your chances – you might discover the next Fringe hit!

Roughly equal parts street performance, theatre and party, this is the kind of affordable festival where there's something for everybody – performers and patrons alike. Clowns, jugglers, poets and multi-media artists all share performance spaces, bringing both classics and new works to the stage. The offerings range from light-hearted sketch comedies to challenging performance pieces. Artists are selected on a non-juried basis by lottery. They are encouraged to produce whatever work tickles their fancy, are provided with a schedule of performances in a venue with professional technicians and all the basic requirements for theatre. As a reward for their hard work, 100 per cent of the ticket sales are returned to the artist.

Those interested in such an arrangement for the indoor stage spots are chosen by a lottery system. Applications come from all across Canada and all over the world. Fifty per cent of the assignments are made to local producers from the greater Edmonton region, 30 per cent to other Canadian and United States applicants and 20 per cent to outside Canada and the United States. No jury is involved and the budding theatre companies can try out whatever they think might work. This is what gives the Fringe its freshness and innovative appeal and why it's one of Edmonton's most beloved summer events.

The Edmonton Fringe Festival was the first Fringe festival in North America and remains the largest. The catalyst for the current 23 Fringe festivals spread around the continent, it began in 1982 and was modelled after the Edinburgh Fringe Festival with the major difference (as far as theatre goers are concerned) being that the venues are all located in one area instead of being spread all over the city.

Old Strathcona becomes a wonderful space for people to "hang out" with their friends and allows the bona fide theatre-goers to hop easily from one play to another. Standing in line is part of the Fringe experience, so make sure you join the queue for at least one play.

39 Edmonton International Street Performers Festival

The Edmonton International Street Performers Festival helped launch three other Alberta festivals and remains intimately tied to each one.

Soon after taking the reins in 1999, Shelley Switzer began fielding "How do you do that?" inquiries from Spruce Grove and Grande Prairie. She promised to give both a hand if they could find some seed money. Soon Red Deer came calling as well. All three have since launched annual street fests, with Edmonton serving as their programming partner.

Each of the four festivals has its own flavour and no two have exactly the same lineup, but they share talent when they can. Performers can now fly into Alberta, work the Spruce Grove festival over Canada Day, hit Edmonton the next week, zip up to Grande Prairie around the third week of July and then head down to Red Deer.

All the more reason why the best in street fest talent is bound to head our way.

It's a sparkling day, the summer is young and gaggles of engaged fans give Churchill Square a friendly atmosphere. The Edmonton International Street Performers Festival has descended for 10 days of hijinks and humour, and the city couldn't be happier. Even the crowds that circle each act are shaped like smiles.

To the youngsters giggling at the clowns or holding their collective breath at the high-altitude acrobatics, early July in Edmonton has always meant StreetFest. Part of the city's fabric for more than two decades, this festival of fun is Canada's oldest celebration devoted exclusively to street theatre.

It all started in 1985, when Sheldon Wilner lobbed an idea to kindred spirit Dick Finkel, then living in Winnipeg. Wilner was running Summerfest, an umbrella for the music, theatre and visual art events that have since morphed into the festivals Edmontonians know and love. Blessed with funding for a new stream of programming, Wilner invited Finkel to help take it to the streets.

Back in 1985, most Canadians didn't yet know what

street performance was all about. Taking advantage of that blank slate, Wilner and Finkel sprinkled downtown Edmonton with 20 outlandish, yet highly skilled entertainers, whose sole purpose was to make people laugh. Those who came still recall wire walker Phillipe Petite, who spectacularly crossed Churchill Square high above the trees.

Wilner left Summerfest the next year, but Finkel produced StreetFest through 1999, when Shelley Switzer took over as artistic producer. She is supported by a small summertime crew and more than 200 volunteers.

The world-class Edmonton StreetFest features an all-star lineup of 60 or more performers. For every one who comes, another 10 clamour to experience this festival, where performers' talent is respected, crowds are generous and the sun likes to shine.

Always flexible, the festival now attracts more than 200,000 people a year. The young set enjoys Kids' World, a big tent housing tons of fun. The adventurous can attend "Be Your Own Busker" workshops. Adults pile into Late Night Madness, indoor events that combine performers in unique and synergistic shows. Families enjoy their own sit-down events, with humour that's less risqué.

"The beautiful thing about street performance is that you don't buy a ticket first. You decide what the ticket value is at the end of the performance. And if you don't have money to drop in the hat, your 'thank you' is always appreciated."

Shelley Switzer, Artistic Producer Edmonton International Street Performers Festival

Thanks to sponsorship from EPCOR, Switzer's office also runs Comedy Cares, taking humour to hospitals and care facilities all year round. Family gatherings, corporate meetings and other community groups also tap the festival's database of funny folk, a good number of whom live right here in Alberta.

But the heart of the Edmonton International Street Performers Festival remains the outdoor performances in and around Churchill Square. Here you'll find street acts, roving character actors, dancers, mimes, musicians, puppeteers and performance artists of every kind. Colourful, quirky, entertaining or just plain silly, they're certain to add sparkle to your day.

N
102A Ave
39
102 Ave
101 St
100 St
Rue Hull
Jasper Ave

Street Festing in Style

The festival is free and open to all.

Most days run 11:30 a.m. to 10 p.m., rain or shine.

Stop at the onsite information station for festival guides, performance updates and change for your big bills.

Performers earn their keep by passing the hat. Be generous if you can.

Turn off your cell phone or expect to be shamed.

Location: Sir Winston Churchill Square, 99 Street and 102 A Avenue, Edmonton

Phone: (780) 425-5162

E-mail: info@edmontonstreetfest.com

www.edmontonstreetfest.com

40 Edmonton Oilers in the Dynasty Era

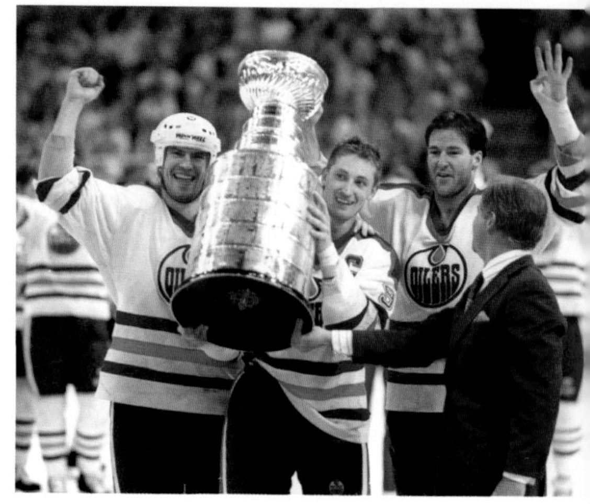

The Edmonton Oilers began life in 1972 as part of the newly formed World Hockey Association. Albertans have always been keen on hockey, whether it was on the farm pond, in the local rinks or in front of the TV on Saturday nights. But the newly formed Edmonton team was a long way from the National Hockey League (NHL). They struggled in the early years and in spite of huge turnouts for games, the Oilers had trouble getting into the playoffs.

In 1977, Peter Pocklington became sole owner of the team and in the next couple of years signed on new players, among them a somewhat gangly 17-year-old named Wayne Gretzky.

Not long afterwards, the Edmonton Oilers became part of the NHL with their focus placed firmly on the Stanley Cup. It took four years of hard work to build a team that could compete at that level, but they were a young, strong team featuring forwards Mark Messier, Glenn Anderson and Jari Kurri, defenceman Paul Coffey, goaltender Grant Fuhr, and Gretzky as its captain. In 1983, they made it to the Stanley Cup final series. They were defeated by the New York Islanders, but the following year, 1984, the Edmonton Oilers won the Stanley Cup.

The Oilers' "dynasty era" had begun. Not only did they win the Stanley Cup five years out of seven (in 1984, 1985, 1987, 1988 and 1990), they constantly broke other records.

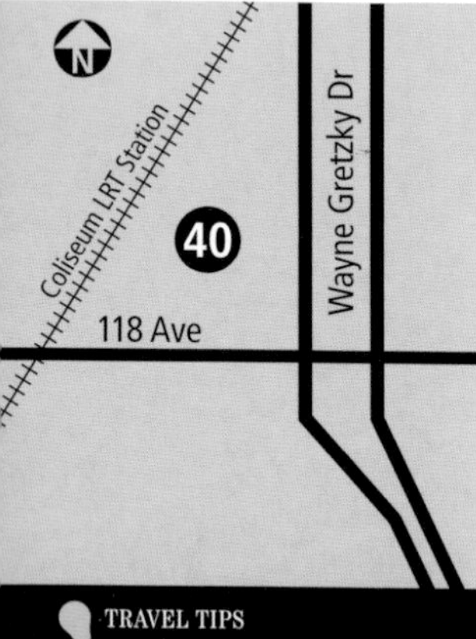

TRAVEL TIPS

Rexall Place, home of the Edmonton Oilers, is open for hockey games and many other special events.

During games, look up into the rafters for the banners celebrating division wins and Stanley Cups.

Look on the Rexall Place north plaza for a life-sized, 6,000-kilogram statue of Wayne Gretzky.

If you call in advance, you can arrange a 30-minute tour of the facility.

Location: Rexall Place, 7424 118 Ave., Edmonton

Phone: Rexall Place: (780) 471-7210

Oilers office: (780) 414-4000

www.edmontonoilers.com

It was an era of records. In the 1983-1984 season, Gretzky broke the NHL record for the most consecutive games with at least one point scored – 51. In November 1984, the Oilers set a record for the longest undefeated streak – 15 games. Another record was set in January 1986 by defenceman Paul Coffey who, in 28 games, scored 16 goals and recorded 39 assists. A few months later, Coffey broke Bobby Orr's record of most goals by a defenceman in a single season by scoring his 46th and 47th goals in one game.

The line-up of records continued in November 1986 with Gretzky scoring his 500th goal in fewer games than any other player. The Oilers set a record for most goals by one team in a playoff game when they defeated Los Angeles 13-3 in 1987, and in May 1988 Grant Fuhr established the single season playoff record by a goalie, winning 16 games.

Gretzky's trade to Los Angeles in August 1988 brought howls of protest from fans and it took the next year to pull the team back together. By the 1990 playoff series, they were ready, and the Oilers, with a team of new young players and without Gretzky, won their fifth Stanley Cup in seven years.

Arguably one of the greatest hockey players ever, Wayne Gretzky was a big part of the glory years of the 1980s.

He won 10 Art Ross Trophies as the NHL's leading scorer, nine Hart Trophies as the league's most valuable player and two Conn Smythe Trophies as most valuable player in the playoffs. He became the NHL's all-time leading goal, assist and point producer for both regular season and playoffs. He also earned five Lady Byng Trophies as the NHL's most gentlemanly player.

His number, 99, is the only one to have been retired by the entire National Hockey League.

Gretzky was inducted into the NHL Hall of Fame immediately on his retirement at the end of the 1998 -1999 season, with the usual five-year waiting period waived. He has his own wing in that hall of fame as well as having a road named after him – the former Capilano Freeway in Edmonton was renamed Wayne Gretzky Drive.

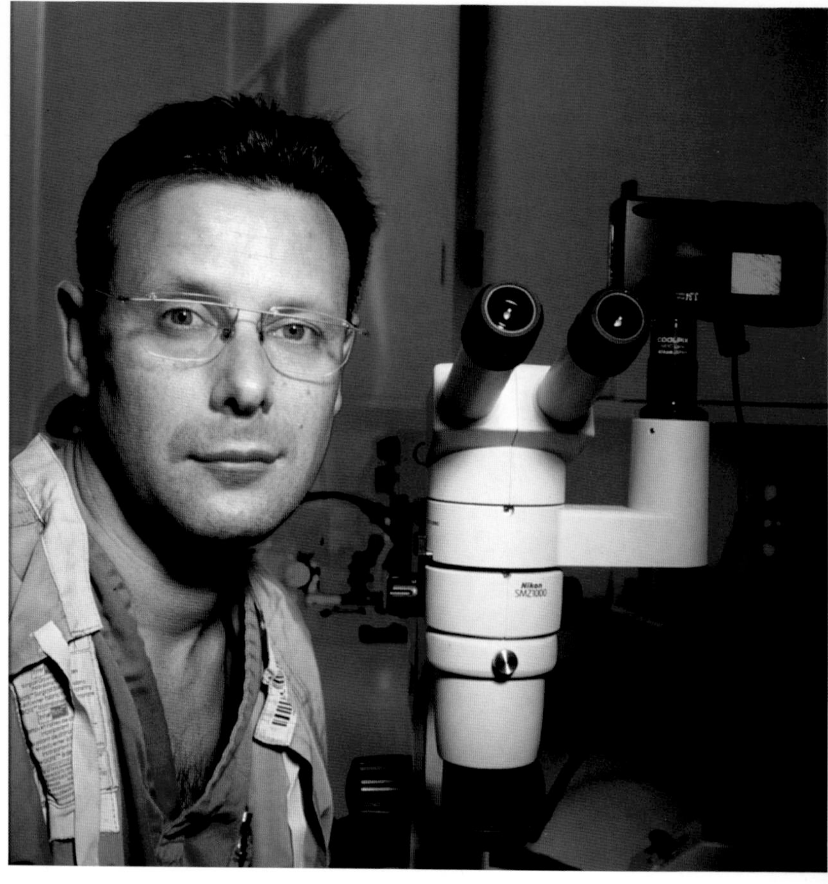

41 Edmonton Protocol

Edmonton Protocol is the name given to a procedure developed by a team of researchers at the University of Alberta for transplanting healthy islet cells into people with Type 1 diabetes.

Diabetes, a metabolic disease that requires medical diagnosis and treatment, occurs when the body can't deal with the glucose or sugar in its blood system. Normally, the pancreas produces the hormone insulin that helps glucose enter the blood stream where it can be used as fuel. Sometimes this system breaks down and the pancreas either stops producing insulin altogether (Type 1 diabetes) or produces some insulin, but not enough (Type 2 diabetes).

In 1922, a major breakthrough in the treatment of diabetes was discovered when the team of Dr. Frederick Banting and Charles Best injected their young patient with an extract from the pancreatic gland, signaling the first treatment for a disease that had always been untreatable and fatal.

The next major breakthrough in this treatment came in 1999 when an Edmonton man received the first clinical trial of the technique that came to be known as the Edmonton Protocol. The research team, headed by Dr. James Shapiro and based at the University of Alberta, had succeeded in transplanting healthy islets, the insulin-producing cells, into a human being. With the help of anti-rejection drugs, the islets went to work and started producing insulin in their new home.

Today, islet transplant does not involve major surgery, which helps the patient recovery relatively quickly from the procedure. The new islets are inserted directly into the liver by needle after the patient has received a local anesthetic. Since the liver has the ability to regenerate itself, when it receives the islets it produces new blood vessels around them. Then the new insulin can get into the blood stream where it is needed.

The University of Alberta team has been working on the project since the early 1980s, and the Edmonton Protocol is acknowledged worldwide as a major leap forward in the treatment of diabetes. However, the struggle isn't over yet. The present procedure is helping patients to stay off insulin injections for years at a time, but not for life. Some have had to go back to the injections, but their bodies still produce some insulin – something that wasn't happening before the islet transplants.

In the first couple of years after the first successful islet transplant, approximately 500 people throughout the world were given a new lease on life. As a result of the success, more money has been directed toward islet transplantation research and better facilities have been built to accommodate it. Aside from the incredible research that is being done, it is the dedication of the scientists, researchers and physicians that has made, and will continue to make, the difference to millions of people suffering from the disease.

With this amazing process now available, it may seem strange that no more than 500 people in the world have been able to take advantage of it. The major problem is the availability of the islets from healthy pancreatic glands. Each patient needs two transplants of the islets for the procedure to be successful, and those islets can only be found after someone has died and donated organs to medicine.

The complete treatment is expensive, partly because of the need for anti-rejection drugs, something the research is now focusing on as well. At present, the drugs may have long-term health effects themselves and so the procedure is not safe for children and is not recommended for those whose diabetes can be controlled with diet and insulin injections.

Visit the University of Alberta website at www.ualberta.ca and search "Edmonton Protocol" for a listing of various articles and other information.

42 Edmonton Radial Railway Society

Peer down – way down – as the streetcar clackety clacks along the upper deck of Edmonton's High Level Bridge, and you're transported back to the earlier era when rail ruled this roost. Directly below glints the North Saskatchewan River, the original fur trade highway. At its edge stands the museum homestead of John Walter, whose ferry predated this bridge; nearby is an ancient burial ground that predates the city.

Besides inviting passengers to time travel, the streetcar provides a handy summertime link between downtown and Old Strathcona.

While aboard, feel free to quiz the friendly pair who take your ticket and operate the car. They'll answer with pride, for they're with the Edmonton Radial Railway Society (ERRS) – the volunteers behind both this vintage crossing and streetcar service at Fort Edmonton Park. The first streetcars rattled along Edmonton streets in 1908, they'll say. That era closed Sept. 2, 1951 with a last run across the bridge, and for awhile the quieter trolley bus was king. All streetcars except No. 1 were sold for use as summer cottages, chicken coops, or worse.

Car No. 1 first returned to operation Thanksgiving weekend 1979 as a salute to Edmonton's 75th birthday. For three memorable days it carted happy passengers across the High Level Bridge, towing a generator car. That successful coming-out spurred volunteers to form the ERRS. They set up shop in Fort Edmonton Park, whose long-term plans already included a streetcar line.

The rest is history, as they say. After building its own workshop, modeled after the 1908 Strathcona streetcar barns, the society laid two kilometres of track and launched streetcar service at Fort Edmonton Park in 1984. The line has carried more than two million passengers, gaining acclaim as a particularly authentic and well operated display.

Whitemud Dr

42

Fox Dr

TRAVEL TIPS

The High Level Bridge streetcar operates 11 a.m. to about 4 p.m. (extended to 10 p.m. during the Fringe Festival) May to mid-October.

The 30-minute round trip runs from 103 Street and 85 Avenue in Old Strathcona to Jasper Avenue between 109 Street and 110 Street.

Fort Edmonton Park streetcar service is free with park admission.

Location: ERRS headquarters is the streetcar workshop, to the left of the steam train platform immediately inside Fort Edmonton Park.

Phone: (780) 437-7721 (High Level Bridge) or (780) 496-7381 (Fort Edmonton Park)

E-mail: info@edmonton-radial-railway.ab.ca

www.edmonton-radial-railway.ab.ca

Meanwhile, the ERRS has restored streetcars from as far away as Japan. Many arrive in sorry states that tug at the heart, particularly for those who grew up with the little engines that could. The society is unique in its ability to build replica parts when no originals are available, addressing a major sticking point in restoration work. It is stockpiling rail with the aim of extending the Fort Edmonton Park line across nearby Whitemud Creek to connect with the LRT. The creek crossing will use a Bailey bridge, named after a Second World War engineer who devised a method of building, repairing and moving bridges in sections.

Speaking of bridges, the society had always dreamed of restoring regular streetcar service across the High Level Bridge, but right-of-way issues, lack of electricity and other hurdles stood in the way. A request by the Fringe Theatre Festival in 1995 to serve outlying sites via streetcar proved the tipping point. A hit in 1995, the streetcar returned for a repeat performance in 1996. That success galvanized volunteers into extending streetcar service north across the bridge.

The first streetcar ever to roll across the High Level Bridge made the journey on Aug. 11, 1913. Streetcars shared the High Level Bridge with the Canadian Pacific Railway: trains on an inner track, streetcars on two outer tracks.

Streetcar trips almost 100 years ago weren't for the faint of heart.

As a concession to passengers nervous about riding North America's highest streetcar river crossing, in 1918 the cars were adapted to ride on the left-hand side of the bridge, so passengers could alight in the centre of the bridge rather than into space in case of emergency. Fortunately, the system never needed to be tested.

Nowadays, ERRS members devote Saturdays to regular maintenance, crucial to its well-oiled service. Having reproduced parts as small as window lifts and as large as an entire chassis, the ERRS shares some of its castings with other museums.

---

43 Elk Island National Park

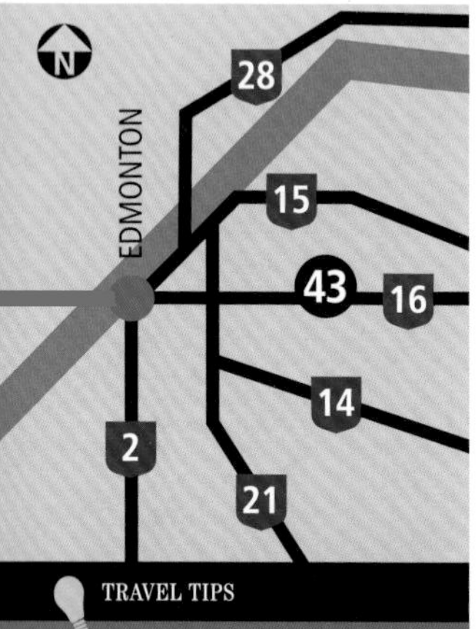

TRAVEL TIPS

The park is open every day of the year, but many services operate only during the summer.

Stay away – at least three bus lengths away – from bison, moose, elk and other large wildlife. Take particular care during breeding season, late July to autumn, and respect trail closures.

Trailhead washrooms, some campsites and a walk near Astotin Lake are accessible to persons with disabilities.

Location: 32 kilometres east of Edmonton on Highway 16

Phone: (780) 922-2950

E-mail: elk.island@pc.gc.ca

www.pc.gc.ca/elkisland

A loon calls, drawing all eyes to the water just in time to see a coyote lope into view, dark against the blazing rays of a setting sun. It's another perfect day at Astotin Lake in the heart of Elk Island National Park: a row on the lake, a stroll on the boardwalk, some sandcastle building, nine holes of golf – and now, an evening campfire with special effects.

All that, and bison too. Elk Island National Park has so many of these majestic beasts that you must always be on the lookout. Nearing the park's main gate on Highway 16, you may see them grazing inside the fence: wood bison south of the highway, plains bison on the north. Separated to avoid interbreeding, they thrive here in such numbers that dozens have been sent to rebuild herds elsewhere. No wonder international visitors bombard their hosts with requests to experience the bison of Elk Island National Park.

Those who linger find not only bison but elk and beaver and moose and porcupine and grebes and grouse – indeed, hundreds of species that make this one of Canada's best spots to view birds as well as beasts. Designated a dark sky preserve in 2006, it's also an excellent place to watch the night sky because artificial lighting is kept to a minimum.

Numerous trails of varying length and difficulty meander through rolling aspen parkland, perfect terrain for hiking and cross country skiing. Camping is an option all year, with your choice of semi-serviced, group or primitive sites. You can explore the islands that dot Astotin Lake in

peace, thanks to a ban on motorized craft. All this adds up to abundant tranquility – as long as you treat the wildlife with respect.

Created in 1906 as Canada's first national game preserve, Elk Island National Park protects some of Canada's most endangered habitat: the Beaver Hills ecosystem. This transitional zone between the boreal forest and the interior grassland plains once stretched vast across the centre portion of the continent, but is now reduced to isolated pockets. Born as an island haven, the park is now recognized as an important link in efforts to ensure an expansive corridor for wildlife movement.

Elk Island National Park preserves intriguing snippets of human heritage as well. At least 224 aboriginal sites provide insights into life as long ago as 5,000 years. The park also is home to Alberta's first forest ranger station.

As dusk turns to dark, new characters take to the stage. An owl hoots, flying squirrels perform acrobatics and the sky to the north begins to crackle with the swirling, multi-coloured pulse of Northern Lights: the perfect close to a kaleidoscope of experience that's new every season, without fail.

Elk Island National Park is situated in the Beaver Hills, an area important to the early fur trade. By the late 1860s, local beaver and bison populations were almost eliminated. The area remained mostly untouched through the homestead period, protected in part by its 1899 designation as the Cooking Lake Forest Reserve.

Although the forest was protected, the elk and mule deer were not. Sport hunting and hunting for meat by settlers posed a threat to wildlife populations at the turn of the century.

In 1906, the federal government created Elk Park and constructed a 2.2-metre fence that included the area around present day Astotin Lake. With elk, mule deer and moose inside those fenced boundaries, Elk Park became the first federally controlled big game sanctuary in Canada, marking a new era in conservation. Now dedicated to both preservation and use by the people of Canada, it's a treasured resource and sanctuary.

44 Ellis Bird Farm

The farm yard at Ellis Bird Farm has been established as a demonstration wildlife habitat area to show others how their own backyards, city or country, can be both beautiful as well as attractive to bees, butterflies, birds and other wildlife.

Butterfly gardens, orchards, native wildflower gardens, hummingbird gardens and water gardens are linked by a network of trails, including an extensive wheelchair path. The site also boasts the world's largest outdoor collection of bluebird boxes.

Charlie and Winnie Ellis spent their time with the birds and other wildlife because that is what they loved. Through education and by example, Ellis Bird Farm continues their legacy, inspiring others, young and old, to appreciate and value nature.

Charlie and Winnie Ellis, brother and sister, took over the operation of the family farm near Lacombe after their parents died in the 1950s. Over the next half century, they built it into a wildlife haven.

Charlie's lifetime interest in birds in general, and the mountain bluebird in particular, began with a nesting box he built from magazine instructions. Nesting boxes for bluebirds, tree swallows, chickadees, purple martins and flickers soon dotted his farm fields.

Charlie and Winnie were true conservationists, turning their farmyard into a wildlife haven for birds, butterflies, deer and other creatures. Ponds, orchards and gardens attracted backyard wildlife, as did a generous bird feeding program.

As they moved into their later years, the Ellises were concerned about who would look after their wild friends after they were gone. Surprisingly, the solution came when it was discovered that Union Carbide was looking for a site in the area to build a new plant. Industry and conservation haven't always been the best of bedfellows, but in the 1980s the Ellises, Union Carbide and others worked out an arrangement that would see the Ellis legacy continue well into the future.

A non-profit organization, Ellis Bird Farm Ltd., was established and incorporated in 1982 with a volunteer board of directors representing MEGlobal Canada (successor to Union Carbide), the Red Deer River Naturalists, the Federation of Alberta Naturalists, the County of Lacombe and the local community. Charlie and Winnie Ellis were honorary life members until their deaths in 1990 and 2004, respectively. The organization's mandate is to carry out a summer nesting program and a winter bird feeding program, to conduct and support scientific research and to develop and deliver public education programs.

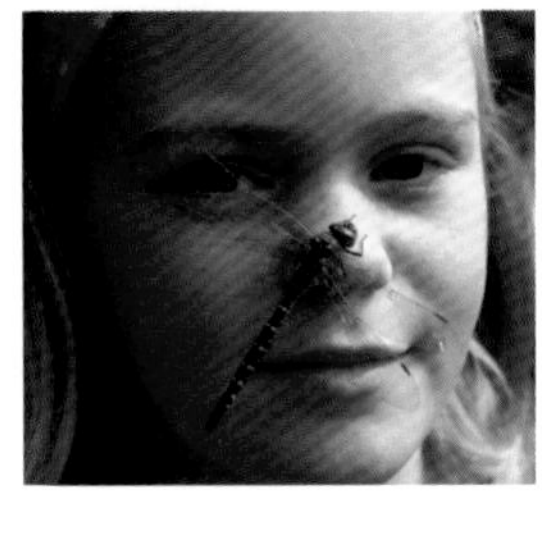

Today, Ellis Bird Farm is both a popular tourist attraction and a well-respected organization. The farm is still a working farm and the old two-storey house that Charlie and Winnie's parents built in 1907 is now a charming tea house.

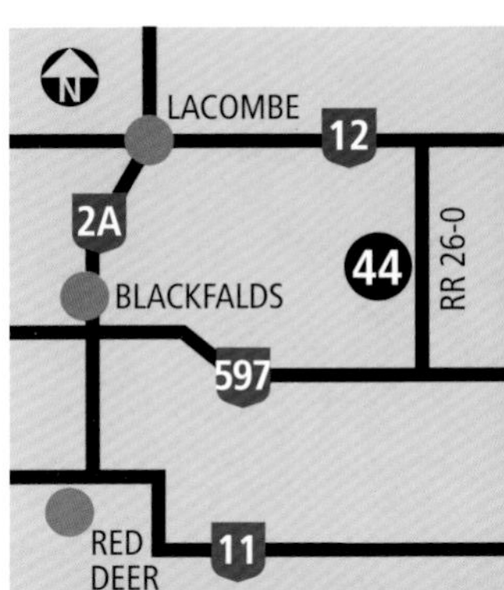

TRAVEL TIPS

The farm is open to visitors 11 a.m. to 5 p.m. Tuesday through Sunday and holiday Mondays from the May long weekend through Labour Day.

Workshops, nature day camps for kids, an annual bluebird festival, an annual seniors' garden party and other special events are held throughout the summer. All events are posted on the website.

Reservations are encouraged for the tea house and required for groups of six or more.

Location: Eight kilometres east of Lacombe on Highway 12 and eight kilometres south on Prentiss Road.

Phone: (403) 346-2211 or (403) 885-4477 (summer only)

E-mail: myrnap@ ellisbirdfarm.ab.ca

www.ellisbirdfarm.ab.ca

P

45 Fairmont Banff Springs

Sir William Cornelius Van Horne had luxury on his mind when he approved the building of a series of hotels along the brand new transcontinental Canadian Pacific Railway. The Banff Springs Hotel was designed to accommodate the wealthy travellers who saw the hot springs of the area as a cure for many ills, travellers who had the time and money to see the world. This destination might be the new frontier, but for the wealthy it couldn't mean sod huts.

The hotel has changed and expanded since its opening in 1888, and has overcome many challenges and setbacks. The first came even before it was completed. When Van Horne arrived to view the construction, he was horrified to see that "someone had blundered" and the building had been turned 180 degrees. The staff would get the million dollar view and the guests wouldn't. He quickly added a new guest section on the side with the view, and construction continued.

Once the hotel was opened, it became a coveted destination. In the early years of the 20th century, thousands were turned away because the hotel was full. In 1911, at the end of the season (the hotel closed every winter until 1969), major expansion began. The centre tower, faced with rundle stone, was added as well as a number of luxurious bathing pools. The tower and other amenities were ready in May 1914 after nearly three years of construction that kept the town of Banff alive.

A fire in April 1926, just at the beginning of the season, destroyed the north wing, the last original section of the 1888 building, and also caused great damage to the centre tower. The replacement of two wings had already been planned for the end of the 1926 and 1927 seasons, and an annex (later used as staff accommodation) had been built to house guests while the old wings were torn down. The fire sped things up a bit.

TRAVEL TIPS

A particularly tasty specialty of The Fairmont Banff Springs is its high tea, served from 2 p.m. to 4 p.m. and including flaky, light scones, Devonshire cream and cakes. You can even add a glass of sparkling wine for a treat.

Location:
405 Spray Ave., Banff

Phone: (403) 762-2211

E-mail: banffsprings@fairmont.com

www.fairmont.com/banffsprings

The period between the wars was an extravagant time, and the hotel was refinished with great care and much expense. The arched glass windows framing the magnificent view were shipped across the country in a custom fitted rail car and great quantities of tyndall stone were shipped from Manitoba to adorn stairways, fireplaces and window sills. Oak wainscoting, terrazzo floors, stained glass and an impressive circular staircase all added to the atmosphere of wealth and abundance. You didn't stay at the Banff Springs Hotel if you were at all concerned about expense.

Today, thousands of visitors annually tour the magnificent grounds and delight in the majestic hotel nestled in its mountain home.

The Second World War saw the closing of the Banff Springs' doors. Europeans were not crossing the ocean and even North American travel was severely restricted. When it opened again after "hostilities ceased," the hotel met with a changed world. More people had vehicles and more people had disposable income. The Banff Springs' days as an exclusive spa and railroad hotel were over. The new era opened its doors to a wider audience – and more people could enjoy the beauty of its setting in the Rocky Mountains.

46 Famous Five

On Oct. 18, 1929, women in Canada became "persons" under the law. For that landmark step toward equality, we can thank five Alberta women who refused to take "No" for an answer: Emily Murphy, Henrietta Muir Edwards, Louise McKinney, Irene Parlby and Nellie McClung.

It started with a put-down. Emily Murphy had barely warmed her chair as the British Empire's first female police magistrate in 1916 when lawyer Eardley Jackson challenged her authority. An 1876 ruling under the British North America (BNA) Act said "Women are persons in matters of pains and penalties, but are not persons in matters of rights and privileges," he argued. "You have no jurisdiction in this court. You're not even a person!"

That objection was overruled as often as it arose in the new magistrate's court, and in 1917 the Alberta Court of Appeal settled the issue for this province by ruling that women are persons. To test whether that opinion held across Canada, Emily Murphy allowed her name to stand for Senate. Prime ministers of the day said they were willing to appoint a female senator but could not, due to the 1876 ruling. Despite growing desire for a woman in Senate, despite a petition signed by half a million seeking Murphy's appointment, the prospect seemed hopeless.

Undaunted, Murphy decided to ask the Supreme Court for clarification regarding female senators under an obscure clause allowing constitutional petitions to be submitted by five citizens. Thus it was that five determined women gathered at her home on Aug. 27, 1927 for tea and signatures.

> *"Canada is not just a map and railroad tracks. We are a song and we must sing it together."*
>
> *Emily Murphy*

Canada's Supreme Court decided against the five

7 Ave SE
1 St SE
46
Stephen Ave SE
Centre St S
MacLeod Tr SE
9 Ave SE
LRT

TRAVEL TIPS

Famous 5 monuments were unveiled at Calgary's Olympic Plaza in 1999 and on Ottawa's Parliament Hill in 2000.

A detail from the Famous 5 monuments was featured on a Canada Post stamp in October 1999 and on the Canadian $50 bill beginning in 2004.

The Famous 5, Heroes for Today (www.abheritage.ca/famous5) pulls together multimedia resources from The Heritage Community Foundation, the Famous 5 Foundation and CKUA.

Location of statue: southwest corner of Olympic Plaza, 228 8th Ave. S.E., Calgary

Famous 5 Foundation

Phone: (403) 253-1927

E-mail: sparksms@telus.net

www.famous5.org

on April 24, 1928, ruling that the word "persons" in Section 24 of the BNA Act did not include females. With the approval of Prime Minister Mackenzie King, the women appealed to the judicial committee of the Privy Council in London.

Remarkably, the Judicial Committee found that women are persons and qualified to be appointed to Senate. It was a key ruling not only for women but for Canadian law, particularly because it declared that the BNA Act "planted in Canada a living tree capable of growth and expansion within its natural limits." To this day, we interpret our constitution in the context of its time.

The ruling paved the way for Cairine Wilson to become Canada's first female senator just five months later, but Emily Murphy never was appointed to Senate. Indeed, Alberta did not have a female senator until Martha Bielish received the nod in 1979, a half century after what has become known as the Persons' Case.

"Get the job done and let them howl."

Nelly McClung

Some question the wisdom of holding the Famous Five up as role models, given some of their less progressive views. In the end, though, they affirmed the personhood of all women. Fallible, ordinary, together they accomplished the extraordinary – and changed the world.

Nearly identical sculptures of the Famous Five stand in Calgary and Ottawa. Sculpted by Alberta's Barbara Paterson, the images reflect the women's diverse personalities.

Nellie McClung, the writer, brandishes a newspaper headlined "Women Are Persons!" The very British Irene Parlby is impeccably dressed yet sporting Alberta rose earrings that hark to her post as Alberta's first female member of cabinet. Louise McKinney's temperance ring flashes as she clasps her hands in a near-prayer position, a nod to her faith and passion. The grandmotherly Henrietta Muir Edwards raises a celebratory toast that also salutes her hobby, painting teacups. Emily Murphy stands judicially beside an empty chair, inviting support.

The empty chair invites us to join the circle, finding courage for the ongoing work of building a just Canada.

47 Fort Chipewyan

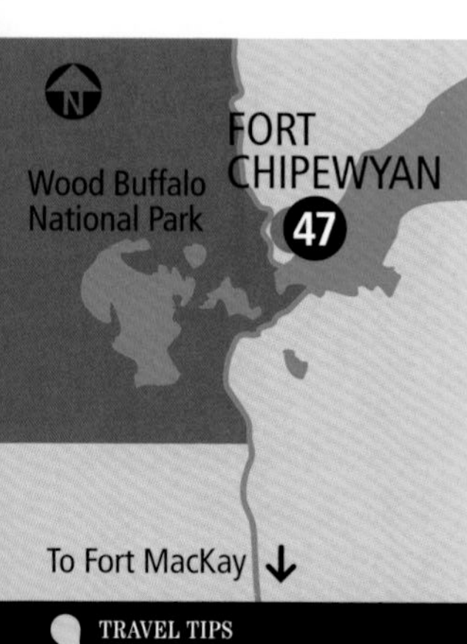

TRAVEL TIPS

You can drive to Fort Chipewyan only in the winter over an ice road.

The community is part of the Regional Municipality of Wood Buffalo, the largest regional municipality in North America. It is connected to Wood Buffalo National Park, Canada's largest national park and one of the world's largest. It was established in 1922 to protect Canada's last remaining herds of bison.

Location: Fort Chip is on the northwestern edge of Lake Athabasca, the fourth largest lake in Canada.

Phone: 1-800-973-9663 or Fort Chipewyan Regional Office at (780) 697-3600

E-mail: webmaster@woodbuffalo.ab.ca

www.woodbuffalo.ab.ca

The oldest European settlement in Alberta, Fort Chipewyan, or Fort Chip as it is generally known, was established in 1788 and was the scene of much violence in those early fur trade years.

Before that, the violence had been between the Beaver and Cree First Nations but they had eventually decided to co-exist peacefully and to trap and trade the furs that were in demand by the fur trade companies in the area.

Later violence was among the fur traders themselves. There were three major companies in the area, all competing for the valuable beaver hides that were still in demand in Europe, and it wasn't until all three companies were eventually amalgamated into one, the Hudson's Bay Company (HBC), that business was conducted without bloodshed.

The Oblate fathers established a mission at Fort Chip in 1851 and in 1874 Bishop Grouard built a convent and a residential school.

A third church, built in 1909, is still in existence thanks to the efforts of the small community and supported by matching grants from the Alberta Historical Resources Foundation. It is decorated in a traditional early western style for churches, with a blue-painted vaulted ceiling decorated with angels and stars. The paintings on the walls depict Bible stories but with a twist – the paintings include York boats, fur traders and aboriginal faces.

The Anglican mission was begun in the 1870s and by 1874 they had built the church that is still in use today. A small school built as an Anglican day school in 1874 is also still standing. All the buildings are now protected by the Provincial Historic Resource Designation.

By the end of the 19th century, the fur trade was in decline and, when the HBC amalgamated its northwestern offices and moved its administration to Edmonton, Fort Chip was left behind. Transportation routes moved south and to this day the options for getting there are limited. A winter or ice road is available (after freeze up) from Fort McMurray (300 kilometres to the south) or Fort Smith (180 kilometres to the north), and the Athabasca River is available in the summer. Flights move people and supplies in from Edmonton and Fort McMurray six days a week, while barges transport larger items in and out during the 'open' times on the river. One bus a week runs from Fort McMurray to Fort Chip during the ice road times.

The main industries at Fort Chipewyan in the 21st century are still trapping, fishing and forestry. Oil sands-related work and tourism have added to the economy despite the difficulty of getting there. Distance education has been an important addition to the community and Keyano College has a Fort Chipewyan campus, offering upgrading and some college courses. There is no question that the remote location is a challenge to the prosperity of the community but its 1,200 residents think it's doing just fine.

The Anglican mission and school buildings at Fort Chipewyan are constructed in the Red River or fur trade style. The fur trade posts or forts were moved often in response to the trading patterns of the First Nations or simply because the trees so necessary to keeping somewhat warm in the winter had been used up. Squared logs were laid horizontally between corner posts so that the whole building could be pulled apart and moved. Many other buildings used this style, too, including the mission church at St. Albert – which had three different locations during its history.

48 Fort Edmonton Park

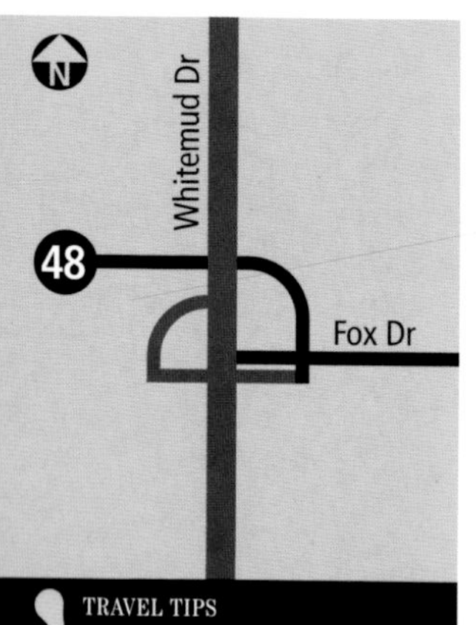

TRAVEL TIPS

The park is open every day from the May long weekend to Labour Day, and Sundays in September. Guided wagon tours are available Monday to Saturday in September; reduced admission in effect.

Plan on spending several hours at the park; your visit will involve lots of walking.

Book a room at the Hotel Selkirk: 1-888-962-2522 or e-mail reservations@hotelselkirk.com.

Location: Whitemud Drive and Fox Drive, Edmonton

Phone: (780) 496-8787

E-mail: attractions@edmonton

www.edmonton.ca/fort

They call the engine huffing at the station as you enter Fort Edmonton Park a vintage locomotive, but it's actually a time machine. It carries you from today to the park's namesake, a key Hudson's Bay Company fur trading post depicted as it was in 1846.

At the fort, one of four distinct eras depicted in this living history park, you enter a world where fur greased the economic wheels as surely as oil does today in Alberta.

There's also 1885 Street, where you'll find early settlers at work on Ottewell Farm or chewing the fat beside their horse-drawn wagons. There's 1905 Street, celebrating the town's first boom, when the railway arrived and Edmonton became the capital city of the fledgling province of Alberta. And there's 1920 Street, where the Al Rashid Mosque and the Ukrainian Bookstore reflect the city's expanding cultural diversity.

More than 75 buildings line these streets - some original, others reconstructed. All existed in Edmonton's past, but not on this spot. The fur trading fort, for example, stood on the river bank below the Alberta legislature building, several bends northeast of the park's location along Whitemud Drive below the Quesnell Bridge.

Chat with any of the costumed characters sprinkled throughout the park and you'll discover tidbits that make each era come alive. Inside the fort, you might find a Cree or Métis woman beading a belt or carpenters building York boats that carried goods by river. At any bedroom door, note the knotted ropes that served as mattresses back then, and the phrase "sleep tight" suddenly makes perfect sense; tighten those knots and you might enjoy a better sleep. Just outside the walls, stop at the teepee encampment to hear what life was like for aboriginal people who came to trade at the fort.

This 64-hectare park invites you to not only see and hear but experience slices of times past. Let the kids loose in the Gyro Park playground, check out the ice cream at Bill's Confectionery, buy a fresh-baked loaf at Lauder's Bakery, aim at the bull's eye in the shooting gallery, play a round of 1920s miniature golf or dress up for a period photo. You can even stay the night at the elegantly reconstructed Hotel Selkirk, where 1920s décor is complemented by modern amenities.

And be sure to take a ride: both the steam train and a streetcar that is the literal centrepiece of 1905 and 1920 Streets are free, and an old-fashioned fee will put you in a stagecoach or wagon – even atop a pony if you fit.

Opened in 1974, the park expands every year, so each visit offers new experiences. One popular addition is a 1920s midway where you can test your skill at various games and ride a beautifully handcrafted carousel. Choose your favourite of the painted ponies and let it carry you back to an era when time ran at carousel pace.

The Hudson's Bay Company built the first Fort Edmonton - named for an estate in Middlesex, England owned by a deputy governor of the company - in 1795.

A shortage of firewood led to its relocation in 1802. Eight years later, the company moved the fort from what is now downtown Edmonton to a site 80 kilometres downstream. They gave that up after only three years, returning to the city area. In 1830, following two damaging floods, the post was moved to higher ground upstream. That fort, located on the grounds of the present legislature building, was dismantled in 1915.

Half a century later, as a Canada centennial project in 1967, reconstruction began. Since then, the Fort Edmonton Foundation has raised more than $20 million for the ongoing development of the park. Owned and operated by the City of Edmonton, the park opened to the public in May 1974.

49 Fort Museum of the North West Mounted Police

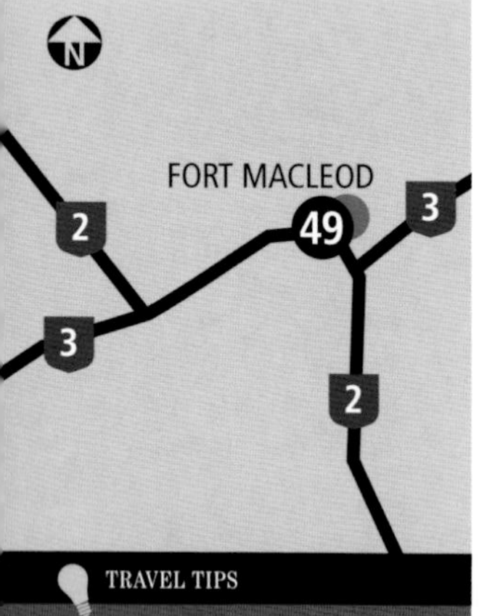

TRAVEL TIPS

The museum is open May 1 through Oct. 15. Hours vary, with the museum open daily 9 a.m. to 6 p.m. from July 1 through Labour Day.

The Musical Ride is performed four times daily most days at the fort in the summer.

On Saturdays and Sundays in summer, active members of the Fort Macleod RCMP become The Red Serge Patrol to welcome you and promote the RCMP.

Location: Westbound Highway 3, 219 25th St., Fort Macleod

Phone: 1-866-273-6841

E-mail: info@nwmpmuseum.com

www.nwmpmuseum.com

Ride into the past at the Fort Museum of the North West Mounted Police (NWMP) in Fort Macleod. Past glory comes to life as summer students, dressed in scarlet tunics and white helmets, carry flags and rein well-trained horses to perform movements from the famous musical ride.

In the main building, marvel at the early history of the renowned police force, now the famed Royal Canadian Mounted Police. The force's 1874 journey from Ontario to southern Alberta was plagued with hardships. Train travel ended in Manitoba, and then the treacherous trail ride, known as the Great March West, began.

Battleford, in what is now Saskatchewan, was a hard-won journey's end for some. The others continued to Fort Whoop-Up near current-day Lethbridge, expecting a battle, but whiskey traders had fled. Only a few Mounties were stationed there to prevent a return to business as usual. Finally, after the 1,288-kilometre trek, the troop stopped to build their own fort by the Oldman River. Throughout the journey, men endured bad water, food shortages, insects, storms, illness and more only to find living at their fort wasn't easy. Hundreds of miles from another settlement, living meant enduring winter cold, summer heat, floods and other privations, but the troupe was commanded by Colonel James Macleod, who earned great respect while ensuring everyone did his job.

Displays convey the importance of Fort Macleod. Between 1876 and 1878, it was headquarters for the NWMP. By 1884, when the original post needed repairs and was again threatened by floods, a new fort was built at a better location. All the while, "getting their man," curtailing violence and other crimes, patrolling the Canadian border lands, fighting prairie fires, helping isolated settlers and bringing music and culture to southern Alberta was a never-ending challenge.

In 1922, the post at Fort Macleod closed. Only two officers remained to enforce the law. But discover the stories for yourself at the museum.

At the fort museum, Colonel Macleod is given special acknowledgement. As assistant commissioner for the NWMP, an honourable man and a man of his word, he earned the confidence of the Blackfoot. For the Government of Canada, that respect translated into a willingness by the Blackfoot to sign Treaty 7.

From 1877 to 1880, he was Commissioner of the NWMP and a magistrate. Later, he was appointed to the Supreme Court of the Northwest Territories. Calgary's Macleod Trail is named after him.

Also honoured is Sir Fredrick Haultain. Authentically restored, his original log cabin, which was both his home and law office, stands in tribute to the first lawyer in Fort Macleod. Eventually becoming the premier of the Northwest Territories, he worked to create the provinces of Alberta and Saskatchewan, but his first home in the West was smaller than many modern-day bedrooms.

The Kanouse Trading Post is another original building, and is on its original site. Inside, find the colourful histories of whiskey trader-turned-businessman Kamoose Taylor and of other early residents of Fort Macleod.

In Fort Macleod, history is everywhere including on the golf course, at the cemeteries and at nearby ranches. Beginning in 1890, residents played golf on grassy flats nearby. Within five years, the Royal Fort Macleod Golf Course was open, making it the oldest golf course on the Prairies west of Manitoba. Today, the nine-hole course along the Oldman River has mature trees and lush fairways.

The Holy Cross Cemetery, consecrated by Father Lacombe in 1888, and the Union Cemetery are two of the oldest in southern Alberta. Forty members of the North West Mounted Police were buried at the Union Cemetery. Also buried here is Jerry Potts, Métis guide and interpreter for the force. Events at the Fort Macleod Ranch Rodeo reflect actual work done on ranches in the late 1800s. Just as it was once done, events like calf branding require team work. A number of the original NWMP took up ranching in the area after their tour of duty.

50 Frank Slide

Exhibits at the Coleman Museum reflect the broader history of the Pass. The museum has outdoor displays, but indoor ones include a blacksmith shop, pioneer room, wildlife room and mining room.

Well-known early photographers of the Crowsnest Pass, Thomas and Evan Gushul, are also featured. Thomas, the father, arrived in the area in 1909 and worked as a miner before taking up photography as a hobby and then establishing a photo business. He and his son, who trained at the National Art School of Chicago, captured the local people and events.

Attracting labour leaders and communist agitators during the Depression, the Pass became a hotbed for mine strikes. Although the Gurshals' collections include many family portraits, they were also able to photographically document labour parades and unrest.

Summer hours are 8 a.m. to 5 p.m. Monday to Saturday. Winter hours are 8 a.m. to 12 noon and 1 p.m. to 5 p.m. Monday to Friday. For information, phone (403) 563-5434.

The landscape around Frank is as memorable for its beauty as the area's history is for its tragedy. On April 29, 1903, the small town of Frank stood in the path of a massive rock avalanche. Shortly after 4 a.m., limestone rock sheered off Turtle Mountain and buried part of the town. The slide is two kilometres wide, and 82 million tonnes of rock are spread over three square kilometres of the valley to an average depth of 14 metres.

Few witness a mountain face crashing to the ground and live to tell about it. At Frank, 23 people who were in the path of the slide survived to share their heart-wrenching personal accounts.

The Frank Slide Interpretive Centre is ready, willing and able to inform and entertain those interested in the slide and other dramatic Crowsnest Pass events such as Canada's worst mine disaster. Situated on a rock bench above the massive piles of debris, the centre features a viewing area, and pathways allow visitors to compare the stunning backdrop of other mountains to the scarred eastern slope of Turtle Mountain.

There, take a few minutes to drink in the silence as you imagine the thunderous event. Walk among the huge boulders and let yourself appreciate nature's formidable power. North America's deadliest rockslide lasted only 100 seconds. The debris carried by the slide

buried some temporary dwellings and a row of miners' cottages in Frank and destroyed the surface workings of the coal mine. The disaster claimed more than 70 lives, transformed a river channel into a lake and buried over a mile of Canadian Pacific Railway track.

What caused the slide? The primary cause was the mountain's unstable geological structure. Underground mining was a contributing factor. Weather and water took their toll. Run-off from melting ice found its way into summit cracks. Temperature extremes caused expansion and contraction. The resulting slide is not simply part of local and western Canadian history, but is recognized as an important event by earth scientists around the globe.

Whether you are simply curious about the slide or want to experience the area's mountain majesty, visiting Frank Slide is a must-see to understand the depth of adversity Albertans have faced in our colourful past. If you have time, stay to discover other dramatic chapters of history in the area. Featured are displays about settlement, coal mining, railways and community life in the Pass.

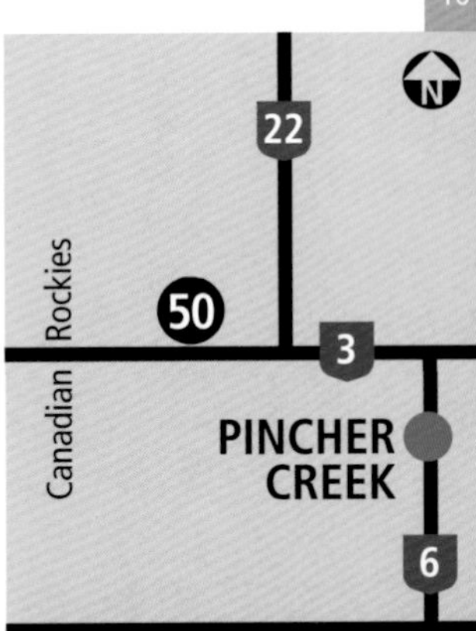

TRAVEL TIPS

Walk the paths in the slide area to get a sense of the massive size of boulders.

From May 15 to Sept. 14, Interpretive Centre hours are 9 a.m. to 6 p.m.

From Sept. 15 to May 14, hours are 10 a.m. to 5 p.m.

The centre is closed Christmas Eve, Christmas Day, New Year's Day and Easter Sunday.

Interpretive Centre displays illustrate the 1903 Frank Slide, railway building, European settlement, early coal mining and community life.

Audio-visual presentations *In the Mountain's Shadow* and *On the Edge of Destruction: The Frank Slide Story* are shown daily.

Location: 1.5 kilometres off Highway 3 in the Municipality of Crowsnest Pass

Phone: Toll free in Alberta 310-0000 then (403) 562-7388

E-mail: info@frankslide.com

www.frankslide.com

51 Glenbow Museum

If you love history and art, Calgary's Glenbow is the place to visit. Its motto, "Where the World Meets the West," describes a fascinating journey of discovery. The facility is an art gallery, library, archives and museum, and the Glenbow does an outstanding job in all four disciplines.

Originally founded and funded by Calgary lawyer Eric Harvie, the museum was the recipient of his eclectic collection of world art, sculptures, historical pieces and collectables. Other philanthropists and many Albertans have donated everything from rare Canadian coins and medals to Buddhist sculptures.

On the main floor, a giant glass sculpture depicting the aurora borealis glitters with light. On the second floor, visitors discover some of the best in Canadian and world art. Displays change, but special exhibits have featured prehistoric wonders, art and artifacts from the ancient Mediterranean world, religious works from Asia and masterpieces of early and contemporary artists.

On the third floor, visitors discover or rediscover the Canadian west. Staff have worked extensively with aboriginal people, and valued artifacts from Inuit and other First Nations' cultures await. Reputed to have the best Blackfoot collection in the world, the Glenbow can boast of an outstanding Blackfoot Gallery where treasured artifacts are showcased.

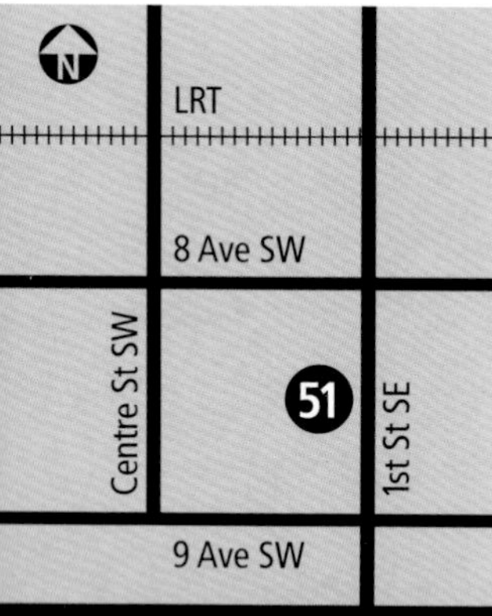

TRAVEL TIPS

Hours are 10 a.m. to 5 p.m. Tuesday through Friday. The library and archives are closed Mondays and weekends.

If you enjoy dabbling in art or have children in your group, stop by the Discovery Room, an art-based studio open during museum hours.

The gift shop has a great selection of art and history books and offers unique jewelry and gifts.

Location: 130 9th Ave. S.E., Calgary

Phone: (403) 268-4100

E-mail: glenbow@glenbow.org

www.glenbow.org

Settlement history is well represented, too. Opening in 2007, *Mavericks: an Incorrigible History of Alberta* is another must see for your list. *Mavericks* will invite you to explore Alberta's history through the dynamic stories of more than 40 mavericks from Western Canada's past.

On the fourth floor, you'll find more surprises. One gallery focuses on the experiences of the warrior, including displays as divergent as the suits of armour worn by Japanese samurai and uniforms worn by First and Second World War nurses. Elsewhere on the floor, marvel at mineral displays.

If you need help researching Canadian or family history, the library and archives on the sixth floor have outstanding collections of documents, books, photographs, recordings and films. The Glenbow archives has always been a front runner in using technology to share its wealth of ephemeral or paper-based collections, so you can browse through thousands of the historical photos online at the museum or on the web.

There's more to this outstanding facility than world-class exhibits, collections and resources. There, those who love Canadian history and art will find a spiritual home.

Extend your visit to the area with a wander along Stephen Avenue Mall. Huge, modern buildings speak of the present, but take note of the few remaining sandstone buildings from an era past. Offering a sense of permanence, the golden brown buildings evoke visions of our forefathers. In recent years, the city has recognized the importance of saving and restoring them as heritage buildings while modern businesses and organizations make use of the interior space.

After a fire in 1886 that devastated the wooden structures of downtown, Calgary rebuilt as the "Sandstone City." A superior building material in a landscape threatened by prairie fires, sandstone was readily available from about 15 nearby quarries. For decades, those working at the quarries and as stone masons made up a significant part of the Calgary workforce.

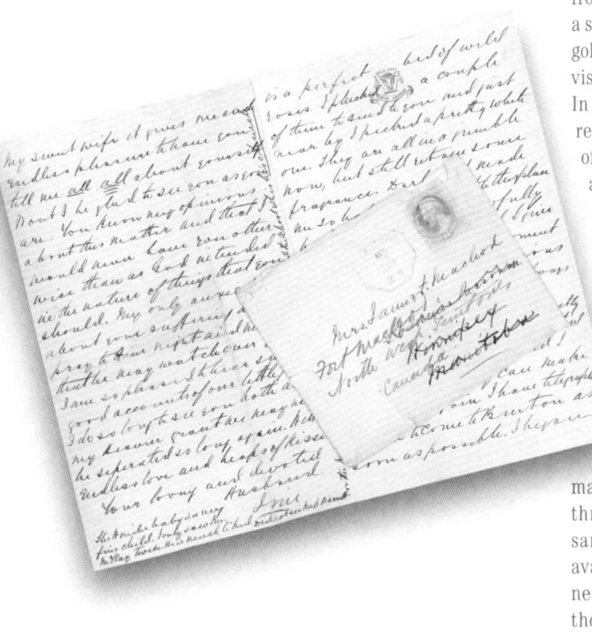

52 Grande Cache

Little did Ignace Glasson know that when he stored a large cache of furs over a winter around 1820, he was making history – but that's how Grande Cache got its name and is still so called nearly 200 years later.

Grande Cache is a town now and has the amenities of the 21st century. But its special placement atop a 1,280-metre plateau surrounded by panoramic views of 21 mountain peaks and two river valleys means people visit Grande Cache to take advantage of some active outdoor activities.

In the summer they come for the incredible whitewater rafting and trail riding, as well as "heli" everything – hiking, camping, rafting and skiing. Golf enthusiasts will feel right at home here as well. For something different, try the Passport to the Peaks hiking program.

The winter offers its own rewards. While the rest of the world is burrowing into warm quilts, Grande Cache is offering snowshoeing, cross country and telemark skiing.

Grande Cache is also home of the Canadian Death Race (they haven't lost anyone yet), which involves running over 125 kilometres of trails and three mountain summits and, with all the ups and downs of those trails, climbing almost 5,200 metres. To add to the adventure, runners have to cross a major river by boat. Part of the race is at night. It's an intense experience and there are even training camps for potential participants. For the not-quite-so-tough, the race can be done by a relay team and for the under-16 crowd there's a kid's version – quite a feather in the cap to have completed this one.

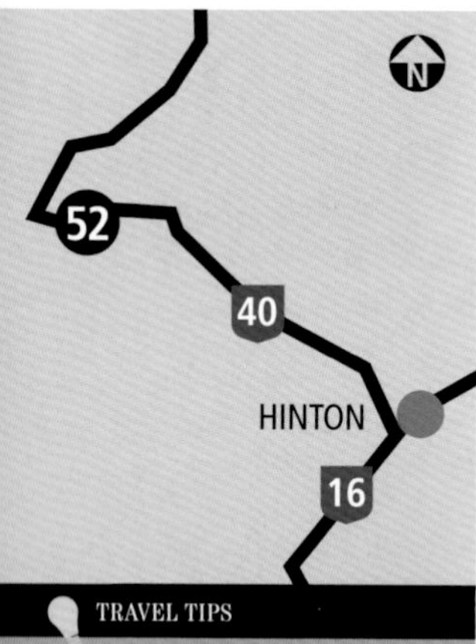

TRAVEL TIPS

The Grande Cache Tourism & Interpretive Centre is a 'first stop' for travellers with its maps and information, gift shop, exhibits, displays and local art work.

Visit the spectacular Sulphur Gates at the confluence of the Smoky and Sulphur rivers, only a 15-minute drive from town.

Location: About 437 kilometres northwest of Edmonton, 180 kilometres south of Grande Prairie and 140 kilometres north of Hinton on Highway 40.

Phone: 1-888-827-3790

E-mail: tourism@grandecache.ca

www.grandecache.ca

In town, Grande Cache is a wonderful spot for a slower pace of life – no rush hour traffic, not even a traffic light. And for still quieter contemplation, Grande Cache is the gate to Willmore Wilderness Park. The park is provincially operated and allows no motorized vehicles – feet and hooves only. There are 750 kilometres of trails and no facilities, so you have to know what you're doing in the great outdoors when you visit Willmore.

Of course, this quiet contemplation will be shared by four-footed thinkers – deer, elk and even the threatened woodland caribou might be browsing. In the higher elevations you can see the impressive big-horn sheep and lower down there are black bears and grizzlies. Again, you have to know what you're doing in this wonderful place.

And if you don't have time to linger, Grande Cache claims that its Highway 40 is a "much more scenic route to Alaska."

The Grande Cache Lake picnic area is the site of an aboriginal camp where much archeological work has been done, showing that people had camped at this site for about 10,000 years.

Another ancient site is between the old communities of Susa Creek and Muskeg, about 11 kilometres from town where a tiny graveyard also illustrates that these were popular stopping places for thousands of years before Europeans came.

As for the future, the Grande Cache Coal Corporation has been launched to re-activate coal mining in the area. The mine site, about 20 kilometres north of Grande Cache, was already producing and selling coal by 2004.

Foothills Forest Products, a successful small pine panel board company out of British Columbia, purchased and reopened the local lumber mill in April 2005.

EnCana, Canada's largest gas developer, has set up operations in Grande Cache, estimating it will be their second largest play, comparable to Grande Prairie, and sustainable over the long term.

53 Head-Smashed-In Buffalo Jump

TRAVEL TIPS

The centre is open daily except Christmas Eve, Christmas Day, New Year's Day and Easter Sunday. Hours vary.

In July and August, watch for dance and drum performances every Wednesday.

Special events are held annually on National Aboriginal Day, June 21.

Every year on July 23, special performances celebrate the 1987 opening of the centre.

Location: about 18 kilometres north and west of Fort Macleod on Highway 785

Phone: Toll free 310-0000, then dial (403) 553-2731

Email: info@head-smashed-in.com

www.head-smashed-in.com

For an awe-inspiring experience, visit the site of one of the world's oldest, largest and best preserved buffalo jumps. In continuous use by First Nations for more than 5,500 years, Head-Smashed-In Buffalo Jump was named a UNESCO World Heritage Site by the United Nations in 1981.

Even the landscape of the surrounding Porcupine Hills is dramatic and beautiful. Blending into the sandstone cliff where the drama unfolded, the interpretive centre helps captivate the buffalo culture and spirit. Here were the culminating moments in many Blackfoot buffalo hunts. Here, thousands of bison died so that the First Nations might live.

Although *bison* is the scientific and contemporary Canadian term for the vast herds of animals that once roamed the Canadian and American prairies, officially the site name is *buffalo* jump, the American term for the great animals. The territory of the Blackfoot, called Blackfeet in the United States, extended south to the Yellow Stone River, west to the continental divide, north to present-day Edmonton and east to present-day Regina, Sask. They moved back and forth following the seasons, so both names were accepted, but their own term for the animal they hunted was *iinnii* (singular) or *iniiksii* (plural).

The herds numbering thousands of animals were the primary food source for the Blackfoot. Especially in the fall for the long winter ahead, the people needed vast quantities of meat, much of which they made into pemmican. Working together, they herded small groups of buffalo towards the cliffs and then stampeded them. Not able to see the 300 metre-deep precipice ahead, the buffalo fell. The jump was the most efficient means of performing the hunt before the arrival of guns and horses. Once the animals had fallen, hunters with bows and arrows, atlatls (wooden weapons that allowed darts to be thrown harder) and spears ensured their quick deaths. Much of the hardest work was to follow. At the base of the cliff, meat preparation began and hides were scraped.

The bison also provided clothing, shelter and ceremonial and ritual opportunities. Tanned hides were made into teepee covers and clothing. Bones and horns were transformed into household items, tools and other ceremonial or useful items.

The interpretation staff and displays at the centre demonstrate how the work was done, but they also give insights into the lifestyle, customs and spiritual beliefs of the Blackfoot. You will discover life among the people before contact with Europeans, as well as the impact of the recent arrivals on the culture of the First Nations.

Whether you use the Canadian spelling *teepee* or the American spelling *tipi*, the experience will be the same. Head Smashed-In calls it "tipi camping," and the program means you are in luck if you love the outdoors.

If you want a taste of the traditional Blackfoot lifestyle with quiet, cool nights, dark skies and counting stars, here's your chance.

No, you don't sleep on a buffalo robe. Air mattresses are provided. Bring your own sleeping bag or rent one. You can bring other camping gear but no private tents or dogs. Given the luxury of a small camp stove, wood is provided for it, but arrive with rain gear, day pack, sturdy shoes and water bottle.

Several tipi camping packages are available, some more rustic or longer than others. You could even learn how to erect your tipi! Investigate your options and book early.

The name for the site has an interesting story, too. One year, a young Blackfoot hunter wondered what the scene of the stampeding bison must look like from the base of the cliff. He waited and watched, but he didn't live to tell the story. In his memory, the Blackfoot named the site Head-Smashed-In.

As a World Heritage Site, Head-Smashed-In is as important as the pyramids and Stonehenge in conveying world history, and it is right here in Alberta.

54 Heritage Park

At Heritage Park in Calgary, you are transported to an earlier time. First built in 1964, the park is a "living" village presenting life as it was in Alberta before 1914.

Here, you can talk to a blacksmith, enjoy fresh buns from the bakery, take a ride in a horse-drawn wagon, catch a ride on an antique gas-powered bus, rattle through the park on a steam train, tour the reservoir on the S.S. Moyie paddlewheeler or just soak in the period costumes and the coming-and-going of old delivery trucks. Three-quarters of the buildings are right out of Alberta's history; for example, the Prince House, the park's largest and most majestic home, is the original house, moved to the park from Prince's Island in Calgary.

The 27-hectare park is situated on Glenmore Reservoir. From the lower parking lot, you can take the streetcar to the entrance. If the upper lot isn't full, the walk is much shorter.

Near the entrance is the trading post for gifts, but you will find mementoes and knick-knacks in shops on Main Street, too. If you arrive between 9 a.m. and 10 a.m., regular admission includes a free pancake breakfast!

Otherwise, a great place to start is on the train. Once you have your ticket, plan to board or disembark at any of the three stations as often as you like. If your first stop is the 1891 Laggan Station, you will step into Alberta's earliest history. Visit the teepee, cabins, Hudson's Bay fort and saloon.

Walk to the farm, and be sure not to miss the small sod house. Just imagine how dark but cool it was on hot

---

When you've completed your visit to Heritage Park, take time to visit Glenmore Park, one of the most beautiful areas in Calgary. Glenmore Reservoir is the focal point of the park. Drink in the idyllic scene of water, sailboats and distant mountains. Created by the damming of the Elbow River, the reservoir is part of the city's water source. From some areas of the park, the public can launch canoes, kayaks and sailboats, but no swimming or motorboats are allowed.

An extensive pathway system leads around the reservoir. Some paths are very near the water; others veer away from it, meandering through trees and hills to Fish Creek Park or through residential areas.

The park is a great place to see native flora as well as birds, gophers, frogs, beaver or rabbits. Other animals such as deer follow the river valley into the park.

---

summer days. Cabins and mansions beckon, too. On Main Street, don't miss the Claresholm General Store c. 1905. Consider how technology has changed when you see the newspaper office, bank, dental office, Chinese laundry, drugstore and hospital. Early law and order is represented at the 1887 Banff Mounted Police barracks. Take a moment at the church and at the 1910 Barons Snooker Parlour, a reminder of a time when playing pool was living on the wild side.

Check out the elevator and fire hall, as well as the drilling rig, a replica of the one used at the Dingman site near Turner Valley where the first significant gas field was discovered in Alberta. Gasoline Alley has memorabilia related to early motor vehicles.

If you have little ones with you, the rides and booths at the antique midway are a great midday or final stop. To thrill-seeking youth, the rides of yesteryear may seem tame, but younger and older visitors will enjoy the working ferris wheel, merry-go-round, whip, caterpillar and dangling swings.

Be tempted by tasty snacks and meals at various locations, but if you prefer a family picnic, you will find plenty of open space and some picnic tables.

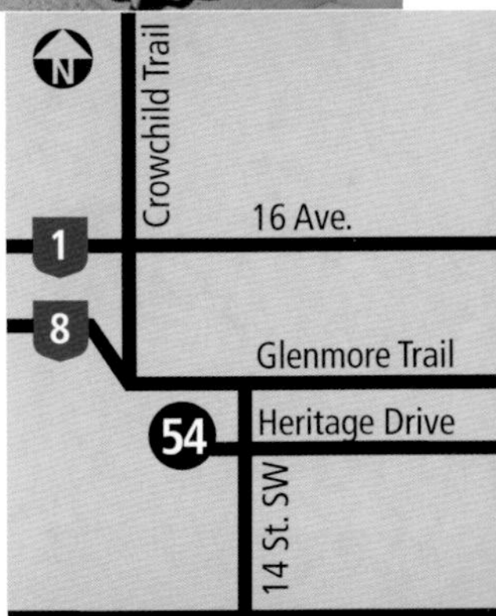

TRAVEL TIPS

The park is open 9 a.m. to 5 p.m. daily from the May long weekend through the September Labour Day long weekend.

It remains open weekends until Thanksgiving and also opens for special events.

Heritage Park will maintain its opening hours during a planned 2008 expansion. The Gasoline Alley interpretive exhibit will be open year round.

Location: 1900 Heritage Dr. S.W., Calgary

Phone: (403) 268-8500

E-mail: info@heritagepark.ab.ca

www.HeritagePark.ca

55 Highway 41 - Medicine Hat to Oyen

Named the Buffalo Trail or Trail of the Buffalo, Highway 41 in eastern Alberta extends from the United States border south of the Cypress Hills to La Corey just beyond Cold Lake. If you dream of experiencing Alberta's grassland the way it once was, be sure to travel the section from Medicine Hat to Oyen. The journey offers open prairie at its best and, for most travellers, the short-grass country seems never-ending. Stretches are table-top flat, but you also pass through the gently rolling Middle Sand Hills.

Here, sky becomes as impressive as land. Some days, the Mediterranean-blue sky overhead is cloudless. Other days, clouds billow and race across it. As you drive up one hill after another, you almost feel you're driving into that vast blue of sky or those billowing clouds.

In fact, you are travelling the eastern boundary of an area known to many simply as "The Block." Bounded on the south by Highway 1, west by Highway 39 and north by Highway 9, the block reveals the prairie landscape as it must have looked before settlement. At night motoring along this lonesome highway, you can imagine the howl of a lonely coyote or feel irresistibly compelled to marvel at stars and constellations.

Within the tract, Canadian Forces Base Suffield operates a huge training base. As well, the Suffield National Wildlife Area is home to 1,100 species of plants and animals. Fourteen species are endangered, threatened or

OYEN
9
55
41
1
MEDICINE HAT

TRAVEL TIPS

Fill your gas tank at Medicine Hat and Oyen. Elsewhere, gas stations are scarce or may be closed.

Sandy Point District Park, with its small campsite, is just south of the blue bridge over the South Saskatchewan River. Watch closely. It is easy to miss.

Consider taking your cell phone, snacks and pop or water.

Drop by the Crossroads Museum in Oyen. Also, a large sculpted pronghorn is in Friendship Park at Oyen.

Location: Highway 41, Medicine Hat to Oyen

Phone: 1-800-252-3782

E-mail: travelinfo@travelalberta.com

www.travelalberta.com

of special concern, but they survive because the block is an unploughed, mixed- and dry-grass ecosystem.

If you're lucky, you might catch a glimpse of pronghorn antelope. As the most specialized and representative wild mammal of the region, antelope thrive only on native prairie grassland. Not surprisingly, the antelope's colouring provides perfect camouflage. The herds aren't always easy to spot, so be alert.

Here, too, the last of Alberta's herds of wild horses once grazed. Stories of the stallions and mares ranging freely captivated hearts and minds. Were they feral horses who had wandered from early ranches or from First Nations' and settlers' camps? Was theirs the noble heritage of mustangs that, over thousands of years, migrated north from early Spanish settlements? Grazing on rangeland across North America, wild horses once numbered in the hundreds of thousands. With changing conditions and hunting, numbers plummeted and only a few small herds remained. The last round-up of Alberta's wild-horses was staged on the Suffield range in 1994 to protect the endangered habitat of "real" wildlife. Still, did the wild horses have the right to be protected like other wildlife? Emotions ran high, and today, many still wish they could see horses running free.

If you head south, consider carrying on past Medicine Hat to the Cypress Hills or the American border. If you head north, stop at Oyen or continue north to the end of the Buffalo Trail, more than 400 kilometres away!

The name Buffalo Trail honours the vast herds of bison that once grazed this landscape. The great mammals symbolizing the prairie were estimated to have once surpassed 60 million on the North American plains.

Then, between 1830 and 1870, with a demand for buffalo robes, commercial hunting killed off herds. Also, settlement that encroached on grazing land dealt a powerful blow.

By about 1880, few free-ranging bison remained on the prairie. Already by 1907, the Canadian government began re-introducing the beloved prairie bison, and between 1907 and 1909, about 400 head were shipped from Montana. More arrived later to the National Buffalo Park Reserve near Wainwright.

Years later, with the population flourishing beyond wildest expectations, animals were culled, and some were sent to Wood Buffalo National Park. However, along the Buffalo Trail, the abiding vision of pre-settlement days in the early West remains an image of millions of buffalo ranging freely on the plains.

---

56 Hillcrest Mine Disaster

TRAVEL TIPS

There are no facilities at the cemetery and mine site.

Accommodation is limited in Crowsnest Pass and fills up quickly in summer, so book ahead if you would like to stay in the area.

Location: Just south of Highway 3 in the Crowsnest Pass. Exit is well marked.

Phone: (403) 562-7388 (Frank Slide Interpretive Centre)

E-mail: info@frankslide.com

www.frankslide.com

P

Visiting the Hillcrest Cemetery is a moving experience, and a place to discover the depths of character of our people and our province. Experiencing the Crowsnest Pass area starts with an understanding of time, place and adversity. Explosions at many mines in the Crowsnest Pass claimed lives, but the Hillcrest explosion was the worst mining disaster in Canadian history.

Already by 1900, coal was king throughout the Pass; within 14 years, about 1,000 people lived in the hamlet of Hillcrest. At the mine, 377 members of the United Mine Workers of America were on the payroll, and average pay was about $125 per month. Most miners were between 20 and 30, but ages ranged from 16 to 63.

On June 19, 1914, 237 men hiked the trail to the mine for the morning shift. Soon 235 of them had gone below ground. The fireboss had posted a warning of low-level methane gas, which wasn't unusual. To be dangerous, levels had to rise to between five and 15 per cent, but the Hillcrest operation was considered the safest and best-run mine in the valley.

Then, at 9:30 a.m., without warning, a thunderous explosion rocked the mine site. Disaster had just added a terrible chapter to our history. Of the 189 deaths, some were the direct result of the explosion, but most men died from lack of oxygen. A father who escaped after the explosion went back to save his three sons. All four died. Another miner who had survived the Frank Slide

lost his life at Hillcrest. As well, the tragedy widowed 130 women and left 400 children fatherless.

In time, the Hillcrest mine resumed operations. Then, in 1926, another explosion claimed two lives. In 1939, Hillcrest and Mohawk Collieries amalgamated, and the buildings at Hillcrest were not used again.

Year after year, countless travellers pay their respects by visiting the three mass graves at the Hillcrest Cemetery, a Provincial Historic Site. Surrounded by special fencing, the graves are well-kept tributes. Here, too, is the nine-foot Hillcrest Mine Disaster Memorial. The only monument of its kind in Canada, it lists names of those who died in the Hillcrest explosion, as well as names of those across Canada who died in other mine disasters.

Down the highway, in the theatre at the Frank Slide Interpretive Centre, three films explore the tragic history. Through photos, commentary and details, *Disaster of the Century*, *Canada's Worst Mine Disaster* and *The Devil's Breath* convey the poignancy. Interpretive programs also bring this sad chapter of history to life. From these presentations, you learn of the rescue attempts, and inevitably you walk away gripped by the tragedy while appreciating afresh the true meaning of heroism.

Crowsnest Mountain stands apart from other mountains. To photographers and hikers, it is distinctive, but hiking the mountain takes excellent conditioning. Your reward awaits you at the top of the Crowsnest Mountain hike where panoramic views of the valley and the High Rock Range in British Columbia will take your breath away.

To drink in those views, you first have to tackle the 1,040 metres of elevation gain from the trailhead. Although the trail does not require actual rock-climbing, it is on the verge of requiring these skills – even for experienced hikers. The trail is six kilometres, beginning with wide, gentle paths. But it narrows as it climbs. On scree slopes, the trail becomes less clear and it's easy to lose your footing on the thousands of loose stones. Finally, the steep chimney at the base of the cliff face appears.

Hiking time is 3½ to four hours. Be sure to check a hiking guide for detailed information.

57 Lois Hole

Lois Hole was real. When she gave you a hug, it was real. When she said "Put your garden in early," that was real. When she nudged leaders to pay more heed to education and health care, that, too, was heartfelt and real. Lois Hole had numerous titles before and after her name, yet she never lost the down-to-earth sincerity that made her the love of Alberta.

Earthiness was an apt quality for a woman whose family nurtured the largest retail greenhouse and gardening centre in western Canada. Lois Hole loved to recall how she and husband Ted struggled at first to make a living on their 81 hectares beside the Sturgeon River near St. Albert. Only when passersby started begging to buy the farm's excess cucumbers and carrots did the perfect answer take shape. Soon a greenhouse sprouted next to the farm's big red barn, and demand for the farm's produce soared.

Sons Bill and Jim both grew to love the farm, initiating the shift from vegetable gardening to today's greenhouse business. Later they were joined by Bill's wife, Valerie, who stuck with the Holes despite being stranded in the field picking vegetables while the family rushed Ted to the hospital with a broken leg.

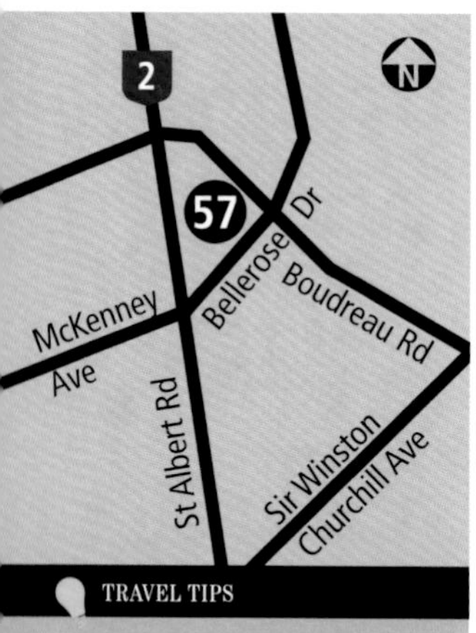

TRAVEL TIPS

Hole's Greenhouses and Gardens is open daily, and open evenings seasonally.

Greenhouses and display gardens attract busloads of gardening aficionados to gaze as well as buy.

Location: 101 Bellerose Dr., St. Albert

Phone: 1-888-88HOLES or (780) 419-6800

E-mail: info@holesonline.com

www.holesonline.com

Word spread that Lois Hole had a knack for giving excellent gardening advice, spiced with homespun humour. She became the voice of Hole's Greenhouses, spinning instructive tales that spared no one, herself included. Did you hear how the pigs taught her to harrow by rolling in a newly planted carrot patch? To her surprise, the carrots came up fine, weedless where the pigs had rolled. "You can do the same thing with the back of a rake," she said. "Works like a charm."

"The heart and soul of Alberta doesn't lie in the rich farmland, the majestic Rockies, the precious oilfields or bustling cities. As wondrous and important as those features may be, that heart resides in our people."

Lois Hole

Transferred to print, Lois's words became a set of best-selling northern-climate garden books. She also wrote a folksy memoir, *I'll Never Marry a Farmer,* taking its title from a vow she made to her mother as a girl in Saskatchewan. It's one of the few vows she's known to have broken.

Through it all, the Holes modeled generosity of spirit, donating to more than a thousand organizations a year. Lois was equally generous with her time, serving three decades as school trustee in St. Albert.

In the late '90s, leaders began to recognize what a gem Alberta had in Lois Hole. Elected chancellor of the University of Alberta in 1998, she was named a member of the Order of Canada in 1999. The next year, in 2000, she became lieutenant-governor of Alberta, the second woman to hold that post. Forthright as always, she continued to speak her mind about topics close to her heart.

In March 2003, Ted succumbed to cancer; Lois followed less than two years later, at age 71. Tributes poured in, and numerous agencies began planning Lois Hole tributes. Besides carrying on with Hole's Greenhouses and Gardens, her family faces the truly monumental task of ensuring that the many good works being done in her name keep her memory forever real.

58 Jasper National Park

TRAVEL TIPS

Jasper has many private home accommodations, like B&Bs but without breakfast; see www.stayinjasper.com.

Some campgrounds take reservations via www.pccamping.ca or 1-877-737-3783.

Check out Alpine Club of Canada backcountry huts at (403) 678-3200, info@AlpineClubofCanada.ca, www.alpineclubofcanada.ca.

Book lodging ahead during peak camping and ski seasons.

Miette Hot Springs, open May to early October, 1-800-767-1611, www.hotsprings.ca.

Location: Jasper Information Centre: 500 Connaught Dr., Jasper townsite

Phone: (780) 852-6176

E-mail: jnp@pc.gc.ca

www.pc.gc.ca/jasper

Jasper is a place that grows on you. Entered from the east via the Yellowhead (Highway 16), Jasper National Park begins as understated front ranges, low-slung mountains separated by a broad, stream-threaded valley. Drive another half hour to the Jasper townsite, and you find a laid-back retreat that doesn't shout but rather whispers "stay awhile," with small-town charm that belies its world-class amenities. Continue down the Icefields Parkway or head off the beaten path, and now the mountains grow tall and near, capped by shimmering icefields and pale blue glaciers. Here, along the Continental Divide, stands the highest peak in Alberta: the 3,747-metre Mount Columbia.

The largest and most northerly of Canada's mountain national parks, Jasper protects more than 10,000 square kilometres of threatened life while offering four-season recreation for every interest and ability: camping, hiking, climbing, skiing, cycling, swimming, fishing, golfing, theatre, dining and more. You might begin with a ride on the Jasper Tramway (open mid-April to mid-October) for a panoramic overview of the townsite, the Athabasca River, numerous glacier-fed lakes and six mountain ranges.

Jasper is particularly known for its network of backcountry trails, many of which could tell tales of use by the region's earliest people. Numerous campsites, cabins and lodges along those trails range from do-it-yourself to fully catered.

Those who'd rather explore within hailing distance of a road have plenty of choices as well. A favourite destination is the majestic 3,300-metre Mount Edith Cavell, south of town at the end of a winding 14-kilometre road that becomes an unofficial ski trail in winter. You can view the mountain's aptly named Angel Glacier via a short interpretive trail – or climb into the meadows to travel with marmots, pikas and tender alpine flowers.

Exquisitely hued lakes also make Jasper a special place. Near the historic (and luxurious) Jasper Park Lodge, you'll find scenic swimming at lakes Edith, Annette and Beauvert. On the plateau behind town, Patricia and Pyramid lakes make a fine destination for biking and hiking. Further away are such options as the mysterious Medicine Lake, which empties in winter through Canada's most extensive underground "karst" or cave system.

Much of the water from Medicine Lake eventually reaches Maligne Canyon, itself a must-see. A short interpretive trail over four bridges provides excellent views of the thundering Maligne River carving potholes in rock deep below. Keep walking to the fifth and sixth bridges, and you'll pass Jasper's foremost rock climbing zone. In winter, descend into the canyon with a guide to view waterfalls in their sculpted winter attire. Continue on to the famous Maligne Lake, a sparkling gem surrounding Spirit Island, one of the Rockies' most photographed spots.

After an active day, what better tonic than the Miette Hot Springs, the Rockies' hottest. For a century and more, bathers have climbed the scenic Miette Rd. to rejuvenate in the Rockies' hottest mineral spring. An interpretive trail leads to the springs' source; continue beyond to experience east Jasper, a fine place to park awhile.

Jasper Forest Reserve was born in 1907 to protect the Athabasca Valley amid the advance of two transcontinental railways. By 1911, both the Grand Trunk Pacific Railway and Canadian Northern Railway had reached what was then termed Fitzhugh station. The station was later renamed in honour of fur trade factor Jasper Hawes.

Now part of the Canadian Rocky Mountain Parks World Heritage Site, Jasper contains five national historic sites:

- The Jasper Information Centre, built in 1914 and still a key information hub.
- Yellowhead Pass, used to transport leather. A viewpoint stands 9.5 kilometres west of Jasper townsite.
- Jasper House, a fur trading post as early as 1813, recalled on a plaque 35 kilometres east of town on the Yellowhead.
- Athabasca Pass, a fur trading gate described at a picnic area 19 kilometres south of town on Highway 93A.
- Henry House, built in 1811 to support Athabasca Pass; plaque is on the Yellowhead as it bypasses town.

59 Kalyna Country

In the formative period of prairie development, when there was widespread concern that the mostly unsettled West might be taken over by the United States, the Canadian government offered cheap or free land to anyone, particularly small farmers, who would come and work it. Immigrants poured in from all over Europe, some escaping religious persecution, some with so little hope in their own land that they had nothing to lose, and others just seeking a better life to pass on to their children.

The migration to the area east and north of Edmonton created a multicultural patchwork of settlements, many formed by newcomers from Eastern Europe. Organized in 1992 into an ecomuseum, or heritage district, these rural communities continue to preserve the flavours and celebrate the customs the first settlers brought with them from Ukraine, Poland, Romania, Britain and other parts of the world. The region is actually Canada's largest Ukrainian settlement and the world's largest ecomuseum.

Kalyna Country, as the region has been dubbed, from the Ukrainian word for the highbush cranberry native to the area, embraces nine counties and more than 50 communities including First Nations reserves and a Métis settlement.

It makes a delightful place to visit, take a walk back in time or check out all the "largest" claims. You've probably heard of the giant *pysanka*, or Ukrainian Easter egg, in Vegreville. There are also

TRAVEL TIPS

Order a free copy of the Kalyna Country Visitor's & Events Guide or the Victoria Trail guide online, by e-mailing or phoning.

There are more than 20 visitor centres throughout the region to help you get the most from your explorations.

Location: Kalyna Country is a 20,000-square-kilometre region in east central Alberta, bordering Edmonton to the west, Lloydminster to the east, Wainwright to the south and Kikino Métis settlement to the north.

Phone: 1-888-452-5962

E-mail: info@kalynacountry.com

www.kalynacountry.com

six-metre mushrooms in Vilna, a larger-than-life Peter Fidler monument in Elk Point and Mundare's sausage that is almost 13 metres high and weighs about six tonnes! With more than 10 of these unique roadside attractions in the region, you'll need a checklist to keep track.

At the Saddle Lake reserve, a steel sculpture of a warrior on horseback strikingly symbolizes the vibrant spirit of the modern-day Cree Nation. At the evocative Ribstones Historic Site southeast of Viking, you can commune with the ghosts of ancient aboriginal buffalo hunters and with them pay homage to their life-giving prey.

In the village of Andrew, a well-preserved grain elevator is available for exploring, and a second one is being restored in the hamlet of Radway.

If the weather isn't cooperating, you can always spend quality time indoors at your choice of more than 40 local museums and historic sites throughout the region. Of course, if a pleasant workout in the great outdoors is what you're looking for, you can go canoeing or jet boating along the scenic and historic North Saskatchewan River or take in a stretch of the Iron Horse Trail between Heinsburg and Waskatenau.

A special feature of Kalyna Country is its historic churches, many of them beautiful onion-domed sanctuaries built by the Ukrainian pioneers and lovingly maintained by their descendants. Scattered throughout the countryside, they are popular destinations for organized tours and favourite subjects of photographers and painters. Whatever your reason for coming to rural east central Alberta, you are sure to find many things to see and do.

Kalyna country isn't just for summer.

Winter offers wonderful adventures such as skiing across more than 100 kilometres of groomed and ungroomed trails in the Cooking Lake/Blackfoot Provincial Recreation Area. Elk Island National Park also has four trails for cross-country skiing as well as seven for snowshoeing and hiking.

If you need to rent equipment, Strathcona Wilderness Centre has everything you need for cross-country or snowshoeing; the centre also offers lessons for the novice.

If you prefer downhill skiing, head out to Long Lake Ski Area and its 12 downhill and snowboarding runs. The best months for snowmobiling in the area are December to March. The 500 kilometres of snowmobile trails will surely tempt you away from hibernating in front of the fire.

60 Kananaskis Country

If golf is your passion, Kananaskis Country is a premier destination. Two stunning 18-hole golf courses take their names from the surrounding mountains. Mount Kidd, a Robert Trent Jones course, with its many elevated tees, offers breathtaking views of the surrounding mountains. Its signature par three hole is much photographed. Mount Lorette, Kidd's sister course, is arguably more challenging and just as breathtaking. Thirteen holes are laid out along and over the Kananaskis River. Mount Kidd is known for its sand and Mount Lorette for its water.

From the complimentary valet service to ever-friendly staff, Kananaskis Country Golf Course is a must for every Alberta golfer from professional to beginner.

Whatever the season, Kananaskis Country calls. Treasured by conservationists and outdoor enthusiasts, Kananaskis Country lures vacationers, artists, athletes, golfers, anglers and those simply seeking outstanding beauty and serenity. Kananaskis Country encompasses numerous park and protected areas including six provincial parks – Peter Lougheed, Spray Valley, Sheep River, Bragg Creek, Canmore Nordic Centre and Bow Valley – with Peter Lougheed Provincial Park the largest – and four wildland parks – Bow Valley, Elbow-Sheep, Bluerock and Don Getty.

Running through the mountain paradise are the Kananaskis, Elbow, Sheep and Highwood rivers. It's little wonder that kayakers come to challenge the rapids while smaller lakes invite canoeists to float peacefully. Seeking the sting of bracing mountain water, others set off on thrilling whitewater raft trips while the gentler fun seekers dangle toes in ice-cold lakes.

For climbers, the Barrier Crag, Yamnuska and Wasootch Slabs offer more than 100 climbing options with varying degrees of difficulty.

Hikers will discover countless trails for exploring meadows, creeks and mountain tops. Want to invest a few hours in an experience that will rejuvenate you for weeks? Treat yourself to a great half-day, full-day or backpack adventure. At park visitor information centres, pick up trail maps and be sure to ask about bears. This is grizzly and black bear territory, but you are more likely to see sheep, elk, deer or coyotes.

There are more than a thousand kilometres of trails in Kananaskis Country. The trail along Galatea Creek to Lillian Lake is one of many gems. It's considered moderate for experienced hikers and offers rewards of outstanding scenery. On such high altitude trails, knee-deep snow lingers until late June and may reappear in September, so July and August are the best bets. No tea houses top these peaks. You eat and drink what you pack.

The backcountry campground at Lillian Lake is a great base for backpackers. It is one of 18 backcountry campgrounds located in Kananaskis Country. RV and auto campers also have choices but demand soars on summer weekends. Even at the Lower Lake or Elkwood Campgrounds near the Lower Kananaskis Lake, with more than 100 sites each, arrive early! Some vehicle access campgrounds, such as Mt. Kidd RV Park with 229 sites, offer reservations.

Oh, yes! Don't forget the Highwood Pass, especially in early fall. On a sunny autumn day, the blue of sky and river, green of spruce trees and brilliant yellow-orange of larch inspire artists and photographers. Approaching from the south, the highway follows the Highwood River, a great haunt for anglers. Further north, in the Kananaskis Valley, trail rides transform city slickers into cowpunchers.

In winter, cross-country skiers love the multitude of groomed trails found at several locations in Kananaskis Country, and down-hill skiing has long been a lure. Mount Allan's Nakiska hosted Olympic Winter Games competitions in 1988. Its variable natural snow pack is augmented by extensive snow-making coverage.

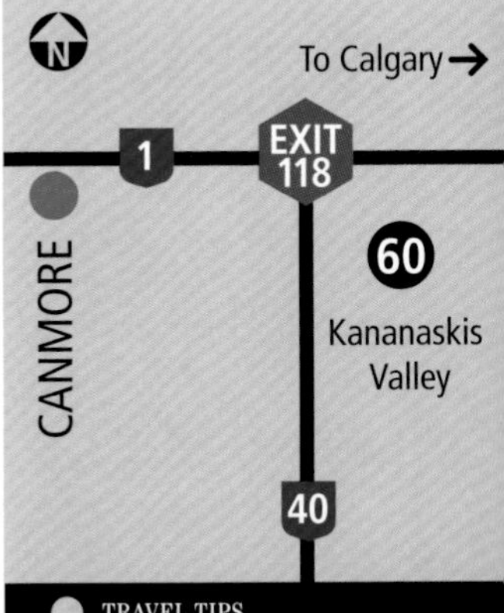

TRAVEL TIPS

Prepare for your day by packing energy snacks, liquids, sun screen and insect spray.

Hats, light jackets and durable shoes are a must.

To determine wheelchair accessibility for specific facilities, call William Watson Lodge toll free in Alberta 310-0000, then (403) 591-7227.

Location: South off Highway 1 onto Highway 40 (90 kilometres from Calgary)

Phone: Travel Alberta 1-800-252-3782

E-mail: travelinfo@travelalberta.com

www.cd.gov.ab.ca/parks/kananaskis

61 Lac La Biche Mission

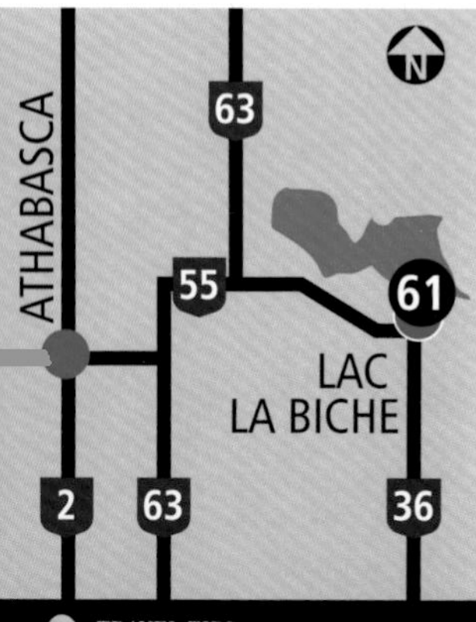

TRAVEL TIPS

The Lac La Biche Mission is open from the May long weekend through Labour Day in September.

The mission includes the restored convent (the oldest standing sawn lumber building in Alberta), the church and displays. The visitor centre is wheelchair accessible.

Location: 10 kilometres northwest of Lac La Biche

E-mail: libmiss@telusplanet.net

www.townllb.com or www.laclabicheregion.com

In 1798, David Thompson of the North West Company became the first European explorer to arrive on the shores of Lac La Biche. Peter Fidler of the Hudson's Bay Company (HBC) followed Thompson's route to the area only one year later, in 1799.

The geographic importance of the area became apparent over the next several decades, and its significance as a settlement took a major step forward in 1844 with the arrival of the first Roman Catholic priest, Rev. J.B. Thibeault, who answered the invitation of retired voyageur Joseph Cardinal to visit Lac La Biche.

The Lac La Biche Mission is situated near Portage La Biche, the area between the Churchill Basin, which drains into Hudson's Bay, and the Athabasca-Mackenzie Basin, which flows to the Arctic Sea. The mission is located in the Athabasca-Mackenzie Basin.

Portage La Biche, which became known as a passage to the Pacific Ocean and the gateway to the southern Athabasca country, was a crucial link in Canada's first transcontinental route.

The first permanent mission was founded by Father Rene Remas, Oblate of Mary Immaculate (OMI), beside the HBC post. In 1855-56, the Oblate missionaries moved the Lac La Biche Mission, given the name of Our Lady of Victories, from alongside the HBC Post to its present site.

Later in 1856, the missionaries cut a cart trail from the mission to Fort Pitt, northwest of present-day Lloydminster, connecting Lac La Biche by an overland route to the Red River Settlement near present-day Winnipeg. The mission earned the title of the "Warehouse of the North," becoming a pivotal point in a transportation system that supplied the northern missions as far north as Fort Good Hope in the present-day Northwest Territories.

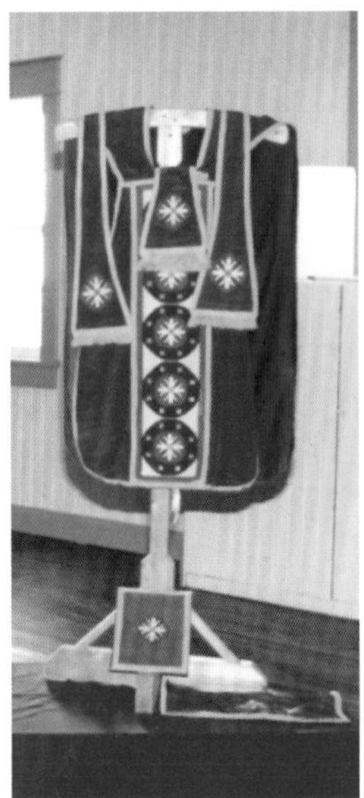

The arrival of the Grey Nuns at the mission in 1862 added further depth to the community. They established Alberta's first residential school, a hospice and an orphanage in the stone-built convent. The Grey Nuns left in 1898; Les Filles de Jesus took up their duties in 1905 and stayed at the mission until 1963.

As well as providing a crucial transportation link across a vast territory, the mission also made a lasting impact on the local community. The missionaries introduced agriculture to nearby residents, changing their traditional nomadic lifestyle to an agrarian community because the bison were disappearing. Initially, residents grew root crops, and then produced sufficient quantities of wheat to supply flour to the northern missions.

In fact, Lac La Biche and its mission were first in Alberta to grow wheat in commercial quantities. The area boasts other firsts as well. With the residents' assistance, the missionaries built Alberta's first powered sawmill in 1871. Father E.Grouard introduced Alberta's first printing press in 1877, and it worked hard to publish religious texts in syllabics for the aboriginal community.

With the arrival of the railway and steamboats, the mission declined in importance as a key transportation link. Modern life and technology had shunned the community that had once been key to survival in the northwest.

The nearby town of Lac La Biche, with a population of 2,700, is the gateway to Lakeland and Sir Winston Churchill provincial parks. Nearby is a golf course as well as many lakes, campgrounds, birding sites and cultural attractions.

Lac La Biche, home of Portage College, has a diversified economy with gas exploration, forestry, tourism and mixed farming sectors.

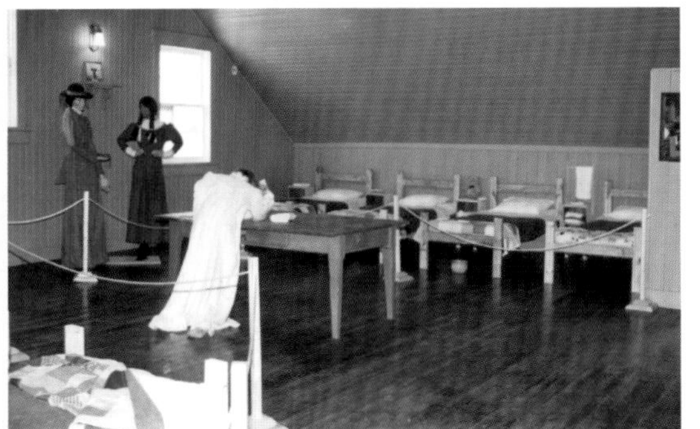

62 Lac Ste. Anne Pilgrimage

TRAVEL TIPS

Pilgrimage dates vary but usually include Ste. Anne's feast day, July 26.

If you're staying overnight, be prepared to camp.

For those who need assistance, a small shuttle makes regular runs between the shrine and the campsites.

Location: About 80 kilometres northwest of Edmonton off Highway 43

Phone: (780) 459-2586 or (780) 460-6927

E-mail: diane.lamoureux@telus.net

www.lsap.ca

For a week each July, Lac Ste. Anne becomes awash with pilgrims as thousands of Catholics, mostly aboriginal, gather to visit old friends, seek healing and be renewed in their faith. Begun more than a hundred years ago, this pilgrimage has become the largest annual gathering of Aboriginal peoples in Canada. In 2004, its significance was recognized as Lac Ste. Anne became a National Historic Site of Canada.

If Lac Ste. Anne could talk, she would tell of ceremonies on these shores stretching back millennia. Then known as Manito Sakahigan or Spirit Lake, she called people back from their winter traplines for the buffalo hunt each summer. Father Jean-Baptiste Thibault, who arrived here in 1844, gave the lake its current name, fulfilling a vow to call his first mission after his patron saint, Ste. Anne.

The first permanent Catholic mission west of Winnipeg, Lac Ste. Anne gained respect and followers as the early missionaries proved their mettle by caring for the sick and standing between warring parties. By the late 1840s, the Oblate Missionaries, an order of Catholic priests and brothers, had made their way into what is now Alberta, and soon their members staffed most of the Catholic missions there. Father Remas, Oblate of Mary Immaculate (OMI), one of the first Oblates at Lac Ste. Anne and known for great holiness, is legendary for once quieting a fierce storm that threatened to swamp a flotilla of fishing boats. Standing on the shore, he sprinkled the angry lake with holy water and commanded it to be still.

By 1887, the buffalo had disappeared and the lake had lost its status as a gathering place. The mission was slated to close until its pastor, Father Lestanc, OMI, visited the Shrine of Ste. Anne d'Aury in France. As he prayed, God powerfully revealed that he must not close the mission, but instead build a shrine honouring Ste. Anne - a place for pilgrims to receive spiritual help.

The first pilgrimage to Lac Ste. Anne occurred just two years later, with 400 attending. Now as many as 40,000 come during the week surrounding July 26, the feast day of Ste. Anne. Most arrive in vehicles these days, but some still make the journey on foot, walking hours, days and even months to reach their destination. A tent city springs up where you might see racks of meat and fish drying alongside campers and motor homes, all within earshot of hymns and prayers.

Mass is offered frequently during the week, in Cree, Chipweyan, Blackfoot and Dene, as well as English. Candlelit processions and stations depicting scenes from creation and Christ's passion invite prayer and meditation. The waters are blessed and then pilgrims wade in, trusting they will be healed in spirit and soul, if not in body. It's a solemn and prayerful, yet joyful, scene as children splash in the water while the infirm receive whatever help they need. Above it all stands the huge shrine to Ste. Anne, which can seat 3,000 or more.

The lake is still a place of meeting, drawing people from all four directions and many nations. Nobody leaves untouched.

Ste. Anne was Mary's mother and Jesus' grandmother. Neither she nor her husband Joachim is mentioned in the Bible, but the two do appear in early Christian writings. Her feast day, July 26, recalls the caring grandmother, a figure honoured in many Aboriginal societies.

July 26 is also a busy day at the church of Ste.-Anne-De-Beaupre near Quebec City. In 1658, a workman was reported miraculously cured during construction of the first Ste. Anne shrine on this site. Other cures followed and today the stone basilica attracts 250,000 pilgrims a year.

Lake Louise

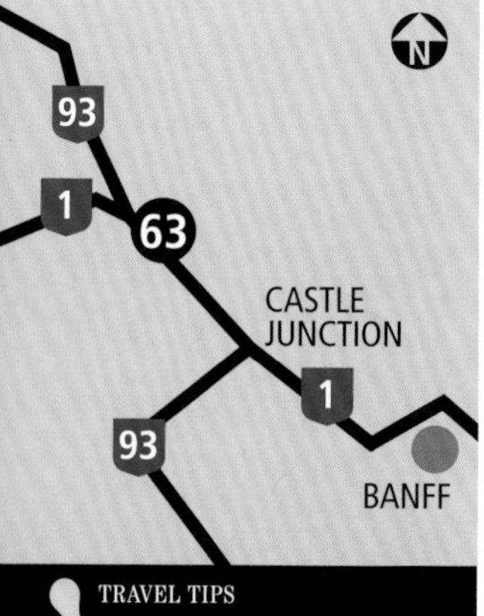

TRAVEL TIPS

Stop downtown at the Lake Louise information centre for maps, brochures, backcountry permits, interpretive program times and reports on any hazards.

Nearby accommodations include campgrounds, hotels, bed and breakfasts and the Lake Louise Alpine Centre (a top-of-line hostel).

Location: The hamlet of Lake Louise is on the Trans-Canada Highway 185 kilometres west of Calgary and 56 kilometres west of Banff.

Phone: (403) 522-3833

E-mail: ll.info@pc.gc.ca

www.pc.gc.ca/banff

www.banfflakelouise.com

Located in the heart of Banff National Park, Lake Louise has multiple personalities. You could be confused by that – or simply enjoy the fact that this gem has facets to fit any inclination. First there's the obvious: Lake Louise is both a hamlet and a lake. What's more, the lake is not adjacent to the hamlet, but several kilometres up a steep (albeit paved) winding road.

Follow Lake Louise Drive to its conclusion on a summer day, and you'll first experience the lake as a crowd pleaser. Parking is often scarce by mid-morning and throngs swarm the boardwalk, each seeking the perfect shot of the Canadian Rockies' most famous lake – and of the huge and historic chateau that overlooks it.

Walk a few paces forward, perch on a rock and already you can begin to drink in the beauty that draws millions here. The sparkling water leads your eye to a dramatic array of peaks and glaciers behind dusky mountain shoulders. It's an intriguing conglomeration of triangles, echoed on a calm day in a mirror of turquoise water. The water's beautiful blue-green colour is caused by "rock flour," bedrock ground so finely by moving glaciers that it remains suspended when entering the lake with glacial runoff.

Options abound for exploring the two Louises. You can hike or ski between the hamlet and the lake via the tramline and Louise Creek trails, which combine to form a seven-kilometre loop. In summer, canoes are available for rent at the lake boathouse. In winter, skating on the lake is free. Cycling routes are also available; see www.pc.gc.ca.

Several adult female grizzly bears live in the Lake Louise area. To avoid unwanted encounters, stay on trails, be alert and obey all trail closures.

Lake Louise is a great base for exploring two scenic parkways: Icefields Parkway to Jasper townsite and Bow Valley Parkway to Banff townsite. Nearby Moraine Lake is also spectacular. The 15-kilometre road to this lake begins about two-thirds of the way up Lake Louise Drive. You may recognize the lake from the backs of older Canadian $20 bills.

Wander the path around the lake, and soon you'll leave the crowds behind. Or hike a few kilometres up steep switchbacks to Lake Agnes where you can toast your tenacity at a teahouse perched nearby. You're now enjoying one of the first hikes built here after the Canadian Pacific Railway (CPR) reached these parts in 1885. To attract passengers, the CPR built successively more elaborate accommodations at numerous scenic destinations, Lake Louise included. Its employees, in turn, helped design the network of trails that made this rugged alpine landscape the birthplace of recreational hiking in the Canadian Rockies.

For an aerial view of the lake and the town and their magnificent surroundings, ride a gondola or chairlift at the Lake Louise ski hill (open June to September). This world-class ski resort sports its own intriguing history of business dreams built and dashed, but it's now bigger than ever. In winter, this is where you'll find the throngs. That's when those seeking the tranquil side of Lake Louise strap on cross country skis or snowshoes and find a trail far afield. Or head to the lake for a skate amid the ice sculptures and a hot chocolate by the outdoor fire.

Leduc No. 1

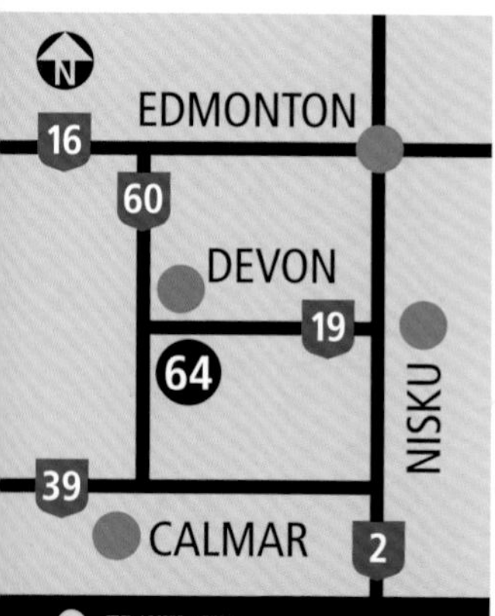

TRAVEL TIPS

The Canadian Petroleum Discovery Centre, on the site of Leduc No. 1, is open daily from 9 a.m. to 5 p.m. year round.

The addition of more than 2,100 square metres of exhibit space, a cafeteria and patio area will add to the experience.

You can guide yourself around the facility or arrange for a tour.

Location: Two kilometres south of Devon on Highway 60, just south of the Highway 19 junction

Phone: 1-866-987-4323 or (780) 987-4323

E-mail: ldohs@c-pic.org

www.c-pic.org

Leduc No. 1, the gusher that started Alberta's "black gold" odyssey, is in one of the most unlikely locations for a rich oil find. At least that's what engineers of the time thought.

Looking for oil in Alberta, Imperial Oil had drilled 133 dry – or unsuccessful – wells before No. 1 "came in" in 1947. Conventional geological wisdom led crews to search for oil in the Western Canadian Sedimentary Basin where oil deposits were situated relatively close to the surface. Either the oil literally seeped to the surface through land faults or was contained in gooey oil sands such as those near Fort McMurray.

Areas including the Leduc region were not geological "hot spots" for oil because it was not thought that oil deposits would be found a mile or more underground.

A seismic test revealed an anomaly, a "one-point-high" and the company decided to give it one more try before calling it quits. Originally the drilling at Leduc had been considered exploratory, a "wildcat" in oil parlance. Imperial had not drilled within an 80-kilometre radius of

Leduc when they started in November of 1946. The drill crew thought at first it was a natural gas discovery, but going deeper, they found oil in the reservoir rock.

"Bringing in" an oil well was a time for ceremony. Pushed for a date, the crew selected Feb. 13, 1947 and pulled out all the stops to bring it in on time. Breakdowns the night before meant that the dignitaries gathered for the 1 p.m. ceremony got very cold waiting for the gush of oil. Some of them went home but those who stayed were amply rewarded at 4 p.m. when the promise of Leduc No. 1 became reality and "she came in with a roar."

The find was the beginning of Alberta's booming oil economy. By the end of that year, 147 more wells had been drilled in the Leduc area. Imperial Oil realized that workers and their families would need homes and proceeded to build the town of Devon (named for the Devonian Reef formation that contains the oil) close to the oil field. The need for services for both the oil field and the town led to more growth.

Leduc No. 1 changed the economic face of Alberta and Canada's oil industry forever as it opened up vast new drilling opportunities in Alberta and Western Canada.

The Canadian Petroleum Discovery Centre & Hall of Fame near Leduc houses displays of the oil drilling process as well as the history of oil exploration in Alberta. Models, dioramas and displays tell the stories of those involved. Interactive computers help you test your knowledge of the industry, and a video entitled *A Mile Below the Wheat* tells the story of Leduc No. 1 and its relationship to the rest of the industry.

Before the Second World War, approximately half of Alberta's income was tied to agriculture. By the time Leduc No. 1 was capped in the early 1970s, agriculture accounted for 15 per cent and resource mining was responsible for 40 per cent of Alberta's wealth. With the addition of the oil sands development, Alberta's economy is assured for many years to come.

65 Lesser Slave Lake Bird Observatory

It began in 1993 with a small group of dedicated bird watchers and conservationists who realized there was something special about the shores of Lesser Slave Lake in north central Alberta.

Apparently, migratory birds don't enjoy flying across the large, open lake to the west, so they veer away from it. Marten Mountain stops them going to the east, so the birds end up in a north-south funnel along the shore.

The Lesser Slave Lake Bird Observatory (LSLBO) is the northernmost migration monitoring station in Canada and is in a perfect spot to collect critical information on migratory birds in their breeding grounds. It was incorporated in 1997 and continues to be run by local volunteers who hire seasonal staff for research and the education programs that are so essential to conservationists of any kind. Since its founding, LSLBO has banded more than 45,000 birds of more than 240 different species. Besides the banding, LSLBO is responsible for many projects, including an owl monitoring program and a tundra swan survey.

Why do we have bird observatories? It's all part of the attempt to preserve our environment and its occupants, right down to the smallest. Scientists need to know whether different species are increasing or decreasing, whether they're taking new routes on their migrations and whether their breeding grounds have changed. With this information, they can determine whether the habitat of the birds has been altered and whether steps need to be taken to protect that habitat. Counting and keeping track of the numbers of such little characters may seem a

N
88
2
65
SLAVE LAKE
33

TRAVEL TIPS

Lesser Slave Lake Provincial Park is a 2.5-hour drive northwest of Edmonton.

The Boreal Centre for Bird Conservation is open year round, welcoming visitors seven days a week in summer.

Scheduled tours of the research facility are also available.

Location: From the junction of Highway 2 and Highway 88, drive another 18.5 kilometres north on Highway 88, look for a large blue Boreal Centre for Bird Conservation sign and turn west.

Phone: (780) 849-8240

E-mail: info@borealbirdcentre.ca

www.lslbo.org and www.borealbirdcentre.ca

difficult task, but there are standardized methods used throughout North America so numbers and changes can be compared.

In the fall of 2006, the new Boreal Centre for Bird Conservation opened its doors. It's a 560-square-metre complex with space for a laboratory, research library and offices for staff, volunteers, visiting experts and educators. You can also find indoor and outdoor exhibits.

The centre is a dream come true for the hard-working group and took years of planning and collaboration with Alberta Community Development. The new centre allows expanded summer programs such as having kids build birdhouses, dip in the lake for bugs and get banded like the birds. Adults are busy touring the facilities and going on walks, hikes and races, the latter with a prize for the best costume.

The building itself is glorious. Its inverted roofline is designed to suggest a bird in flight. While conducting their research and offering their education programs, the LSLBO is committed to disturbing the environment a little as possible. That task belongs to the songbirds.

The desire to design a building with as little impact on the surrounding environment as possible led to the adoption of a high standard of sustainable building design called LEED™ - Leadership in Energy and Environmental Design. LEED™ gives points in six major categories of building construction, and then after the project has been completed and is operational, awards certification based on a review of the building's performance. The categories are sustainable sites, water efficiency, energy and atmosphere, materials and resources, indoor environmental quality and innovation and design process.

The Boreal Centre for Bird Conservation has been built with these categories in mind and therefore includes features such as commercial grade composting toilets and waterless urinals, a rainwater capture and treatment system and a geothermal pump system for heating. As well, sustainable building products were used in its construction.

66 Lethbridge High Level Bridge

TRAVEL TIPS

On the east side of the river, you'll find great views from the Sir Alexander Galt Museum and Archives and nearby pathways. Access view points on the west side of the river are at the University of Lethbridge or Bull Trail Park North.

A map of river valley parks and pathways is available at City Hall and www.lethbridge.ca.

Location: Near Heritage Heights on the west side of the river and 1st Street and Scenic Drive on the east side of the river

Phone: 1-800-661-1222

www.lethbridge.ca

Visiting Lethbridge means marvelling at the superstructure erected there by the Canadian Pacific Railway (CPR). At 96 metres high and with a span of 1.6 kilometres, the High Level Bridge stretches from the riverbank coulees on one side of the Oldman River to those on the other side.

Historically, only a narrow gauge railway operated between Lethbridge and Montana. With the city far from the CPR main line, freight headed any direction but south had to be hauled up and down the steep coulees. Recognizing available coal, livestock, produce and grain in the region, the CPR acknowledged the economic benefit of better transportation, but it planned a major branch line only from Medicine Hat through the Crowsnest Pass to southern British Columbia. Lethbridge was out of luck.

Eventually, low level river crossings on that line deteriorated. It was time to upgrade, so the CPR decided to add a branch linking Lethbridge to the east-west line. For the community, the world looked brighter. The new line involved building a massive railway bridge. It was nicknamed "The Big Bridge Over the Belly River," but something wasn't right. Was it the Belly or the Oldman? In 1909, surveyors got it right. The main riverbed was the Oldman, and its tributary was the Belly. The bridge would be over the Oldman River.

Lethbridge embraced the idea and lobbied for a traffic lane, too. The lobby was unsuccessful, perhaps because of the challenges facing builders. The bridge must span from one side of the coulee to the other. The coulee was

deep and slopes were unstable. Then, too, there was the famous Lethbridge wind!

The massive undertaking was completed in June 1909, and Lethbridge celebrated.

The first train crossed the bridge Oct. 23, 1909. Full tonnage freight trains were soon to follow. Sometimes referred to as "The Big Bridge," "The Big CPR Bridge" and "The CPR Trestle," the bridge's construction had cost a whopping $1.3 million at a time when most shoes cost about $2. But by taking the train, travellers could make the trip between Fort Macleod and Lethbridge in one hour rather than two.

Upon the official opening of the bridge in November 1909, the *Winnipeg Free Press* called it "One of the wonders of the world!" The phrase was hyperbole, but Albertans and locals loved it, and the claim stuck. After all, at the time it was the longest and highest bridge of its type – for which engineers had used a steel viaduct style of construction.

Numerous trains still make daily crossings. The bridge, though, is much more to the people of Lethbridge. A response to local geography, the bridge is part of the city's settlement and industrial development. The area under the first span of the bridge was a hobo jungle in the 1930s, speaking to good times and hard times. Not surprisingly, a 1969 design incorporating the bridge image was copyrighted and is still used to represent the city.

Lethbridge offers everything available in larger cities. A city of nearly 80,000 people with a university, community college, malls, theatres, historical attractions, regional airport, libraries, art gallery, arts centre, symphony orchestra and many recreational facilities, there is something for everyone. Somehow, the community still manages to keep a little of the small town atmosphere, too. Expect a well-educated population with nearly 45 per cent of residents between 20 and 50 years old.

Able to boast of about 24,000 hours of sunlight in a year with temperate winters and minimal snowfall and rain, Lethbridge is a great place to go almost any time of year. As a business centre, it serves southern Alberta, British Columbia and Montana communities. Its access to three border crossings makes it ideal for travellers. Coutts (a 24-hour United States border crossing), Carway and Del Bonita are all about a one- to 1.5-hour drive. Waterton Lakes National Park is about the same driving distance.

67 Lethbridge Scenic Drive

TRAVEL TIPS

Because traffic can be busy on sections of Scenic Drive, choose places to park and stop.

Location: Scenic Drive, on the north side of the river, begins at the intersection of 24 Avenue S. and Mayor Magrath Drive and winds northwest to Whoop Up Drive.

Phone: (403) 320-3995

www.lethbridge.ca

P

For a drive that offers the best in Lethbridge scenery and passes the city's most important attractions, take the route along the east side of the Oldman River. Aptly named Scenic Drive, the winding street offers magnificent views of the High Level Bridge and the coulee, the deep ravine through which the river flows.

A short section of the drive is north of Highway 3. Here, as you look to the west, you see a landscape that was once a busy coal mining area. Most of the Scenic Drive is south of the highway. It passes under the High Level Bridge and near the busy downtown area. At 1st Avenue, you catch a glimpse of the brewery gardens, a reminder of a time when the successful Lethbridge Brewing Company made Lethbridge Pilsner the beer of choice for many Albertans. The plant is now closed but the garden offers a pleasurable walk.

Next, Scenic Drive meanders south along the top of the coulee. Lethbridge Lodge offers accommodation overlooking the river, and nearby is the Lethbridge Centre for shopping.

Only one block south, you'll find the Sir Alexander Galt Museum and Archives, named for the man whose coal mining and other ventures were instrumental in building the city. Before becoming home to the museum and archives, the old brick building was the Galt Hospital. Recent renovations have added space and transformed the facility. The Viewing Gallery and Events Hall has glass walls, offering magnificent views of the river, coulees, the High Level Bridge and the University of Lethbridge.

Outside the museum, just enjoy standing on the pathway and looking across the river valley and down to the Oldman far below. You will love the vista spreading before your eyes – as long as the famous Lethbridge wind isn't creating near gale-force winds around you.

As you continue your driving tour along Scenic Drive, the impressive views of the deep ravine and coulee slopes with their fascinating shapes will transport you back to the region's earliest history. Most are sand-coloured formations dating to the early glacial erosion that took place thousands of years ago. Other brownish slopes have been shaped by the wind, rain, floods and snow-melt of more recent years. Where the coulees look red, colour was created by slow-burning slag heaps from coal mining.

Eventually, Scenic Drive passes a cemetery and takes travellers through residential areas to Mayor Magrath Drive, one of the busiest thoroughfares in the city.

You will long remember your time driving along the top of the coulee. The river, its valley and fascinating shapes are reminders of an era when bull-trains had to cross that river and lumber up and down the coulee, when early speculators developed coal reserves, when bridges were built and when a community accepted dry land conditions but was determined to prosper.

For a closer look at Lethbridge's natural environment and its tie to history, take Whoop-Up Drive to the river bottom parks. Go north through Indian Battle Park. Find the commemorative Coal Banks Kiosk. Stop and look up at the bridge.

Continue to the Helen Schuler Coulee Centre and Lethbridge Nature Preserve. Enjoy the native flora and fauna in this 82-hectare reserve where you will find self-guided and unmarked trails for walking, running and cycling. In the river's flood plain, moisture means cotton wood groves and saskatoon bushes flourish. Tough enough for the prairie heat, on the dry slopes of the coulees, prickly pear cactus, short grasses and prairie flowers reign. If you're interested in reptiles, from spring to fall, the arid slopes become the domain of rattlesnakes, but garter snakes are more common!

The preserve is open throughout the year except on Mondays. The centre has seasonal hours. Check Helen Schuler Coulee Centre at (403) 320-3064 or www.city.lethbridge.ab.ca/leisure/hscc.

Grant MacEwan

Grant MacEwan started writing at a very early age, keeping a journal in small pocket books or even on scraps of paper. Later in his life he went back to these jottings, tidied them up a bit and added some more mature thoughts to what had happened. He wrote his journals until the 1960s and his son-in-law, Max Foran, edited them for publication in 1986. The book is simply called *Grant MacEwan's Journals* and shows a lot of what he was like as a young man: introspective, frugal, hardworking and with a sense of humour that made him enjoy life.

Two of his most appealing books are *Fifty Mighty Men* and *And Mighty Women Too: Stories of Notable Western Canadian Women. Watershed: Reflections on Water*, was his 49th and final book, published after his death.

The YMCA was his favourite place to stay, and peanut butter was his favourite food. Greyhound Canada bus lines named a bus in his honour.

Mention Grant MacEwan to youngsters in Calgary and they'll probably think of an elementary school. Young people from the Edmonton region may call to mind the towers at the downtown Grant MacEwan College campus, and slightly older folk will remember him as the engaging lieutenant-governor of the 1960s and '70s. But for people who knew him, had occasion to speak to him, or have read his books, he was a man of unbounded energy, eloquent words and a passion for the history of "his" Prairies.

He knew all three of the Prairie provinces. Born on a homestead near Brandon, Man. and raised on farms in Manitoba and near Melfort, Sask., he attended the Ontario Agricultural College in Guelph, Ont. and Iowa State College before returning to become a professor at the University of Saskatchewan's School of Agriculture. His move to Alberta came in June 1952 and within four years he had a seat on Calgary City Council and another in the provincial legislative assembly.

Grant MacEwan went on to many other accomplishments and honours, but none of them seemed to change his attitude to life in general. Elitist he was not, and even in his later years, he preferred riding the bus instead of flying or driving to get to faraway destinations in order to give himself more writing time. His philosophy of life made him a conservationist. He said it was his way of connecting to a greater spirit, whatever that spirit was called.

Recipient of five honorary degrees and author of more than 49 books, his early writings were often about some practical aspect of work on the farm. A hobby he developed while spending time with the Canadian historian A.S. Morton became a passion and he started writing about the history of western Canada. He feared that the stories of the early days would be lost if someone didn't get them written down. He was sometimes criticized for the non-academic tone of his histories, but he knew that wasn't what he was after. He wanted ordinary stories for ordinary people – something to make the history come alive – and that's what he wrote.

His interest in individuals and his sense of humour attracted people of all ages. At the same time, his energy and efficiency amazed them. Even in his 80s he would start working early in the morning, move quickly from one area of his life to another, and still be going strong when the rest of the world was sleeping.

In 2000, just over a month before he died at the age of 97, Grant MacEwan was presented with the Writers Guild of Alberta's Golden Pen Life-time Achievement Award for "significant literary contribution." He brought so much to our knowledge of the lives of ordinary people in the early days of the province. But it was his enthusiasm and excitement about life in general, and the western Canadian life in particular, that endeared him to a whole province.

107 Ave
105 Ave
104 Ave
68
109 St
105 St
Jasper Ave
N

TRAVEL TIPS

Grant MacEwan participated in the 1970 Miles for Million walkathon; his hiking boots from the trek are on display in the MacEwan Room at Grant MacEwan College's City Centre Campus.

The college celebrates Grant MacEwan Day every February to remember Dr. MacEwan and to recognize staff and faculty who have excelled.

Location: Grant MacEwan College City Centre Campus is at 10700 – 104 Avenue, Edmonton

Phone: (780) 497-5040

E-mail: boardofgovernors@macewan.ca

www.macewan.ca

69 MacKay's Ice Cream

This family-owned business dates back to 1948 when James and Christina MacKay decided to add homemade ice cream to the line of goods at their general store in Cochrane. They experimented with new and original flavours but the most important aspect of the ice cream was the use of the richest and freshest ingredients the MacKays could find – pure cocoa from the Netherlands and fresh fruit and nuts.

That tradition continues more than 50 years later. After James MacKay's death in 1983, his daughters, Rhona and Robyn, took over from their mother and have continued to use the freshest ingredients for all their products, making the ice cream in small batches and adding the candies, nuts and flavourings by hand to preserve that homemade taste.

Since people visit from literally all over the world to sample the delectable frozen treats, a map on the store wall invites customers to mark their home destination. But the majority of visitors, besides local Cochrane residents, make the 20-minute drive from Calgary to treat their taste buds with the featured flavour of the week or flavour of the month.

And flavours there are! The MacKays have the capability to make more than 200 different flavours – everything from saskatoon berry to licorice, from nanaimo bar to watermelon lime cooler. The biggest sellers are still vanilla, chocolate, strawberry and maple walnut, the old stand-bys, but there are still lots of adventuresome types who want to try a new one each time. If you'd rather try sorbet, sherbet or frozen yogurt, Rhona and Robyn have those, too, all made with the same attention to quality they devote to their ice cream.

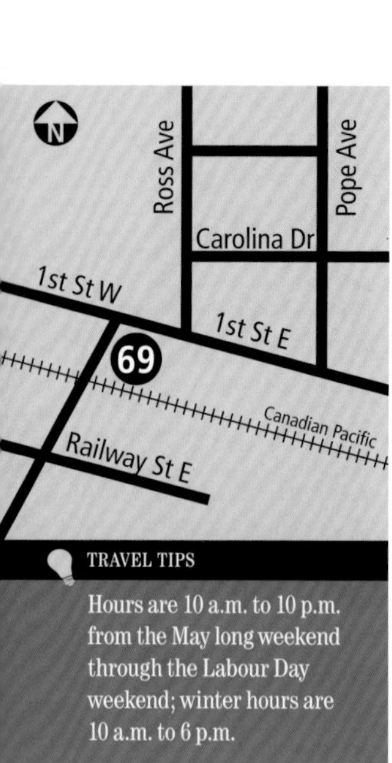

TRAVEL TIPS

Hours are 10 a.m. to 10 p.m. from the May long weekend through the Labour Day weekend; winter hours are 10 a.m. to 6 p.m.

Closed Christmas Day, Boxing Day and New Year's Day.

Location: 220 1st St. W., Cochrane

Phone : (403) 932-2455

E-mail: generalinfo@mackaysicecream.com

www.mackaysicecream.com

The sisters have been part of the business all their lives, but they didn't rely on that background for their expertise. They graduated from the University of Guelph in Ontario as well as completing a special course at Penn State University on ice cream manufacturing. This has helped their credibility in the ice cream business world, dominated by large multinational companies. In 1994, the MacKay sisters were awarded a University of Toronto Rotman Canadian Woman of the Year Award for the huge impact their business has had on the local economy of Cochrane.

Besides the single, double and triple cones, the MacKays sell ice cream cakes and ice cream by the litre and the tub. They have also expanded their business to include wholesale sales to a very special (and lucky) group of restaurants and specialty food stores, as well as other 'scoop' shops in Alberta, British Columbia and Saskatchewan.

A steady diet of the 17 per cent butterfat in this marvelous stuff might not do your waistline a lot of good – but one cone now and again certainly puts a spring in your step. Try it!

So what goes into MacKay's terrific ice cream? There are definitely nuts in the ice cream but not eggs (except in the cookie dough flavour) or gluten. The yogurt is 97.2% fat-free.

And the difference between sherbet and sorbet? Sherbet is still a milk product, but it contains only two per cent butterfat - far less than regular ice cream. Sorbet is totally dairy free and good for people who are lactose intolerant.

The MacKays are still working on an ice cream for diabetic diets.

The ice cream cakes serve nine to 15 people, depending on the generosity of the servings, and come in the decadent flavours of chocolate fudge chunk, cookies and cream, strawberry-vanilla and raspberry cheesecake.

On to Cochrane!

70 Magnificent River Rats Festival

It's the little Canada Day celebration that grew.

Back in the mid-'90s, the Athabasca Rotary Club decided to dish up a set or two of country music to keep families entertained before the Canada Day fireworks. On a shoestring budget, organizers brought in Alberta favourite Danny Hooper in 1996, passing the plate to help make ends meet.

When the dust settled, organizers paid the bills, breathed a sigh of relief, then went scouting for next year's talent. A foot-stompin' performance by Alberta's Duane Steele in 1998 upped the buzz and by 1999, when Juno Award winning Prairie Oyster took to the stage, the grassy riverside site held 7,000 happy fans. Far from running aground, the Magnificent River Rats Festival was fast earning a name as western Canada's largest rural Canada Day event. In 2002, it won Alberta Tourism's ALTO award for tourism excellence.

"From what we can gather, we're the biggest little Canada Day celebration in western Canada."

Grant Grosland
President, Magnificent River Rats Festival Society

After expanding to three days, the festival has settled back to two as a comfortable compromise, with about four main acts a year – country, plus some classic rock. By keeping tabs on who's passing through, the festival snags top acts. Each plays an hour and a half or more, expansive sets by city festival standards. Area talent also gets its share of stage time before the headliners come on at 6 p.m.

But as organizers are quick to point out, there's more to this festival than a two-day outdoor concert. It's a true family outing, with activities for all ages, tot to senior – and no beer garden.

Between 1880 and 1914, Athabasca Landing became a key jumping off place for river traffic connecting to the Arctic Ocean. Located at a point where the Athabasca River loops south before continuing northeast, this landing provided an alternative to often impassable pack routes.

Supplies came north from Fort Edmonton by cart in the summer and by sleigh in the winter. Each spring, there'd be a flurry as Métis labourers constructed scows to ship supplies upriver to Lesser Slave Lake and posts beyond. The landing became even more important when traders began shipping goods and furs out of the northwest via steamboats.

Rapids proved a great frustration on the Athabasca River. Most crews portaged their cargo around the dangerous Grand Rapids, but Métis boat handler Louis Fousseneuve proved that loaded scows could run the rapids. Thus his nickname: "Captain Shot."

Canada Day kicks off with a pancake breakfast and Legion parade and ends with fireworks second to none. There's a "Taste of Athabasca" food court, horse-drawn tours of the town's historic sites, lots of fun for kids, a line-up of bragging-right cars and a craft tent showcasing local talent. Behind all that fun stands strong local support. Both the Town of Athabasca and Athabasca County are main sponsors, and more than 150 volunteers invest about 4,000 hours a year.

While soaking it all in, keep your eye out for Athabaska Dick, the festival mascot. Taking a cue from the Robert Service poem of the same name, the mascot adds yet another element of fun while reminding those with a heritage bent of the town's role in the fur trade.

As some may recall, the Service poem ends with Athabaska Dick exclaiming: "Thank God! The whiskey's saved." It's a good bet he'd be a tad sorry about the festival's lack of a beer garden. Nevertheless, one could think of no better use for the landing that once watched Hudson Bay goods come and go than the Magnificent River Rats Festival.

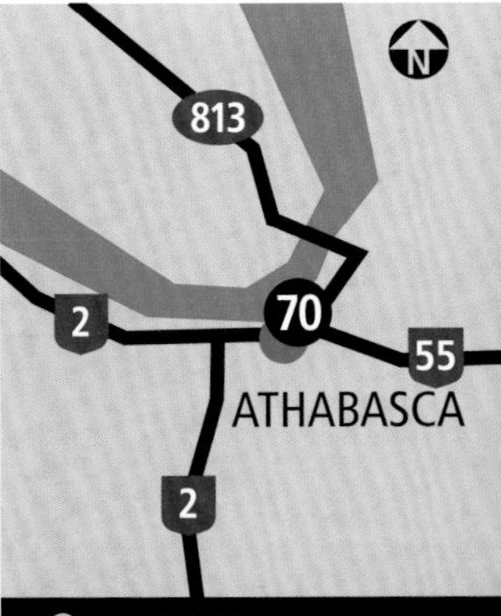

TRAVEL TIPS

No reserved seating. Bring a lawn chair to stake your spot for the day.

Camping is available at Blueberry Hill three kilometres away, plus other designated areas in town.

Frequent shuttle service from campsites and hotels to festival site.

Take a horse-drawn tour of town and learn about Athabasca Landing of 1912.

Location: Along the river near 50 and 50 Street in the Town of Athabasca, 150 kilometres north of Edmonton on Highway 2

Phone: (780) 675-2230

E-mail: tourism@athabascacounty.com

www.mrrf.com

71 Marv's Classic Soda Shop and Diner

Government Rd S
Centre Ave
22
71
1st Ave SW
1st St SW

TRAVEL TIPS

To enjoy the antiques and candy store, plan an hour or more at Marv's Classic Soda Shop. Summer hours are 10 a.m. to 9 p.m. Tuesday to Saturday, and 11 a.m. to 5 p.m. Sunday and Monday. Winter hours are 11 a.m. to 5 p.m. Monday to Sunday.

If you love walking or cycling, follow the three kilometre Friendship Trail connecting Turner Valley and Black Diamond.

Location: 121 Centre Ave., Black Diamond (the mall in the old Moutainview Theatre on Main Street)

Phone: (403) 933-7001

E-mail: marvssoda@telus.net

www.marvsclassics.ca

As you wander along the Cowboy Trail south of Calgary, stop in Black Diamond for a special treat. Everything about Marv's Classic Soda Shop is retro, and the diner brings the 1940s and '50s back to life.

In 2000, Marvin Garriott opened an antique shop. After about a year, he added soda counter specials, beginning with only three flavours of ice cream for malts, milkshakes, floats and other cold treats. Soon he added hot dogs and burgers to his menu. Today, his shop is a full-menu diner with black and pink booths, primary colours of the rock and roll era.

Check out an original nickelodeon, which plays the popular hits of the time. Enjoy the Beach Boys with their California and surfing songs, Elvis hits and a host of others on the 1957 juke box. Just listening to such music offers the chance to "Relive Old Memories and Create New Memories," Marv's motto for the soda shop. If you're lucky, Marv might treat you to a song, too, especially one of his Elvis favourites. When his guitar is nearby, he may even provide accompaniment.

Servers decked out in nostalgic costumes hustle your treats to your table. Doing things in the old-fashioned way, Marv not only does the '40s and '50s well, he can boast recipes for ice cream treats that date back to between 1905 and 1915. At first you might think of just having an ice cream, but when the atmosphere reminds you of the old-fashioned floats, malts and shakes, be ready to change your mind. Marv has the cherry cokes, banana splits and ice cream sundaes that you loved in your childhood and will want your children or grandchildren to enjoy, too.

Marv has an original soda fountain in working order and uses a Hamilton Beach mixer for malts, but getting parts for the old machines is a challenge. More durable are the metal containers called "tin cups" used for mixing. As in the '40s, '50s and even '60s, Marv serves the malts and sodas in the proper glass and leaves you with the tin cup that holds what remains.

Don't leave without some old-fashioned candy, much of it on display in candy jars. You will find cinnamon toothpicks, Smith Brothers candies, Black Jack and Beemans gum, newly purchased but old-style chocolate bars, soap candy, chicken bones, Dutch salted licorice and a favourite of many – black anise jaw breakers. Have a cough? Ask for Victory V lozenges, which some think were made of ether but are actually produced from linseed oil. Many of the candies are specially imported, so don't miss your chance to enjoy the flavours of the old days.

As well, purchase a souvenir for yourself or a great retro gift for one of those friends who aren't sure they want others to know about that next big birthday.

Named for its coal resources, Black Diamond has a huge diamond-shaped coal sculpture as a reminder of its heritage. In 1899, the fossil fuel was discovered by a land surveyor digging an irrigation ditch. The industry boomed, but, more recently, black gold in the form of petroleum has fuelled the economic engine.

Already in the 1890s, ranching flourished and, today, Black Diamond is an ideal place to begin a trail ride into the foothills. Trail rides and pack trips mean the pleasure of sharing cowboy cooking, cowboy poetry, cowboy tall tales and cowboy music around the campfire. You may come home saddle sore, but you will have experienced life as it was in the Old West.

For more on Black Diamond, email: info@town.blackdiamond.ab.ca or check www.town.blackdiamond.ab.ca.

72 Medicine Hat Clay Industries Historic District

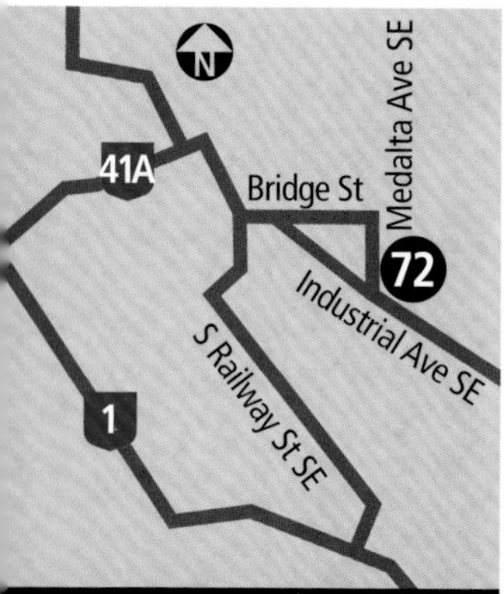

Visiting the Medicine Hat Clay Industries National Historic District illustrates how the community, with its entrepreneurial spirit, natural resources and strategic location, turned dreams to reality.

Here, available clay became a building block for the community, and in 1886, a small brickyard opened. Plentiful gas allowed for inexpensive fuel to fire the kilns. Access to the Canadian Pacific Railway mainline meant reliable transportation. Hoping to attract businesses, the city offered free water, building sites and tax concessions to new industries.

American investors responded and Alberta Clay Products Co. Ltd. was born. In 1910, with a plant built with bricks made by its own workers, the company opened its doors. Two years later, the plant was the second largest of its type in North America. Dominating the Canadian market in sales of brick, tile and clay pipe for decades, the company was the only manufacturer of clay pipe in western Canada. Eventually, its production output was 80,000 bricks and 24,000 sewer pipes daily. By 1918, with innovative Nova Scotia-born businessmen Harry Clinton Yuill and son J.H.Yuill at the helm, future success was guaranteed.

Companies were bought and sold, re-organized and renamed, but by the late 1920s, Medalta Potteries Ltd. was becoming recognized as the giant in the industry.

Throughout the years, other porcelain, china and pottery facilities opened, and business boomed. Even during the Depression, many clay businesses made money. By 1938, the Yuills opened Medicine Hat Potteries in direct competition with Medalta Potteries.

In 1947, with electrical and telephone transmissions increasingly important, National Porcelain Co. began production of insulators. Although post-war trade opened the market to plastics, metal and glass, some companies survived. Hycroft China was formed from the former Medicine Hat Potteries in 1955 and continued production of its successful artware, domestic china and, later, toilets under the ownership of flamboyant Medicine Hat mayor Harry Veiner.

Effective early technology and methods were central to success. The kiln fireboxes burned gas but could be converted to coal if gas became scarce. Kilns were the beehive type in which heat was conducted up the curved walls to the dome-like roof and then drawn back down through the interior of the kiln into chambers beneath

Medalta Ave SE
41A
Bridge St
72
Industrial Ave SE
S Railway St SE
1

TRAVEL TIPS

The interpretive centre at the Medalta site tells the story of the Historic Clay District.

The exhibit galleries and gift shop are open year round. For summer and winter hours and tour times, call or check the website.

All routes from the TransCanada Highway and Highway 41A boast improved signage, making the Historic Clay District easy to find.

Location: Medalta Site, Historic Clay District, 713 Medalta Ave. S.E., Medicine Hat

Phone: (403) 529-1070

E-mail: info@medalta.org

www.medalta.org

the floor and up the chimney. At Alberta Clay Products, rock salt injected into the heated kilns for making sewer pipe helped form an excellent and distinctive glaze.

The clay district's historical importance forms another chapter in the Medicine Hat story. Medalta Potteries is protected as a Provincial and National Historic Site. Hycroft China became a Provincial Historic Site and, eventually, the entire Historic Clay District encompassing 60.7 hectares was designated a National Historic Site.

Today, that district includes active businesses. I-XL Industries continues to manufacture bricks on the site of the earliest brick company, and Plainsman Clay Products is a working plant.

The interpretive centre operates a tourism and educational complex with a working pottery museum and an international artist in residency program; as well, it is developing a centre for contemporary pottery.

The outstanding Medalta pottery line was first manufactured by Medalta Stoneware Ltd. in 1915 under the ownership of Charles Pratt, William Creer and Ulysses Sherman Grant who took over the building and equipment of the fledgling Medicine Hat Pottery Co. Unaware that the required raw materials were available locally, Medicine Hat Pottery Co. had been importing clay from Washington. Medalta Stoneware Ltd. reduced costs and became profitable by using an Eastend, Sask. supplier.

In 1921, Medalta Stoneware Ltd. was the first industry in western Canada to ship manufactured goods to eastern Canada. By 1924, now renamed Medalta Potteries Ltd., its stoneware crocks, churns, bowls, jugs, flower pots and vases appeared in households from Vancouver to Montreal.

By the late 1920s, the company was producing three-quarters of Canada's stoneware and providing jugs for prairie liquor control boards.

Once performing utilitarian uses, today Medalta products are treasured collectibles.

73 Meeting Creek Coulee

TRAVEL TIPS

Donalda and District Museum is open 9 a.m. to 5 p.m. Monday through Friday year round, and also open 11 a.m. to 5 p.m. weekends from mid-May to mid-October.

You can visit the grain elevator and the railway station anytime. Just pick up the keys at Half Diamond Sales or call the Camrose Railway Station at (780) 672-3099.

Location: Meeting Creek is on Highway 56 about 50 kilometres south of Camrose. From there, travel further south on Highway 56, then east on Highway 53 to Donalda.

Phone: Village of Donalda (403) 883-2345

E-mail: vdonalda@telusplanet.net

www. village.donalda.ab.ca

The Meeting Creek Coulee area is one of Alberta's little-known gems, with attractions and interests for the whole family. The small town of Donalda is known locally as the Lamp Capital of Canada because of its collection of more than 900 kerosene lamps at the Donalda and District Museum. And you can't miss one giant lamp standing at the end of the main street and overlooking the coulee.

There's a delightful little tea shop called Nutcracker Suite that serves loose teas and amazing desserts; try something with their saskatoon berry sauce.

Check out a designated historic resource in the town of Meeting Creek, further north on the coulee. The Alberta Pacific Grain elevator, an all-wood elevator designed to grade, weigh, store and ship grain, was built in 1917 in what is known as the Prairie Vernacular style. It has an attached shed, once used as the office, and another small outbuilding. At one time, you would have seen one or more of these elevators in most prairie towns, but they slowly started to disappear as transportation improved and bigger, more centralized elevators were built. Not

many of these old elevators have survived, as both time and the occasional fire have taken their toll on the old wood. The Meeting Creek elevator is now protected and visitors can view the grain handling artifacts inside and see how grain was handled in the early days.

Meeting Creek also has a railway station that you should definitely add to your visit agenda. You can take a self-guided tour through this 1913 building and see what life for the railway agent and his family would have been like. As well, there are displays of photographs that feature not only a number of western Canadian railway station designs, but also the once-plentiful Canadian grain elevators.

Then there's the beautiful Meeting Creek coulee itself. Years of erosion have worked their magic on the Paskapoo sandstone rock formations to create something more like a moonscape than the Alberta prairie. It is believed that parts of the coulee were used in the early buffalo hunts and, if you're lucky, you may find an arrow or hammer head that was left behind when the buffalo were no more. In season, you may share the areas with duck, goose or deer hunters but generally it's a wonderfully peaceful place, attractive to hikers, artists and photographers. If you listen carefully, you may just hear the distant echo of thousands of buffalo hooves.

Another Donalda attraction is the Imperial Bank of Commerce building, a registered historic resource that overlooks the coulee and hosts the Donalda Gallery for the Arts. The gallery, open throughout the summer, exhibits the work of many central Alberta artists and art clubs.

As well, be sure to visit an old creamery that opened in 1924. Thirteen years later, a group of local farmers bought the creamery, issued share certificates to the group and hired a manager – and the Donalda Co-operative Creamery was born. Some of the pioneer farmers served on the board of directors for more than 25 years, seeing the creamery through an attempted takeover by the "big boys" and overseeing the production of the award-winning "Donalda Maid Butter" that was in production for more than 40 years.

The building has been maintained and designated a registered historic resource. You can arrange tours through the museum and see how things were done in the old days.

74 Mile 0 of the Mackenzie Highway

Exploring Alberta, what better place to begin than Grimshaw, Mile 0 of the 999-kilometre Mackenzie Highway? Called Highway 35 in Alberta and Highway 1 in the Northwest Territories, it's the road less travelled, promising unrivaled vistas, roaming wildlife, intriguing history, spectacular waterfalls and enough side trips to keep you rolling until the ice roads form.

The highway follows numerous rivers, most notably the mighty Mackenzie, to the very end of the summer road in Wrigley, N.W.T. Coming back, you can loop west through British Columbia on the Liard Trail. Do the whole circle, and you've driven the Deh Cho (big river) Trail, whose name recalls the aboriginal term for the Mackenzie River.

As you depart Grimshaw up Highway 35 past a mix of fertile farmland and forest, nearly every town offers cause to pause: the Pioneer Village and Museum at Lac Cardinal, the trading post in Dixonville, the 1918 Latvian homestead in North Star, the bird sanctuary in Deadwood, the Manning museum that started life as the Battle River Hospital – to name a few.

A short detour east on Highway 697 takes you across the Peace River by ferry, through unexpectedly lush farm lands to La Crete, a predominantly Mennonite community, then on to Fort Vermilion, which vies with Fort Chipewyan as Alberta's oldest settlement. Highway 58 brings you back on course at scenically situated High Level, a midway point on the Mackenzie Highway and home of the Mackenzie Crossroads Museum and Visitors Centre - and of the most northerly grain elevators in the world. Follow the Hay River north past Indian Cabins, where a native cemetery dotted with spirit houses offers a taste of the aboriginal, fur-trading and pioneer history found all along this route.

TRAVEL TIPS

The Mackenzie Highway crosses three free summer ferries that operate daylight hours only. The largest, near Fort Providence, is slated to be replaced by a bridge. In winter, weather permitting, the crossings become ice roads.

Location: Grimshaw is 440 kilometres northwest of Edmonton. The Mile 0 marker stands at the intersection of Highways 2, 2A and 35.

Phone: Tourist Booth: (780) 332-2200 (May to September);
Town (780) 332-4626

E-mail:
grimshaw@telusplanet.net

www.dehchotravel.com

Fourteen kilometers later, you enter the Northwest Territories. Stop at the visitor centre, and you'll walk away with proof: a North of 60 Certificate. This side of the parallel, the Mackenzie Highway is called the Waterfalls Route; you'll see why at must-see Twin Falls Territorial Park and many other stops.

Nearing Great Slave Lake, source of the Mackenzie River, more detours beckon. Turn east onto Highway 5 to Fort Smith, where you will find outfitters and information about entering Wood Buffalo National Park. Take Highway 3 through the Mackenzie Bison Sanctuary (scrunching dung pies as you go) to reach Yellowknife, the territory's capital.

"The Mackenzie Highway is still Canada's only all-weather overland route into the Northwest Territories."

Carmen Johnson, Grimshaw Tourism Booth

Back on Highway 1, watch the Mackenzie River swell as creeks and waterfalls bubble and thunder into the flow. Past Checkpoint, you soon reach Fort Simpson, staging point for trips on the wild waters of Nahanni National Park. Catch spectacular views of the Mackenzie River as you continue on to Wrigley, the starting point for winter ice roads to such outposts as Norman Wells and Fort Good Hope.

If you're doing the full Deh Cho loop, return to Checkpoint and follow the well-gravelled Liard Trail (Moose Highway) past forts Liard (check out the hotsprings), Nelson and St. John. Then it's back to Grimshaw - or perhaps south to the Rockies, just hours away.

Highway 35 from Grimshaw began as the Battle River settlers' trail and served as a winter caterpillar route to Great Slave Lake in the late '30s. After the Second World War, it was speedily rebuilt as the Mackenzie Highway for all-weather access to mining and fishing resources.

Grimshaw's Mile 0 marker is surrounded by evidence of the town's links to the highway. The nearby Grimshaw Tourist Booth inhabits a caboose, recalling the town's birth as "the stop" along the Central Canada Railway and later years when goods shifted from rail car to caterpillar train here. Just steps away, the Mile 0 Mackenzie Highway Antique Truck Museum amply depicts the highway's birth and early years.

Sir Alexander Mackenzie discovered Mackenzie River while searching for a route to the Pacific. Arriving at the Arctic instead, he termed this the "River of Disappointment." Arctic Explorer Sir John Franklin gave the river its current name.

75 W. O. Mitchell

A language for our prairie landscape: that's what acclaimed writer W.O. Mitchell gave us. Indeed, he had a genius for transforming the people and places and habits he knew so well into tales that draw an "aha" of recognition even in those removed from prairie life.

That gift surfaced in 1947 with the novel whose very title has become a Canadian icon: *Who Has Seen the Wind.* In a close parallel to Brian O'Connal in that tale, William Ormond Mitchell was born in Saskatchewan in 1914 and lost his pharmacist father at the early age of seven. This prairie landscape was indelibly imprinted on him and became the setting for his *Jake and the Kid* stories (1961) and for his evocative novel, *How I Spent My Summer Holidays* (1981).

During the Depression years, Mitchell attended the University of Manitoba, travelled to England and France one summer, and then to Seattle where he took a playwriting course. When he returned to Canada, he survived by doing odd jobs in Alberta including selling insurance and radio ad time; he even worked as a carnival high diver clown. During this time, he began acting in the Calgary Theatre Guild.

Trying school again at the University of Alberta, he earned a BA and a teaching certificate in 1942. Professor F. M. Slater, who became Mitchell's mentor, urged the

N
2
HIGH RIVER
543
75
23
2A
2

TRAVEL TIPS

W. O. Mitchell lived in High River from 1945 to 1968.

A downtown wall painting of the author commemorates his years here.

He and his wife, Merna, are both buried in the High River Cemetery.

Location: High River is about 40 kilometres south of Calgary on Highway 2

young man to write about what he knew. Mitchell took the advice to heart, developing and later teaching his "freefall" method of writing.

In Edmonton he also met and married Merna Hirtle, with whom he had three children.

"...his books will always exist like a Rosetta stone for the rediscovery of Western Canadian rural life..."

Fred Stenson

Mitchell taught high school in small Alberta towns, moving to High River in 1945 where he did some supply teaching while publishing in magazines such as *Queen's Quarterly* and *Maclean's.*

Following the stellar success of *Who Has Seen the Wind,* he became *Maclean's* fiction editor for three years while developing *Jake and the Kid,* a side-splitting CBC radio series that ran about 200 episodes. Both Mitchell and his cast of characters were household names by 1951, when the family moved back to High River. The series concluded in 1956 and, in 1962, he published *The Kite,* his first novel set in foothills country. His other foothills novels include *The Vanishing Point* (1973), *Since Daisy Creek* (1984), and *Roses Are Difficult Here* (1990).

He supplemented his novel writing with television writing and a series of semi-autobiographical sketches that became the basis for his public performances. Those sketches gave us Mitchell as the loveable, comic, sometimes bawdy storyteller – Canada's Mark Twain.

Increasingly in demand as a mentor, Mitchell moved to Calgary in 1968 to take the first of several writer-in-residence posts across Canada. He continued to write, producing seven more novels and a number of stage, film and television scripts. He also continued to perform widely across Canada until 1996.

W.O. Mitchell died in Calgary on Feb. 25, 1998, just short of his 84th birthday. Cancer claimed his life, but the foothills and prairie landscapes he created most certainly persist.

W.O. Mitchell's literary awards are as impressive as the writer himself. They include honorary doctorates from eight Canadian universities, appointment as Officer of the Order of Canada in 1973 and being named Honorary Member of the Privy Council in 1992.

As well, he won the prestigious Chalmers Award for *Back to Beulah* (1976) and the Stephen Leacock Award for Humour in 1962 for *Jake and the Kid* and in 1990 for *According to Jake and the Kid* (1989). In 1989, W.O. Mitchell received the Sir Frederick Haultain Prize for "exceptional accomplishments and outstanding contributions to the people and the province of Alberta."

For more information, see the recently published biographies by Barbara and Ormond Mitchell, *W.O.: The Life of W.O. Mitchell, Beginnings to* Who Has Seen the Wind. Toronto: McClelland & Stewart, 1999, and *Mitchell: The Life of W.O. Mitchell: The Years of Fame 1948-1998.* Toronto: McClelland & Stewart, 2005 or visit www.ucalgary.ca/lib-old/SpecColl/mitchell.

76 Nikka Yuko Japanese Garden

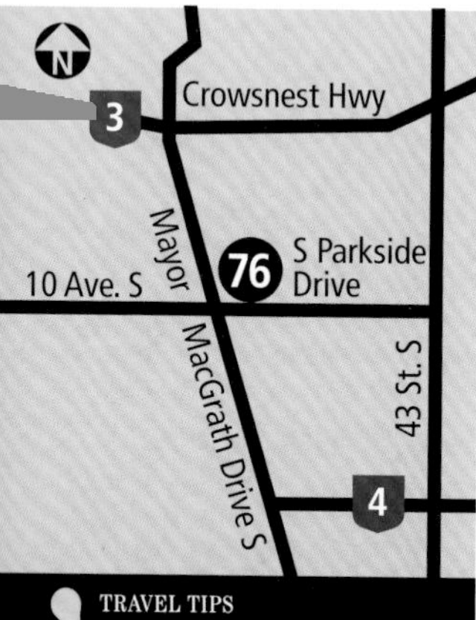

TRAVEL TIPS

Hours are 9 a.m. to 8 p.m. daily from July to early September, and 9 a.m. to 5 p.m. spring and fall.

Admission fee includes a half-hour tour by a yukata-clad host or hostess.

Special events on Saturdays at the pavilion may include traditional music, crafts and a Sunday tea ceremony beginning at 2 p.m.

Check for moonlight viewing, scheduled the Saturday of the full moon week from May through September, when the garden is open until midnight and illuminated by floodlights.

Location: Henderson Lake Park at 9th Avenue and Mayor Magrath Drive, Lethbridge

Phone: (403) 328-3511

E-mail: info@nikkayuko.com

www.nikkayuko.com

If your spirit needs calming or inspiration, take time to meander through the Nikka Yuko Japanese Garden in Lethbridge. The paths are designed as a journey of mental reflection, especially when you glance into the large pond and lake to find sky, nature and yourself reflected from the water's surface.

Even its name speaks to the importance of harmony. *Ni* means *Japan*. *Ka* means *Canada*, and *Yuko* means *friendship*. Also called the Japanese Canadian Friendship Garden, it symbolizes a difficult historical journey for Japanese immigrants to Canada, Canadian-born Japanese and other Canadians, but the journey ended in greater understanding.

Alberta has long been home to Japanese immigrants, many of whom have farmed in the province since the early 1900s. Then, too, the Japanese population in southern Alberta increased when many of Japanese heritage were moved from the British Columbia coast to southern Alberta internment camps during the Second World War. In the Lethbridge area, internees worked on farms and in sugar beet fields, and after the war, many families stayed. Years later during Canada's centennial in 1967, the Nikka Yuko Japanese Garden was opened.

Acknowledging the Japanese contribution to the region and country, the 1.6-hectare garden refreshes the soul. It offers a chance to appreciate traditional Japanese gardening, but it was designed for the Alberta landscape. Five different types of traditional Japanese styles were incorporated into the design. To fulfil the spirit of a Japanese garden, designs must incorporate scenic effects, sensory effects and cultural values so designers needed to make the local landscape and Canadian cultural values part of the whole.

The garden is experienced and understood through subtle visual effects regarding order, composition and decoration. The foot bridges, gates, pagoda, bell tower and pavilion were built by Japanese artisans, imported and reassembled in Lethbridge. The floor and finishings of the pavilion, a re-creation of 16th century architecture, are of Taiwanese cypress wood. From it, you view a dry rock garden, a form used for centuries by Zen monks and spiritual devotees as a means of meditation.

Paths, streams, ponds and shrubbery evoke Japan. Yet the garden is transformed by the landscape and culture of the region. The prairie garden area in the northeast corner offers the best views of Henderson Lake. The stepping stone path takes visitors to the Ariso Beach area, where the pebbles were hand-picked for shape, uniformity and smoothness and then placed on the beach.

Elsewhere, there is an adaptation to Canadian culture. In Japan, the type of bell in the tower would only be used in a temple. In Lethbridge, any visitor can ring the Ceremonial Friendship Bell, and its gong will carry for five kilometres on a calm day. Even the structure seems to have a message. Removal of the bell would mean the structure would collapse, as if to say the removal of friendship, such as that between Japan and Canada, can make relationships fail.

Henderson Lake Park has a 24-hectare man-made lake as its focal point. Amazingly, all trees have been planted in the semi-arid landscape that, historically, was treeless. Today, with many mature trees in the park, walking paths and picnic sites are beautiful.

The lake can be used by fishermen and those with small boats. Great flower gardens, campgrounds and recreation facilities are drawing cards, too. An outdoor swimming pool, horseshoe pits, tennis courts and baseball stadium offer added recreations.

Also in the park, you will find the Henderson Lake Golf Club, which is open to the public. This 18-hole championship course has all the challenge and facilities you could want. Fairways are level, but because they wind along the lake, water hazards provide challenge. The other challenge is the sand frequently in play and the odd windy day. Mature trees mean shade from heat in summer. Check www.hendersonlakegolfclub.com.

77 Nordegg Heritage Centre and Brazeau Collieries Mine Site

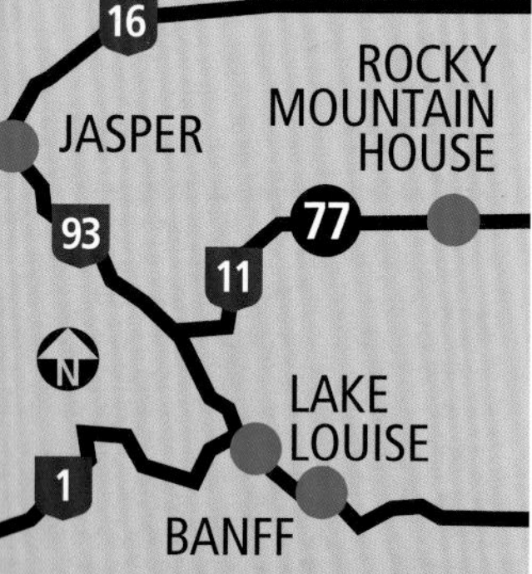

TRAVEL TIPS

Nordegg is part of Alberta's last frontier; don't expect many amenities.

Guided tours to the mine site are offered daily in summer.

The Nordegg Heritage Centre Museum tells the story of the area's history.

A non-denominational church service is held at 11 a.m. every Sunday in the original Nordegg church, in the Ghost Town.

Location: Nordegg is about 95 kilometres west of Rocky Mountain House on Highway 11, or about 167 kilometres west of Red Deer.

Phone: (403) 721-2625 or (403) 845-4444

www.nordegghistoricalsociety.8m.com

The Nordegg Heritage Centre and Brazeau Collieries Mine Site bring the colourful tale of the area's industrial heritage to life.

Martin Nordegg, born Martin Cohn, reached Canada in 1906 on invitation from a Canadian member of Parliament. Cohn represented German investment interests, the Deutsches Kanada Syndikat, later absorbed into the larger German Development Company with Canadian investors.

In 1909, this company joined the Canadian Northern Railway, uniting several coalfields and creating Brazeau Collieries with the objective of forming a mining empire that could control the prairie coal supply. These coalfields stretched from Mount Allen in Kananaskis Country to Grande Cache. The Nordegg coalfield, staked 1911, became headquarters for the 154-square-kilometre fledgling mining empire.

When Nordegg was planning his town, the railway's Mackenzie and Mann were building Montreal's Mount Royal district. Nordegg liked that community's semicircular plan so he designed his town like Mount Royal's western section.

Construction began after the railway reached the town. Nordegg wanted a beautiful town with pleasing colours. Most buildings, including commercial, were operational by late 1914. The Bighorn Trading Company store carried groceries, dry goods, clothing and furniture, and traded in fur hides as requested.

Four- and five-room homes were built and, during the 1940s, some three-room houses increased the size of the town. All buildings had electricity supplied from the mine site. Nordegg intended all homes to have water and sewer, but 1914 mine officials believed this was unnecessary. The compromise: five-room homes had water, while four-room homes had a stand-pipe on each street.

And what's a thriving town without a hospital? Nordegg had consulted with University of Toronto medical authorities, and Nordegg's hospital became Alberta's best outside Calgary and Edmonton, with mine employees paying the doctor $1 per month.

The outbreak of the First World War in 1914 made Martin Nordegg an enemy alien, however, and Ottawa recalled him in 1915. He never again lived in Nordegg.

Although his dreams of a coal mining empire died, the mine and town became major players in resource-based Canada. In 1937, Brazeau Collieries experimented with a process that, by the late 1940s, saw Brazeau become Canada's largest, and North America's second largest, coal briquette supplier.

In June 1950, however, fire destroyed the processing buildings. Rebuilding took 18 months. Brazeau tried increasing Kananaskis' output, but most coal orders dropped. In 1952, the new, high-tech plant (now the industrial museum) began production, but other fuels were taking over transportation technology. In 1955, the mine and town were closed, although Brazeau Collieries wasn't dissolved until 1996. Ownership transferred to the Alberta government because of unpaid rebuilding debts; in 1963, a minimum-security prison, a Bowden institution satellite, opened on the site.

In the early 1980s, discussions regarding leveling and clearing the mine site began. Volunteers worked frantically to save this record of Alberta's development, but expenses mounted. In 1992, Clearwater County took over, and preservation continued under the Nordegg Historical Society.

In 1993, the Brazeau Collieries Industrial Mine Site Museum became a Provincial Historic Resource, and a National Historic Site in 2002.

The old Ghost Town is up the hill from the Heritage Centre. Request a map of the town from the tourist desk; site information is given on the back.

Are there ghosts in the Ghost Town? Paranormal Investigators of Edmonton and the Calgary Association of Paranormal Investigators both say yes.

There is something special about Nordegg. From old timers to first-time visitors, everyone feels it. Many interesting stories have been told of those who lived and died here, leaving an essence of themselves behind. This feeling is more likely to be felt at the mine site in the upper, or old, section, but the heritage centre, built as the new Nordegg School in 1945, can also be an "interesting" place. But everyone is friendly here - even the ghosts.

78 Reynolds-Alberta Museum

Stan Reynolds inherited a love of collecting from his father, whose 1905 Oldsmobile never left the family (and now stands in the museum). Concerned that Alberta was letting her past rust away, it wasn't unusual to spot Stan on airborne reconnaissance, examining farmers' fields. He once dropped down to make an offer for a tractor, only to be rebuffed with "Stan Reynolds offered me more than that!"

Typical of the rescue tales is the one about the 1911 Hupp-Yeats Electric Coach. The lady who purchased the car drove it 652 kilometres, then parked it inside her garage. When she had an aviary installed in front of the garage doors for her pet parrot, she stipulated the bird could not be disturbed. To extract the car, they took the garage apart.

In 1981, Stan donated hundreds of pieces to the Province of Alberta in return for the promise of a public facility to house them. The resulting museum opened in 1992.

Reynolds-Alberta Museum celebrates the "spirit of the machine," and it's not hard to imagine a few ghosts hovering about as you explore its eclectic array of cars, trucks, bikes, aircraft, farm equipment and industrial engines. You'll find those machines in various states of being, from rust to high buff – and that makes the wander all the more interesting.

Start in the museum's expansive main hall, which charts a highway from the 1890s to the 1970s in a spirit that's infectiously interactive. Here, you can discover how machines have shaped our lives by putting your own hands to the plough. Experience the theory behind the Model T factory by racing the clock as you "work the line." Make rope the old-fashioned, hand-cranked way. Peer through the glass at the restoration shop and imagine how you might get your hands dirty there.

Only a sampling of the museum's 8,000 machines is on exhibit in the main gallery. Among the jewels is a 1929 Duesenburg Phaeton Royale Model J. One of a kind and beautifully restored, it's a "Doozie" – literally!

As well, the museum warehouse is a treasure trove of machines, from a 1913 Chevrolet touring car just as rusty as the day it was found, to a beautiful 1966 Meteor Montcalm in its original mint condition. The warehouse is also home to an Avro Arrow replica that starred in a TV miniseries chronicling the rise and fall from favour of this sleek Canadian design. Call ahead to book a tour, or watch for the annual warehouse open house.

Other special events include the Harvest Festival on the Labour Day weekend and vehicle restoration courses each February.

You'll certainly want to visit the on-site Aviation Display Hangar, home to Canada's Aviation Hall of Fame and numerous vintage aircraft. In summer, you can get there in style aboard a Model T or a classic Chev. Ask your driver to swing past the outdoor displays, including the world's largest and oldest surface mining dragline, vintage 1917. Take note of the Wetaskiwin Airport next door; some folks have been known to use it to fly in for a visit.

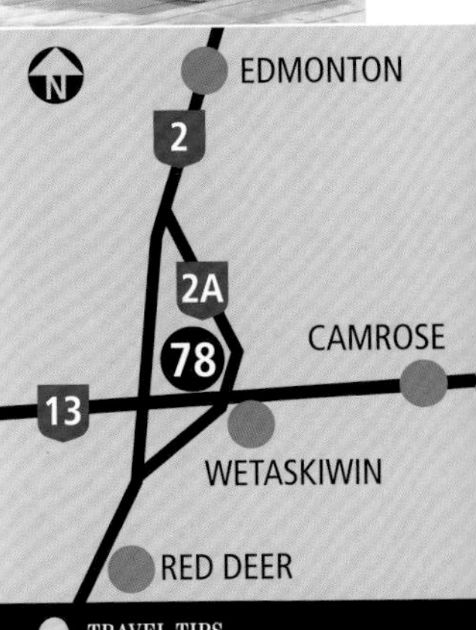

TRAVEL TIPS

Open daily in the summer with extended hours in July and August.

Closed Mondays off-season, September to May.

Book museum warehouse tours a week ahead.

Annual events include the History Road car show and vintage vehicle parade in June.

Ask about unique open cockpit biplane rides.

Location: Two kilometres west of Wetaskiwin on Highway 13

Phone: 1-800-661-4726 or (780) 361-1351

E-mail: ram@gov.ab.ca

www.machinemuseum.net

79 Rosebud Theatre

Rosebud Theatre offers a delightful mix of dynamic plays paired with good food in a picturesque small town setting. Since its humble beginnings in an old community hall in 1983, the theatre has been producing plays that have drawn a host of people from across Alberta and even further afield to experience something now coined as "an adventure of the heart." A full season of plays is produced in an elegantly renovated 220-seat performance venue called the Opera House.

The theatre company employs a resident company of professional actors, musicians and artisans. It is also committed to grooming new theatre talent by providing opportunities for young actors to apprentice in a professional theatre setting. Between March and December, it performs four plays on the Opera House stage and one more intimate play on the 70-seat Studio Stage. Throughout the year, the Studio Stage is also host to additional productions by Rosebud School of the Arts, a vibrant post-secondary theatre training guild school also in Rosebud.

The Opera House has a history of its own after its inauspicious start as a granary belonging to the Alberta Pacific Railway. Rather than tearing it down in 1946 when its useful life as a storage receptacle was over, the people of Rosebud decided it could be converted into a community hall; thus, it was cut in half and moved into town. It became the Rosebud Memorial Hall and was used for dances and concerts and 16-millimetre movie shows. The old hall was sidelined when the Rosebud school became available as a community centre and remained empty until 1984 when Rosebud School of the Arts saw its potential as a theatre.

The story didn't end there. The old hall was drafty and cold and people were known to have taken blankets to plays performed during the colder months. In 1991, Rosebud Theatre began a renovation project of gigantic proportions, putting in a new sloped floor with tiered seating, a lobby area and redesigned stage, and adding

TRAVEL TIPS

Besides the galleries and gift shops, you can also find the Centennial Museum, once the local laundry, and a nine-hole golf course.

Location: Rosebud Theatre is in the village of Rosebud on secondary Highway 840, 35 kilometres southwest of Drumheller.

Phone: 1-800-267-7553 or (403) 677-2001 for reservations; (403) 677-2350 for the office

E-mail: info@rosebudtheatre.com

www.rosebudtheatre.com

everything else from indoor plumbing and heating to lighting and sound requirements. The building also received much-needed insulation and a new roof. The Opera House, which now lived up to its name, re-opened in 1993.

Theatre tickets include the price of dinner and a buffet at the Mercantile Dining Room. Since the theatre company is very much a part of the community, your visit will probably also include a casual chat with actors, musicians, designers or technicians before or after performances.

Rosebud itself is a charming and cozy community. It may not have a gas station, but it does have places to stay – two bed and breakfasts, a guest house and a luxurious country inn. A delightful range of local and regional crafts are also available. A historic church has been converted to an art gallery and recording studio. And check out the Rosebud Café for another flavour of the community.

Rosebud Theatre's mission is best explained in its own words: "Rosebud Theatre's choice of plays varies from lighthearted to serious, comic to tragic, and common to noble. Our intent is to produce a full spectrum of family programming which uplifts and strengthens the participant. It is our belief that values, ideals and noble dreams are not born by chance or promoted by luck. People of good will must be inspired to live them. And as theatre artists, we must be inspired to tell stories that grapple with them. Ultimately, our plays are illustrations of the beauty and complexity of life and the reality of issues and choices facing humanity."

80 Royal Alberta Museum

Make the most of your visit to the museum. Stop by the Museum Café for light meals; let yourself be tempted by a selection of fresh baked muffins, cookies and buns.

After your rest, take a tour through the Museum Shop and choose from clothing, gifts and collectibles that have been inspired by museum exhibitions and artisans. Books and posters focus on natural history or human history, and educational games and activities take their cue from exhibits. Jewelry and local crafts are also available.

And you might meet Moe, the museum's cuddly mascot, a woolly mammoth hailing from a time before the last Ice Age but definitely comfortable in today's warmer climate!

Proceeds from the museum shop go directly toward supporting the museum and all its activities.

The Royal Alberta Museum is well aware of the competition for people's leisure time, but that just spurs the organization on to create bigger and better exhibitions and activities for people of all ages.

The museum was a gleam in someone's eye as early as the 1950s, but was not actually open for business until December 1967 when it was known as the Provincial Museum of Alberta (PMA).

The earliest displays portrayed Alberta's pre-settlement days, focusing on Aboriginal artifacts while other galleries showed scale models of planned future dioramas depicting Alberta's industry, history and agriculture. In the 1960s and '70s, the scale models became life-size dioramas of Alberta's natural regions, and exhibitions on Alberta's settlement were added.

The museum's galleries continue to evolve. The Syncrude Gallery of Aboriginal Culture is one of North America's largest explorations of First Peoples' history with stories spanning 11,000 years and 500 generations. More than 3,000 artifacts and recorded voices tell the aboriginal stories in their words.

In 2002, the museum updated its Habitat Gallery to reflect Alberta's vast biodiversity. With a goal of encouraging visitors to see the wild through different eyes, Wild Alberta presents animals in their natural habitats in 17 spectacular dioramas.

The museum also showcases an exquisite selection of gems and minerals. As well, the Bird Gallery, with its impressive mounts, offers a three-dimensional guide to the birds of Alberta.

The Royal Alberta Museum mission: To preserve and tell the story of Alberta – the experience of people and places over time – and inspire Albertans to explore and understand the world around them.

The museum is host to many national and international travelling exhibitions ranging from robotic dinosaurs to photographs by the late Linda McCartney to ancient Rome, Syria and even Genghis Khan.

The museum continues to be a favourite destination for school field trips with every gallery accommodating learning opportunities. The Bug Room and Fossils! – Creatures from the Depth of Time are particular favourites. Opened in 2001, the popular Museum School offers week-long onsite studies.

The museum started with human and natural history, but now there are programs ranging from Archaeology to Zoology. The museum is committed to building and preserving collections documenting Alberta's biodiversity, landscapes and human history. Recently the museum was successful in securing 29 artifacts collected by the 9th Earl of Southesk when he travelled through Rupert's Land in 1859. After this exquisite collection's time as a feature exhibition, it will become part of the long term displays.

The Royal Museum of Alberta is always changing and growing. Queen Elizabeth II consented to its "Royal" designation when Her Majesty visited in 2005. At the same time, federal and provincial government funding was announced as a five-year centennial project to take the Royal Alberta Museum into the future with a substantial expansion.

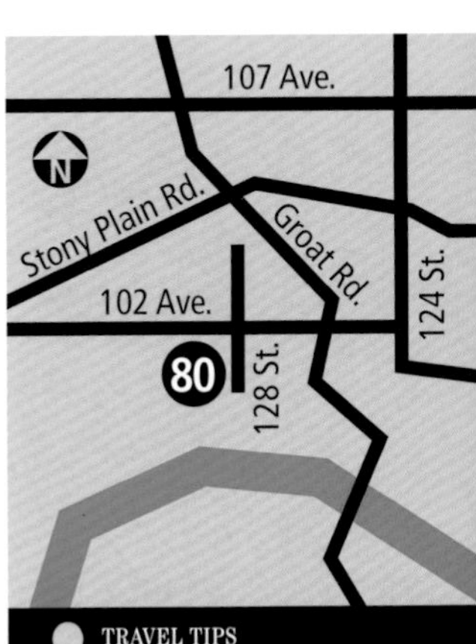

TRAVEL TIPS

Hours of operation are 9 a.m. to 5 p.m. daily; the museum is closed Christmas Eve Day and Christmas Day.

To appreciate all the stories in the galleries, plan to spend at least two hours at the museum.

Location: 12845 - 102 Avenue, Edmonton

Phone: Toll-free in Alberta, call 310-0000 then follow the instructions or (780) 453-9100

E-mail: PMA.Webeditor@gov.ab.ca

Website: www.royalalbertamuseum.ca

81 Royal Tyrrell Museum of Palaeontology

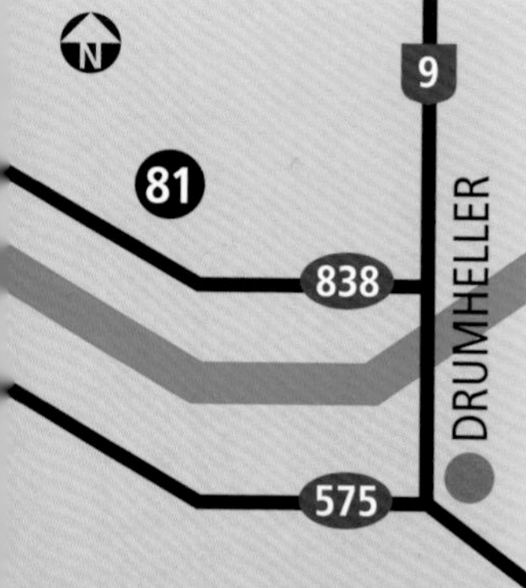

TRAVEL TIPS

The museum and its exhibits can take three hours or more to explore thoroughly.

Audio guides of exhibit highlights are available in six languages.

Summer visitors can participate in a variety of programs including fossil casting, guided hikes, prospecting tours and simulated digs.

Closed Mondays from mid-October to May.

Hiking and biking trails leave from directly outside the museum door.

Location: Six kilometres northwest of Drumheller on Highway 838

Phone: In Alberta, toll free 310-000, then (403) 823-7707

E-mail: info@tyrellmuseum.com

www.tyrrellmuseum.com

Why does Alberta have a world-class dinosaur museum? Because it's home to world-class dinosaurs. Hidden within the sculpted beauty of the southern Alberta badlands is a treasure trove of dinosaur bones. The Royal Tyrrell Museum of Palaeontology collects, preserves, studies and presents these fossil remains. Opened in 1985, the museum now attracts about 350,000 people a year from around the world.

Visitors are struck first by how well the Tyrrell blends into its badlands surroundings. Inside the museum, hands-on activities and dynamic displays celebrate the spectacular history and diversity of life on Earth. The museum galleries draw you forward through millions of years – from the aquatic origins of life to the earliest land-based organisms, through the rise and fall of the dinosaurs and into the Age of Mammals.

One highlight is the world famous Dinosaur Hall. Galleries also feature flying reptiles, prehistoric mammals and marine invertebrates from the ancient Bearpaw Sea, an immense body of water that once stretched from Manitoba to Alberta's Cypress Hills. A large window into the museum's preparation lab allows you to watch technicians in action, painstakingly removing rock to expose new fossils.

The museum houses one of the world's largest collections of dinosaurs, including childhood favourites such as *Tyrannosaurus rex* and *Triceratops*. Stop to admire *T. rex's* cousin *Albertosaurus*, the species whose skull first brought the dinosaurs of this valley to light.

Joseph Burr Tyrrell, the man for whom this museum is named, discovered that skull while searching for coal deposits along the Red Deer River in 1884. One of several explorers sent by the Geological Survey of Canada to find fuel for the west's expanding railway network, he also found numerous invertebrate fossils that proved more useful in interpreting western Canada's geology. But it was the dinosaur that sparked widespread imagination.

Tyrrell's discovery helped spawn the Great Canadian Dinosaur Rush. Between 1911 and 1925, more than 300 skeletons found their way from Alberta into the displays of museums around the world.

The Royal Tyrrell Museum is not only Canada's premier palaeontology museum – it is also an internationally recognized research facility with a full-time team of dedicated scientists whose work informs all of the museum's exhibits and educational programs. Every summer, crews hunt for new fossils to add to the 120,000 specimens in the Tyrrell collection. As new findings emerge, we are realizing that dinosaurs are not all extinct. Indeed, thousands of their descendants live among us today. We call them birds.

Alberta was once a dinosaur paradise. Lush vegetation fed herds of herbivores that became ample food for carnivores. The bones of dead animals lay in river channels or mud flats to be buried in layers of sand and debris.

With the passage of 75 million years or so, the remains became fossilized, covered by more sediment and then massive sheets of ice.

As the latest Ice Age ended 13,000 years ago, glaciers scraped off the covering rock and flood waters carved the Red Deer River valley into today's badlands, exposing one of the world's richest known deposits of fossils.

The Alberta badlands produce new skeletons and fossils every year. More than 300 first-quality dinosaur skeletons have been pulled from a 27-kilometre stretch of the Red Deer River since digging began in the 1880s. Dozens of these are now displayed in museums in 30 cities around the world.

82 St. Ann Ranch

"We are just simply building a town!" Leaving behind a wife, three daughters and a comfortable life in France, Armand Trochu braved deadly cold and a distinct lack of amenities to track down the perfect piece of prairie coulee, find its fabled spring and launch what in 1905 became the Saint Ann Ranch Trading Company. More than a business, the ranch helped spawn a nearby community that still stands today: Trochu.

The railway's promised coming brought a fresh wave of settlers, including the Frère family in 1910. Martha and Ernest Frère bought St. Ann Ranch in 1931, operated it as a farm and sold it four decades later to eldest grandson Louis and his wife Lorene. Asked to write about the ranch for a local history book, Lorene prospected Calgary's Glenbow Archives and hit a goldmine: the addresses of about a dozen Trochu descendants in France, assembled in the '50s by an oil company interested in buying mineral rights. Soon, envelopes addressed to "Armand Trochu Descendants" were winging their way to each of the addresses listed in that file.

Receiving enthusiastic response, Lorene travelled to France in 1989. She returned with a rich bounty of photographs, artwork, artifacts – and, best of all, letters giving rich detail of prairie life as experienced by Armand Trochu and the family that eventually joined him. Now passionate about the ranch's place in Alberta history, the Frère family gained Provincial Historic Site designation for their property and added a museum.

"I am overwhelmed with work. I do not know which way to turn. In addition to all this, they also want to nominate me judge of the peace because it appears that I have a specialty in reconciling people of different nationalities. All that is very nice but where is the life of tranquility that I had dreamed of in the heart of the prairies."

Armand Trochu, 1906

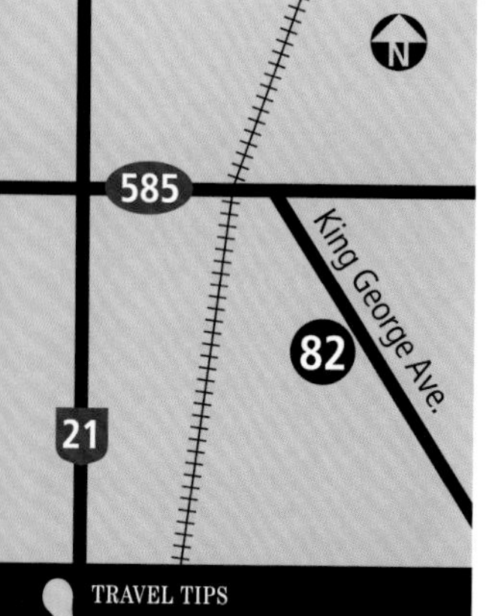

TRAVEL TIPS

Museum buildings open 9 a.m. to 9 p.m. daily year round.

The Country Inn holds 16 in the ranch mansion and five in the pioneer house.

Letters written by Armand Trochu and his teenage daughter to family in France are available online at Glenbow.org.

Location: Follow Highway 585 east through Trochu. Cross the railroad tracks and turn right at the St. Ann Ranch sign.

Phone: 1-888-442-3924 or (403) 442-3924

www.stannranch.com

Drive into the coulee cradling St. Ann Country Inn today, and you'll be greeted by Tom and Holly Frère, another generation in the town's lineage. In addition to a mansion and pioneer house, where you can stay the night and wake to the singing birds, their property still contains some of the buildings that took shape as Armand Trochu and a cadre of mostly disgruntled French cavalrymen carved a home far from home. Along a boardwalk, you march past a post office, chapel, school, hospital, trading post – plus the original 1910 Frère residence, now an interpretive centre displaying Lorene's research. Gems hide everywhere. Inside the interpretive centre, a scrawled addition to a timeline tells you that Armand Trochu just missed sailing on the Titanic in 1912; on the post office wall, a faxed note expresses Grant MacEwan's regrets at missing the ranch's 90th anniversary of incorporation in 1995.

Among those who did attend that celebration were dozens of relatives from France. Addressing the crowd, grandnephew Jacques Bence characterized his great uncle as a man who discarded his identity as a struggling stockbroker with the aim of proving to his eminent family that he could "achieve something by himself." Achieve he did, in roles as arbiter, mayor and postmaster – with a promise of a post as a minister of parliament. Had a failing heart not sent Armand Trochu back to France, who knows what the ranch and Trochu might be today?

Armand Trochu purchased the land that would become St. Ann Ranch from the Hudson's Bay Company in 1903 and joined with Joseph Devilder and Leon Eckenfelder to incorporate the St. Ann Ranch Trading Company Ltd. in 1905. The business was instrumental in the arrival of the first priests, the North West Mounted Police, the Sisters of Charity, the Grand Trunk Pacific Railway and others who formed the original town. Devilder returned to France in 1908 to take over a family banking business and Trochu returned in 1917 due to a failing heart. That left Eckenfelder, originally the junior partner, as the only shareholder remaining in Trochu. The company slowly ceased operations after Trochu's departure and was officially liquidated in 1953.

83 Mary Schäffer Warren

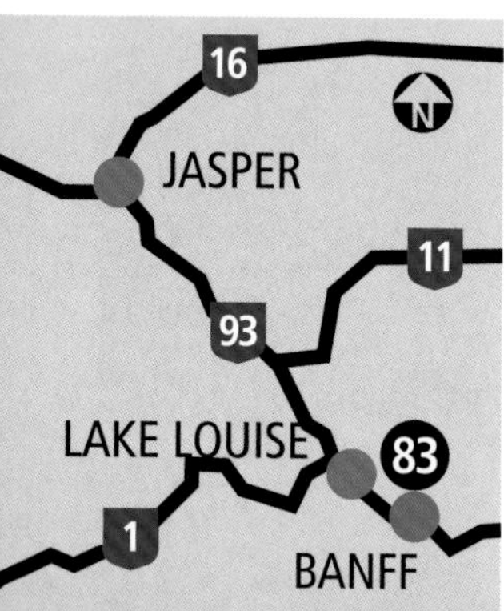

Pieces of Mary

Mary Schäffer Warren's works are held by the Whyte Museum of the Canadian Rockies.

A Hunter of Peace, edited by E.J. Hart (1980), includes *Old Indian Trails* plus Mary's account of the 1911 expedition to Maligne Lake.

Books about Mary include *No Ordinary Woman* by Janice Sanford Beck (2001) and *Off the Beaten Track* by Cyndi Smith (1989).

Mary and Billy are buried together in the cemetery across the road from Tarry-A-While bed and breakfast, 117 Grizzly St.

Location: Whyte Museum: 111 Bear St., Banff

Phone: (403) 762-2291

E-mail: archives@whyte.org

www.whyte.org.

No ordinary woman, Mary Schäffer Warren explored deep into Canada's national parks at a time when no other white woman had. What's more, she left words, photos and paintings that provide a uniquely personal record of early 1900s exploration.

Born to wealthy Quaker parents in Philadelphia, PA, Mary fell in love with our mountains at the Canadian Pacific Railway's Glacier House Hotel at Rogers Pass in 1889. There she also met the charming (albeit considerably older) Charles Schäffer, a Philadelphia medical doctor who, like her, loved botany. Soon married, they made annual excursions to Glacier, Field, Lake Louise and Banff to document Rockies flora, with Mary illustrating the doctor's finds.

In 1903, this happy chapter in Mary's life ended abruptly when her husband and both parents died, leaving little of their wealth behind. As solace, she finished her late husband's study of mountain flora, gradually overcoming a distinct fear of horses and distaste for camping with the help of young guide Billy Warren. The resulting book was published in 1907, written by a respected botanist and amply illustrated by Mary.

That project complete, Mary and travelling mate Mollie Adams defied propriety by setting off to explore little-trod routes in the summers of 1907 and 1908, with Billy Warren again among their guides. Intended destinations included the reputedly beautiful Chaba Imne (Beaver Lake), now known as Maligne Lake. That first summer, they netted one clue: a map drawn by Stoney Samson

Beaver based on a trip to the lake with his father 20 years earlier. Thanks to that map, the following summer's journey climaxed with a slow but elated float across the lake on a rough-hewn raft.

Now known to the Stoneys as Yahe-Weha (Mountain Woman), Mary recounts those journeys in the book *Old Indian Trails of the Canadian Rockies.*

"And they ask if one grows lonely. Lonely? How can one, when all nature sings the evening hymn?"

Mary Schäffer
Old Indian Trails

Three years after Mary's first visit to Maligne Lake, the Geological Survey of Canada asked her to survey the lake, hoping her growing fame would help attract tourists. Happily returning, Mary found Miette and Yellowhead country cluttered with the garbage of westward wanderers. Maligne Lake remained unspoiled, however, setting the scene for a wonderful month of work and pleasure. Again Mary and friends floated across the lake, this time on a boat whose logs were carted over nearby Shovel Pass by pack horse.

Turning 50 and tired of Philadelphia winters, Mary moved to Banff full time. Billy Warren, whom she'd long called "my Chief," built her a house, which she called "Tarry-a-while." In 1915, the two married. In this union, Mary was the elder by far. Mary continued to write, lecture, paint, do needlework, entertain, travel some – and turned a blind eye to Billy's other women friends.

Often consulted by others setting out for wilderness travel, Mary was forthright about the fact that she had followed others' footsteps. "They like to say 'explorer' of me," she once wrote. "No, only a hunter of peace. I found it."

Mary Schäffer's renown is most linked to Maligne Lake, about 45 kilometres southeast of Jasper townsite. Known by the Stoney as Chaba Imne (Beaver Lake), it had been seen by Henry Macleod in 1875, but the arrival of Mary's party in 1908 marked its first recorded visit.

Among the lake's attractions is Spirit Island, one of the Rockies' most photographed spots, still accessible only by boat. Numerous trails near the lake include a short loop named after Mary Schäffer.

While crossing Maligne Lake in 1908, Mary Schäffer named a glacier-draped peak in the Queen Elizabeth Range after Mary Vaux, who had first attracted her to mountain life. Approaching Spirit Island, Mount Mary Vaux (3,201 metres) comes into view along the west side of the valley.

Ironically, major landforms named after Mary Schäffer and her first husband, Charles Schäffer, are not near Maligne Lake, but to the west in Yoho National Park. Mount Schäffer (2,692 metres) and Schäffer Lake are located between Lake O'Hara and Lake McArthur.

84 South Country Fair

Beside the Oldman River in the beautiful countryside of Fort Macleod, experience one of the top five small music festivals in Canada. You are in ranch country, but the three-day South Country Fair is dedicated to diversity in music. One moment, you feel like you've stepped into a hippie revival. The next, you're moved by the folk music of countries around the world. At other times from the stage, you hear the sounds of contemporary music. Many fair-goers expect to hear traditional, ethnic and contemporary folk and they aren't disappointed, but they may also find themselves enjoying rockabilly, blues, jazz, Celtic or even punk music. To date, the fair has showcased everything but opera, but given the eclectic taste of organizers, who knows what might find its way on stage?

Because the South Country Fair is an arts festival, poets and other spoken-word performers present sound, rhythms and words as fascinating as the music offerings. Scheduled word-artists perform on the Lotus Land stage, and if you want to try your work with an audience, times are available for the open microphone.

First held in 1986 with an audience of about 200 people, today the music and arts festival attracts about 2,500 people who have the good fortune of enjoying regional, national and even international entertainers. Acts scheduled for the South Stage are touring groups or individuals, including touring Albertans. The East Stage is dedicated to amateurs and emerging musicians. Then, after the performers end their day, independent films are screened on stage.

N
2
84
3
3
810
FORT MACLEOD
2

TRAVEL TIPS

For this summer festival, many people choose to camp at the Fish and Game Park. Also available are private lots for RVs and camping.

Purchase advance tickets for the festival online.

Location: Fort Macleod Fish and Game Park

Phone: (403) 553-3070

E-mail: asparagus@scfair.ab.ca

www.scfair.ab.ca

As well, the fair has awareness tents, where you can learn about healing arts and details of massage techniques and discover spiritual approaches to health and wellness.

For those bringing a young family, there is fun at Kidz' Kountry where story-tellers, musicians, clowns, puppeteers and other great kids' performers add magical moments to young lives.

Of course, the fair has food vendors, enticing passers-by with the ever-popular hamburgers and hot dogs or spicing things up with a taste of ethnic foods from Africa, Asia and other exotic lands. Count on the vendors at the crafters' mall to display unique items. Although not all the jewelry, clothing, household items and musical instruments are handmade, many are. Other items will be special, too, and not readily available in standard shopping malls.

The entire atmosphere of the fair has a friendly intimacy. In fact, that's what it is all about – creating community. Lifestyles, ideas and taste in music may be similar to your own or quite different. Most important to organizers is that you have a chance to enjoy the company of diverse people, as well as diverse musical styles. "Harmony" and "peace" are watchwords for the festival, and that's really what keeps volunteer organizers dedicated to the festival and keeps fans of the event coming back year after year.

Fort Macleod was incorporated as a town in 1882. By 1910, the population was about 2,500. Currently home to about 3,000, the town has preserved early buildings located on Main Street. Built between 1897 and 1920 and renovated to preserve historical elements, they continue to be places of business.

Of particular interest are the sandstone buildings and those with extensive stone work. Inside, some have pressed metal ceilings. Maybe you want lunch in the Silver Grill Restaurant. Don't miss the giant mirror with a bullet hole and crack that goes back to the early 1900s.

Most impressive is the Empress Theatre. Built in 1912 as an opera house and stage for vaudeville performers, it has been in continuous use ever since. Summer tours take you behind the scenes and you hear about ghosts! The stage is still used by guest artists and theatre groups. Also, special plays are performed for summer tourists. For information, call 1-800-540-9229 or check www.empresstheatre.ab.ca.

85 Spruce Meadows

If you love horses, riders and show jumping competitions, schedule your visit to Calgary around the world-class Spruce Meadows events. Located at the city's southern limits, the site is about a 40-minute drive from downtown.

The first tournament was held on the grounds in 1976, with only a couple of hundred people in the audience. Today, Spruce Meadows has outdoor arenas and paddocks plus more than 20 buildings including two indoor arenas, a tournament centre, stables, offices, additional special event venues and storage buildings. And today, hundreds of thousands attend the competitions.

Regular events begin with indoor competitions in February and end with the Pony Classic in early November, but the highlights of the season are May to September.

In early May, the Spruce Meadows Classic draws many entries and loyal crowds. If the weather is good, the event is outdoors. If not, given the outstanding indoor area and other facilities, the competitions can be held with a roof overhead.

In June, large crowds gather for the National when top athletes compete for $1 million and the title of Spruce Meadows Canadian Champion. June is filled with other events, too, many offering top prize money. If you want something special to do for the Canada Day weekend, enjoy the Canada One events at Spruce Meadows. Extend your visit a few days for the five days of outstanding North American equestrian competitions, when top riders are attracted from all over the continent for purses totalling $1 million.

The Masters, held in early September, is another horse lovers' dream. During the event, the world's best, both riders and horses, vie for more than $2 million in prize money, the highest purse in any show jumping competition. If you want a change of pace while there,

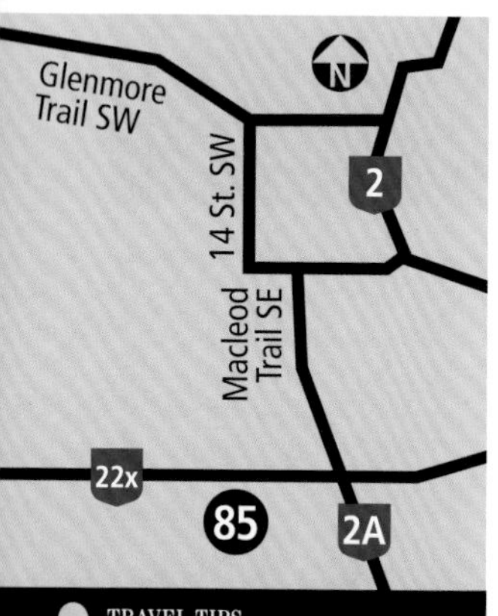

TRAVEL TIPS

Spruce Meadows is open 9 a.m. to 5 p.m., 365 days a year.

Parking is a distance from the tournament rings and other facilities.

During international tournaments and the International Christmas Market, a free shuttle operates from the Bridlewood Somerset LRT station.

Location: On Calgary's southern city limits. From Macleod Trail, Deerfoot Trail North or Highway 2 South, turn west on Spruce Meadows Trail (also known as Highway 22X/Marquis of Lorne Trail).

Phone: (403) 974-4200

E-mail: information@sprucemeadows.com

www.sprucemeadows.com

check out the Festival of Nations entertainment and exhibits. Again, there are so many options of things to do on the grounds, both old and young will enjoy what time they can find to catch their breath and taste the ethnic cuisine offered in conjunction with the festival.

Highlights of the fall include the Harvest Classic, Octoberfest and the International Christmas Market.

Beyond the ring during all the major competitions, Spruce Meadows hosts special performers, offers cultural events and sets up displays. Many are located in or near the International Plaza, which includes a marketplace. Known as the International Market Place, the area is transformed into a country fair, historical village or international marketplace. Clearly, a great time awaits all visitors.

As well as the show jumping competitions, Spruce Meadows hosts the High Country Carriage Driving Competitions in early August. In mid August, the Gadsden Antique Show is held on the grounds. One of the largest antique shows in Alberta, collectors will find thousands of antiques to purchase. Even those who just want to look will have much to see and have a great time, too. In late September, the Canadian-American Western and Equestrian Lifestyles Association holds a trade show at the facility.

For shoppers, the highlight of the year is the Spruce Meadows International Christmas Market in mid-November and offered again days before Christmas. The International Market area is transformed into a Christmas wonderland where you can purchase unique crafts, art, pottery decorations, jewelry, clothing, food and other gifts. A small entrance fee is charged to attend the Christmas Market. Admission for children under 12 is free.

86 Stephansson House

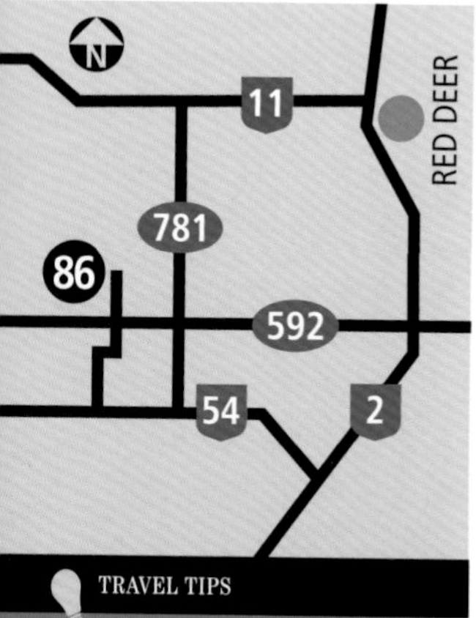

TRAVEL TIPS

Stephansson House is open from 10 a.m. to 6 p.m. daily from May 15 to Labour Day.

Location: Stephansson House is seven kilometres north of Markerville off secondary Highway 592

Phone: (403) 728-3929 summer only; (780) 427-3995 year round

E-mail: stephansson.house@gov.ab.ca

www.cd.gov.ab.ca/sh

Perhaps when the Canadian government was looking for people to homestead its vast western territories in the late 1800s and early 1900s, it should have looked harder at Iceland. The farmers there would at least have been used to the long summer days, the long winter nights and the wide-open spaces.

Stephan G. Stephansson arrived in North Dakota from a farm in Iceland with his parents and his sister and her family when he was 20 years old. He later married and, in 1889 when he was in his mid 30s, he and his family moved to the homestead that today is close to Markerville.

The stay in North Dakota had been very hard, fraught with droughts, fires and frosts that made it almost impossible to make a living. Despite the trials, he managed to farm while honing his skills at writing poetry.

It must have been particularly difficult after putting so much into the effort in North Dakota to leave it all behind and start again in a new territory. His wife, Helga, was pregnant with another child, but with three children and his mother, the family moved north to Canada. Three years after arriving at his new home, the poet was influential in starting a literary society, an unusual choice for the community when there was still no church for some years to come.

Stephansson worked long and hard days and nights as did most homesteaders in those days, but whatever moments he could steal away from ploughing, seeding, harvesting and caring for the farm animals, he devoted to his poetry. He became a premier poet in the Alberta Icelandic community, but he had already established himself as premier poet in his home country of Iceland. Stephansson was a pacifist, and later on his anti-war poetry was to alienate those who had sons fighting in the Great War, but his other poetry was widely read and loved.

The Icelandic community in Alberta was small but it kept its culture alive over the years. Today, the Stephansson homestead enables others to learn about some of its Icelandic specialties. There are school programs for kindergarten and grade school children, and there are day programs for any to enjoy. A poetry day in early summer includes workshops, live entertainment and crafts and, of course, poetry readings. A harvest penny carnival in August invites visitors to shop at the craft market and sample some Icelandic food – not forgetting the poetry reading here either.

Stephansson House has been protected and preserved for other generations to visit and admire, and is indicative of the widely varying backgrounds that have been so cheerfully woven into the cloth that is Alberta.

Stephan did not remember when he actually started composing verse because he was so young. All through his years of farming, he drove himself to complete the farm tasks so he could return to his desk to study more of the meaning of the Icelandic language and to write his poems.

The Icelandic language was not widely used at the time of his birth but his work revitalized it and he published more than 2,000 pages, much more than other Canadian poets of the time. Due to failing health, Stephan in his 60s thankfully turned the farming over to his son Jakob and devoted his remaining years to his writing.

Sutter Family

TRAVEL TIPS

Sutter mementoes will be on display at the Viking arena once it's rebuilt.

For more on the Sutter brothers, visit the Alberta Sports Hall of Fame outside Red Deer.

The Viking hospital, built in 1921, is serving as the local museum where you will find more about the history of Scandinavian settlement in Alberta.

Location: 140 kilometres southeast of Edmonton on Highway 14 at the intersection of Highway 36

Phone: (780) 336-3466

E-mail: laura.arndt@town.viking.ab.ca

www.town.viking.ab.ca

Viking greets visitors with a huge wooden hockey stick and puck proudly proclaiming the "Home of the Sutters."

For hockey fans, explanation isn't necessary. This town of 1,100 is best known for the greatest hockey family in Alberta's history. In the 1980s, six Sutter brothers out of seven – Brian, Darryl, Duane, Brent, Ron and Rich – all played in the National Hockey League (NHL), and all were phenomenal players. Eldest brother Gary also played while growing up in Viking, but chose not to pursue a hockey career beyond his teenage years. Later in life, they continued to be leaders in the hockey world and outstanding coaches. All six brothers who went on to the NHL are honoured in Alberta's Sports Hall of Fame, but those hockey legends were shaped by their rural family life.

Parents Louis and Grace Sutter ran a 566-hectare farm with beef cattle, dairy cattle, hay and grain crops. Their original house, where Louis had grown up, was tiny and without electricity, running water or indoor plumbing.

The Sutter parents raised their boys to demonstrate the spirit and determination that guaranteed success on the family farm. Later, those qualities also ensured success in the NHL. Louis Sutter was a sports junkie but he indulged his passion only when the work was done. He didn't force hard work on his sons but they absorbed the work ethic naturally; they realized early that the whole family honoured discipline and hard work. All the brothers carried on the family traditions. Those in the NHL translated their lessons into finesse manoeuvres on the ice that helped their teams on the scoreboard. They were all feisty, hustling players who always finished the play. As Louis always said, "You don't back down from anybody." They didn't.

Louis died Feb. 10, 2005 in the Viking hospital at the age of 73. The elite of the NHL paid their respects to the family. No one would forget the father of seven amazing brothers who learned the lessons of life and hockey at his knee.

Many of those hockey lessons took place at the Viking arena, the hub of the town's sport and social activities. Named the "Carena" in proud memory of a monthly car raffle in 1950 and 1951 to raise funds to build the rink, it opened in 1952. Here, the Sutter family was a familiar sight as they all laced on the skates. The NHL-bound brothers played their minor hockey here and later donated keepsakes.

In July 2005, the Carena caught fire. The blaze broke out in the north end, which proved lucky because rescuers had time to retrieve the Sutter memorabilia from the south end. Plans are well underway to rebuild the arena where the Sutter family started winning the hearts of Albertans with their loyalty, vigour and talent.

Because of the Sutters, Viking can claim more hockey greats than any other town in Canada. Honouring the on- and off-ice contributions of the family seems as natural as, well, kids playing hockey and dreaming big dreams.

The people of Viking are proud of their Scandinavian heritage. A roadside Viking ship and sculpture of a Viking warrior commemorate the area's Norwegian pioneers. The first Scandinavian settler arrived in 1902.

At Viking Troll Park, located beside the Canadian National Railway station, you will see trees and plants with Scandinavian names. In 2000, Viking placed first in the National Communities in Bloom competition. Also in the park, you will discover a dwarf or two living there. The newest of the trolls is life-sized! Inside the station, enjoy the tea room and art gallery.

Nearby is a First Nations heritage site. On a rise just out of town, you will discover giant stones carved and shaped to appear like the ribs of a large animal, most likely a bison. Called the Ribstones, this site may be about 1,000 years old. The formations are likely related to spiritual ceremonies performed for the buffalo hunt.

88 Taber Cornfest

Across Alberta and even beyond, "Taber" stands for sweet, sweet corn. Late every summer, pickups mounded high with the cigar-shaped bundles of corn head out across the Prairie to become instant roadside stands. Seeing those trucks roll into town, with "Taber corn" blazoned on the side, you know the time of year has come for a mouthwatering meal, with vegetable as the main food group.

Taber is so well known for its super sweet corn that the local Kiwanis Club (joining the province-wide fetish for Big Things in Small Towns) erected an 11-metre metal cornstalk right next to Highway 3, the town's main gate. Every August, that cornstalk serves as a giant welcome to the joy of the Taber Cornfest.

The cornfest celebrates the fruits of this agricultural community with top drawer musical talent, activities for all ages – and of course, corn by the ears full. You've got your cornbread, your corn shuck, your corn stuff, your corn eating contest. Plus, if you're unlucky, your corny jokes onstage.

Talent onstage leans to folks with southern Alberta connections who are proving their chops at home and beyond. You might find Innisfail-born Tammy Gislason celebrating the cowboy heritage, poetic John Wort Hannam celebrating rural routes, Texas Flood paying tribute to the Kings (including the great BB), or rockin' Double Jack from nearby Lethbridge. If you don't like what you're hearing, just take a break and come back in half an hour for the next set.

You'll also find a midway, craft sale, quilt show, obstacle course, car brag, dog show, fun run and lots to do for all. Everybody can eat hearty with a pancake breakfast, a chili cook-off and numerous food vendors. As a final hurrah, there's a round of fireworks beneath that big prairie sky.

N
36
50 St
50 Ave
88

TRAVEL TIPS

The cornfest takes place the last Friday and Saturday of August.

Kick-start the weekend Thursday evening with all-you-can-ride at the midway.

You can camp along the Oldman River at Taber Municipal Park, (403) 223-5500, town@taber.ca or use an RV park along Highway 3. Nearby communities also have campgrounds.

Location: Confederation Park, corner of 50th Street and 50th Avenue, Taber. Arriving on Highway 3, turn north on 50th Street.

Phone: (403) 223-2265

E-mail: chamberoffice@taberchamber.com

www.taberchamber.com/Cornfest/home.htm

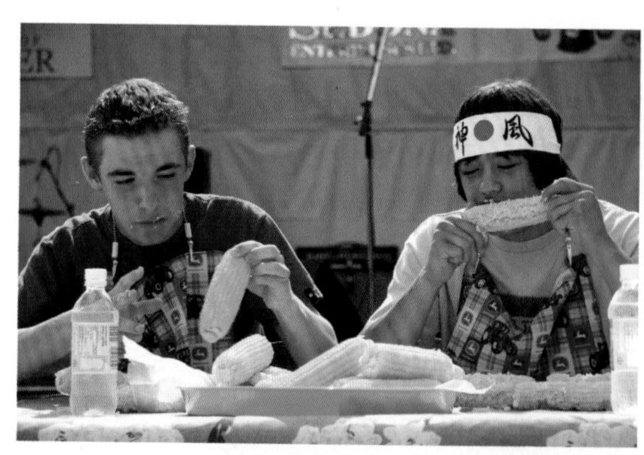

Through the years, the Taber Cornfest has become a time for families and friends from across Canada and the northern United States to reconnect and recollect. The whole town becomes involved, volunteering by the dozens and donating whatever's required. As a result, it's all free. In fact, it's the largest free outdoor festival in southern Alberta. As the good folks in Taber like to put it, "Come for the corn, stay for the fun."

Taber calls itself the heart of southern Alberta's green belt, and irrigation makes it possible.

Born as a range ranching and coal mining town in the late 1890s, the community relied on Oldman River steamers to ship the coal to Medicine Hat until narrow-gauge railway came along. Coal mining declined dramatically in the late 1920s, but the dry years of 1917 and 1920 prompted a push to irrigate, sparking an economic recovery in the early 1930s. With reliable water, this formerly parched land could grow a wide variety of crops, including corn and sugar beets.

By 1950, the town had a beet processing plant that still operates as Roger's Sugar.

For more about the town's past, visit the Taber Irrigation Impact Museum, home to town archives, vintage irrigation machinery and revolving exhibits. Located one block north of the lights on Highway 3 at 50th Street. Phone (403) 223-5708 or e-mail tiimchin@telusplanet.net.

89 David Thompson

David Thompson was born in England in 1770 and and his father died when he was two. His mother was able to enrol him in the Grey Coat Charity School when he was seven but by the time he was 14, he had signed on to apprentice with the Hudson's Bay Company.

When he was 29, he married 13-year-old Charlotte Small, the daughter of a North West Company partner, Patrick Small, and his Cree wife. David and Charlotte had 13 children, five of whom were born out west. Charlotte and the children accompanied Thompson on several occasions.

David and Charlotte died within a few months of each other in 1857 after 57 devoted years together. They are buried in Mount Royal Cemetery in Montreal.

From our 21st century perspective, it is difficult to understand the importance of the work of men like David Thompson. He began his career as a fur trader, but his passion was exploration and mapmaking. After many years with the Hudson's Bay Company (HBC), he became an employee of their chief rival, the North West Company (NWC), when he felt the HBC was not sufficiently interested in opening up new territory or allowing him to pursue his map making.

An important part of his work was his precise skill in plotting and mapping the areas he travelled. His first assignment with the NWC was to chart the actual location of the NWC posts to determine whether they were in Rupert's Land, which included much of modern-day Canada, or in the United States.

Thompson's interest in exploration was probably triggered by the presence of the explorer Samuel Hearne at Churchill Factory the year he joined the HBC, but his skills in plotting and mapping came about as the result of breaking his leg in 1788. It was a bad break, and he spent the whole winter recovering at Cumberland House near Lake Winnipeg. Philip Turnor, the HBC's chief astronomer, happened to be at Cumberland House and, finding Thompson an attentive and keen pupil, taught him the basics of surveying and using the stars as guides. By spring, Thompson had a limp and had lost the sight in one eye, but he was excited by what he had learned.

Thompson spent considerable time at Rocky Mountain House exploring options for passes through the mountains. He also discovered a more direct route to the fur-rich Athabasca country. He wintered at Lac La Biche in 1798 and set out the following spring to explore what is now northern Alberta. He visited Fort Augustus (near present day Edmonton), and then travelled the Pembina and Athabasca Rivers to Lesser Slave Lake, then travelled the Athabasca to the site of present day Fort McMurray. He finished up at Lac Ile-à-la-Crosse where he met and married Charlotte Small.

Thompson is recognized as one of the world's greatest geographers, with his 1814 map of western North America, the Great Map, foretelling the possibility of a nation from sea to sea considered his crowning achievement. Financial problems after he retired, however, led to a life of poverty, with little acknowledgement of all he had accomplished.

His maps and surveys were so accurate they were used by the Canadian government into the 20th century, and his work on the Canada/United States border, along the 49th parallel and from the St. Lawrence River to Lake of the Woods in Ontario, is well recognized.

In his lifetime, David Thompson travelled 88,500 kilometres on foot and canoe and his Great Map covered 3.9 million square kilometres of the continent!

TRAVEL TIPS

Visit the National Historic Site to learn more about David Thompson.

Beginning in 2007, bicentennial celebrations will recognize David Thompson's outstanding achievements, especially along the routes he travelled in the fur trade.

Rocky Mountain House (RMH) will host the Rupert's Land Colloquium (2008) and the fur trade festival.

Location: seven kilometres west of RMH off Highway 11A. RMH is about 82 kilometres west of Red Deer on Highway 11.

Phone: (403) 845-2412

E-mail: rocky.info@pc.gc.ca

www.davidthompson200.org

www.davidthompsonthings.com

90 Turner Valley

TRAVEL TIPS

Guided tours of the Turner Valley Gas Plant are generally available in summer, but it's best to check in advance.

Follow Highway 546 through the Sheep River Valley to see farmland, grassland and parkland.

At Sheep River Provincial Park and Wildlife Sanctuary, 17 different species of raptors have been reported.

Location: Highway 22 or Highway 2 south from Calgary, then Highway 7 west to Turner Valley. The Turner Valley Gas Plant is on the banks of the Sheep River at the edge of town.

For more information, contact the Frank Slide Interpretive Centre.

Phone: In Alberta, toll free 310-0000, then (403) 562-7388

Email info@frankslide.com

www.frankslide.com

Almost a century ago, Turner Valley began a momentous journey. There, the modern age of Alberta's oil and gas industry had its beginnings. Alberta's oil and gas reserves were not the first discovered in Canada but, until the 1940s, Turner Valley's oil field produced the most oil in the British Empire and was the largest and most productive oilfield in Canada.

William Herron, an Okotoks area farmer, discovered gas seeps along the Sheep River and formed Calgary Petroleum Products. Investors included Archibald Dingman, James Lougheed, A.E. Cross and R.B. Bennett. Their drilling rig Dingman No. 1, named after the chief driller, hit pay dirt on May 14, 1914. Gas spewed and Alberta's petroleum industry was off and running. Although the well was not a great producer, the company built a small plant on the site to separate oil and gas. Locals filled their automobile tanks with "skunk gas," so called because the naphtha had enough hydrogen sulphide in it to smell like rotten eggs. Ultimately, costs soared and investors sold to Imperial Oil, which formed a subsidiary, Royalite, to operate the gas plant.

In 1924, Turner Valley's Royalite No. 4 blew wild and a spark ignited the gas. It was weeks before the well was brought under control. The well proved a good one, though. The valuable liquids were captured through a separator, but the waste gas was flared off in a coulee just northeast of town. Other wells directed flares to the same spot to keep production costs down on what they considered the more valuable liquids. The area burned so violently that the ground shook. The seared coulee became known as Hell's Half Acre, where the gas burned like its namesake for many years. When the conditions were right, light from Turner Valley lit up the sky throughout southern Alberta.

Although natural gas was a valuable product, oil filled investors' dreams. The whole nature of Turner Valley production changed in 1936, when Turner Valley Royalties No. 1 hit crude oil just north of Longview.

The Second World War broke out in 1939, and Turner Valley became the centre of a massive expansion. At its peak in 1942, the Turner Valley Oilfield produced more than 10 million barrels of oil to assist the war effort.

The Turner Valley Gas Plant was in operation until 1985. Built on the site of the 1914 discovery, it boasted a number of firsts: the first high pressure absorption gas extraction plant in Canada, Canada's first sour gas scrubbing plants of their type, the first propane plant in Canada and one of the first two sulphur plants.

The locations of tar paper shack communities that housed the workers are part of the area's history, too. Arriving from across the continent, the men were a hardworking, rough and ready lot. Times were wild. Whiskey Row, Dogtown and Poverty Flats are memories, but a free booklet from the Turner Valley Town Office will help you find their history.

The Turner Valley Gas Plant is both a National and Provincial Historic Site.

The Turner Valley Golf and Country Club is located 45 minutes south of Calgary in the Alberta foothills. Beautiful all year round and with a magnificent view of the Rockies, the setting is especially dramatic in early fall.

A mature 18-hole golf course, it boasts sand, water and groves of willow trees, which require accurate shot making from golfers of all levels. Originally this was a nine-hole course developed by the employees of Royalite Oil Company in the early 1930s.

The clubhouse was once the local high school for Turner Valley, and its original design more than accommodates a complete dining facility, pro shop and locker rooms. The view and the food give the visitor a taste of country warmth and hospitality, and the price is reasonable, too. Find the course at 700 Imperial Dr. For tee times, call (403) 933-2212.

91 Ukrainian Cultural Heritage Village

Outdoor or living museums are a real joy on Alberta's sunny summer days and this is one of the best. At the Ukrainian Cultural Heritage Village, 21st century families can wander from one site to another to see how their great-grandparents lived in Alberta if they had come from Ukraine. There are more than 30 historical buildings – churches, a functioning grain elevator, a sod hut or *burdei*, and many other homes from the wealthier Ukrainian situation to the most humble.

The fun part is speaking with the costumed interpreters who host each building or work outside in the gardens. Sometimes you'll see a woman cooking on the wood-burning stove despite the 30 C temperatures outside, sometimes you can chat with a man operating the blacksmith shop, also in the heat. They are all in character and react with amazement when a young person asks where the TV is or what they do in their spare time – a non-existent concept for early settlers.

That's on an ordinary day. There are also special events such as the spring celebration where you can sit on the grass and watch the oh-so-colourful Ukrainian dancing exhibition, from the precision of semi-professional groups to the tentative but equally joyous steps of five- and six-year-olds, all in the brilliant and varied costumes from the different regions of Ukraine.

Ukrainian Day is celebrated in August and encourages you to "live a day the Ukrainian way." The Taste of Ukraine food fair is a real highlight with the ever-popular pyrohy (perogies), hulubti (cabbage roles) and koubasa (Ukrainian garlic sausage), but there are also special performers and church services and the chance to learn how to make the beautiful Ukrainian Easter eggs or *pysanky*.

TRAVEL TIPS

Open 10 a.m. to 6 p.m. daily from the May long weekend to Labour Day. Open 10 a.m. to 6 p.m. weekends only from Labour Day to Thanksgiving.

The special spring weekend is the May long weekend and features more than 500 vibrant Ukrainian dancers.

Location: 35 kilometres east of Edmonton along Highway 16 and three kilometres east of the entrance to Elk Island National Park

Phone: (780) 662-3640

E-mail: uchv@gov.ab.ca

www.cd.gov.ab.ca/uchv

Besides a warm welcome to the village for the public in general, the facility offers education programs tied closely to the school curriculum, giving children an opportunity to interact with the Ukrainian old days in person. Field trips with the schools can be arranged and include guidelines and fact sheets for the teachers to help the kids get as much as possible from the experience.

The week-long Historic Children's Program summer day camp is particularly fun and open to anyone in Grades 2 through 6. The children dress each day in Ukrainian costumes of the time and are sent to board at one of the village homes. There, they experience the life they could have lived, studying in the one-room schoolhouse, playing period games and doing the chores they inevitably had at home. This program, developed over 20 years, is so unique and special that children have come from as far as British Columbia, Ontario, New York and even London, England.

It is truly a wonderful experience to spend a day at the village. If you're driving from Edmonton, there's the added possibility that you might see herds of bison munching close to the highway; they don't know it's the 21st century either.

Each year, more than 1,200 volunteers commit 12,000 hours of their valuable time to virtually every aspect of the village. Areas of support include special events, interpretation, a farm program and the site's museum areas.

Their results are evident in the more than 45,000 visits to the village each year, and through the many awards the Provincial Historic Site has won. These include:

- the 2005 Alberta Tourism Alto Award in the Alberta Pride category,
- 2002 through 2006 Communities in Bloom awards, with Ukrainian Village winning five blooms each year, and
- the 2005 Alberta Museums Association award for on-site driving tours designed for mobility impaired seniors.

92 United Farm Women of Alberta

Every Alberta woman who votes, uses a health clinic or earns a liveable wage has reason to salute the United Farm Women of Alberta (UFWA).

As the names suggest, the UFWA and the United Farmers of Alberta (UFA) are intertwined in history and ideals. The UFA involved women from its birth in 1909 and urged women to organize as early as 1912, noting that farm women were "sharing with the men the burden of the struggle for better conditions." Soon after, the UFA amended its constitution to admit women with equal privileges.

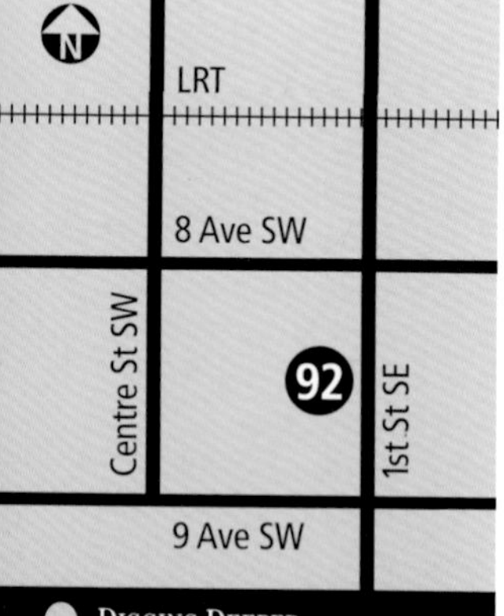

UFA men may have envisioned homemakers' clubs similar to existing government-sponsored Women's Institutes, but the Women's Auxiliary that formed in 1915 and was renamed UFWA in 1916 proved a feistier body. Besides serving as a service-minded gathering place, it played leading roles in battles for women's suffrage, minimum wage and property rights. At its peak in 1921, the movement also campaigned against such evils as venereal disease and child abduction, and sought government commitment to improved mental health services, hospitals, schools and libraries.

Digging Deeper

UFWA and Women of Unifarm records are held by the Glenbow Museum.

Location: 130 9th Ave. S.E., Calgary

Phone: (403) 268-4100

E-mail: glenbow@glenbow.org

www.glenbow.org

To their credit, UFA conventions not only approved but championed most UFWA resolutions. On the other hand, the UFWA was never allowed to carry its proposals to government without UFA sanction.

Alberta's Liberal government passed many reforms sought by the UFWA. Our health care system, for example, took shape in 1917 when UFWA President Irene Parlby pulled farm and municipal leaders together to draft a plan for tax-financed rural hospitals.

Yet not all UFWA campaigns saw success. The push for women's property rights resulted in a weak dower law and even weaker enforcement. A lobby for prairie midwives was blocked by the medical establishment. Repeated briefs calling for "family limitation clinics" bore little fruit.

The Liberals did grant women the vote in 1916. Just a year later, two women won provincial seats: overseas squadrons elected Nurse Roberta MacAdams; rural Alberta elected Louise McKinney of the Non-Partisan League, a self-proclaimed political arm of the UFA.

"Someone asked me what I hope for women to bring into Parliament and I said, 'Well, the most important thing they could bring was themselves, their own viewpoint.'"

Louise McKinney

McKinney pushed for stronger enforcement of anti-liquor legislation, which passed in 1916 with energetic farm support. Despite being linked to a 60-per-cent drop in violent crime, prohibition met with growing distaste, and McKinney was defeated in 1921.

Other UFA/UFWA candidates saw success in 1921, forming the government in Alberta. Among the 38 winners was Irene Parlby, who later joined McKinney as one of the Famous Five. Alberta's first female cabinet member, albeit without portfolio, Parlby ably championed rural and social causes. After serving several terms, she did not run in 1935.

The UFWA returned to its non-partisan roots, changing names over the years as the general farm organizations changed, first to Farm Women's Union of Alberta and finally to Women of Unifarm.

Women of Unifarm disbanded in 2000, yet we continue to benefit from seeds of equality planted in the fertile soil of the prairie frontier, where everyone had to pull together to survive.

The movement that would become UFWA took shape just as the suffrage lobby was being challenged to prove that rural women wanted the right to vote. Knowing that the UFA had called for equal voting rights as early as 1912, suffrage leaders urged the women to build the proof. They accepted the challenge, with gusto.

The future Famous Five were conspicuously onside: Louise McKinney and Irene Parlby (the two with UFWA connections), but also Henrietta Muir Edwards, Emily Murphy and Nellie McClung. A visit from the latter two in 1915 prompted this wry reflection from Premier Sifton: "Mrs. McClung and Mrs. Murphy are very determined women."

Not long after, the UFA received a letter from the premier promising a statute "placing men and women in Alberta on a basis of absolute equality so far as provincial matters are concerned." Alberta passed that bill in April 1916, joining other prairie provinces at the forefront. It would be another five years before most women could vote in federal elections.

93 United Farmers of Alberta

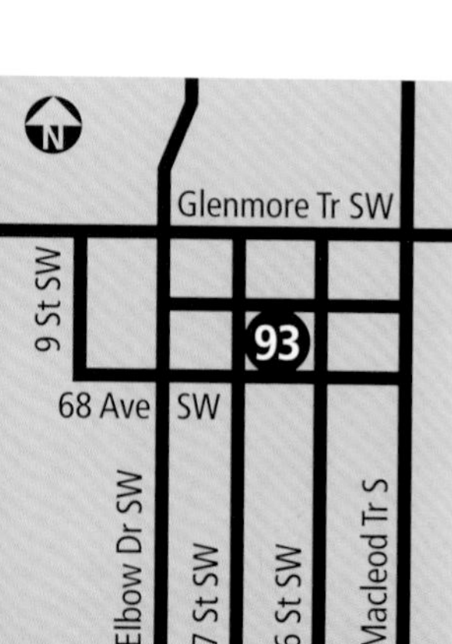

TRAVEL TIPS

In 2003, the United Farmers Historical Society created History in Motion, a mobile museum exhibit that showcases UFA's history since 1909. It rolls into rural and urban communities for special events throughout Alberta.

As well, the Galt Museum, the Grande Prairie 2000 Centre, the Lac Cardinal Pioneer Village Museum, the Glenbow Museum Archives and the United Farmers Historical Society feature the UFA.

Location: UFA head office, 1016 68 Ave. S.W., Calgary

Phone: (403) 258-4500

E-mail: customer.support@ufa.com

www.ufa.net

Wherever you drive in the province, you'll see evidence of the impact of the UFA Co-operative Limited (United Farmers of Alberta). Historically, agriculture helped build the province, with farm families contributing economically and culturally to Alberta through their values, knowledge and commitment to their communities. The UFA even played a significant role in the province's oil and gas industries, fighting successfully to have the province gain control over Alberta's mineral rights in 1930.

The organization had modest beginnings. In 1909, the Alberta Farmers Association and the Canadian Society of Equity merged to form the United Farmers of Alberta. The new member-owned co-operative formed locals throughout Alberta, focusing on agricultural marketing, education, health, social and cultural objectives related to farm families. Many members lived near small or isolated communities, but they showed their collective strength. As a united voice for farmers, the UFA negotiated higher prices for grain, livestock and produce as well as lower prices on farm machinery and supplies. Given its philosophy of co-operation, the organization also encouraged farmers to share their expertise.

By 1919, UFA members agreed that their collective voice should be heard in the Alberta political arena. Reorganizing with a political arm, members canvassed the province for votes during the 1921 election. Passionate speakers drew crowds to community halls and one-room schools. Leaders such as UFA president Henry Wise Wood clarified party objectives for the growing grass-roots movement and the UFA won 38 of 61 seats in the legislature.

Herbert Greenfield, a Westlock farmer, took the helm as premier. The competent and high-profile lawyer John Brownlee became attorney general and the premier's advisor. The elected MLAs were neophytes in the political arena, but among their early accomplishments was the creation of the Alberta Co-operative Wheat Producers Limited, the later-day Alberta Wheat Pool.

Eventually, Greenfield made farming his priority and Brownlee became premier in 1925.

At the time, provinces that had joined Confederation in 1867 controlled their own natural resources and claimed royalties from mineral rights. Western provinces had no such control or claim. The UFA government, like other western provincial governments, lobbied and negotiated for the same rights as eastern provinces. On Dec. 14, 1929, documents were signed as Ottawa agreed to the Alberta Natural Resources Act, conceding some control over natural resources.

By May 30, 1930, royal assent had been given to a broader act that gave complete control over natural resources and provincial public lands, waters, fisheries, parks and historic sites to the provinces. The UFA government drafted the legislation governing royalties – and Albertans have reaped the economic and social rewards ever since.

In 1934, Brownlee resigned and Richard Reid became the next UFA premier. That, along with the Depression and the emergence of the Social Credit party, led to defeat for UFA's political party in the 1935 election. In 1939, members voted to withdraw from politics.

Today, UFA continues as a member-driven co-operative providing farm, ranch and petroleum services and expertise to Albertans.

Today, the UFA Co-operative Limited is dedicated to strengthening agriculture in the province. Serving about 120,000 active members and many more customers, fuel and farm supply outlets operate as far north as High Level and as far south as Milk River. Some outlets have even opened in Saskatchewan and British Columbia.

In 1935, in partnership with Maple Leaf Petroleum, a subsidiary of Imperial Oil, UFA began marketing fuel to Alberta members. Today, the organization markets fuel and other petroleum products to customers at more than 120 outlets. Thirty-five communities are served by farm and ranch supply stores.

UFA has been a proud sponsor of rural communities for almost 100 years, offering direct support to many generations of Albertans. The co-operative's priorities continue to be youth, education, agriculture and rural living as it invests nearly $1 million annually in communities throughout the province.

94 Victoria Settlement

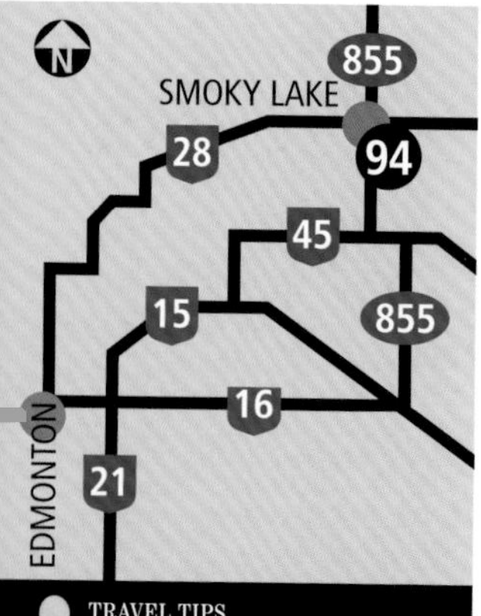

TRAVEL TIPS

The site is open daily from 10 a.m. to 6 p.m. from May 15 through Labour Day.

Take a picnic and drinks as there is no food service available.

Keep your map and sense of direction handy as some of the turn-offs are challenging to find.

Location: About 100 kilometres northeast of Edmonton just off secondary Highway 855. Watch carefully for signs.

Phone: (780) 656-2333 in season or (780) 645-6256 off season

E-mail: victoria.settlement@gov.ab.ca

www.cd.gov.ab.ca/vs

In the mid-19th century, the Carlton Trail spanned western Canada stretching from Fort Garry at modern-day Winnipeg to Fort Edmonton in present-day Alberta. The western most segment of this supply route was known as the Victoria Trail. Prior to the introduction of the Red River cart, supplies destined for the West were delivered by canoe and York boat against the strong flow of the North Saskatchewan River with all the difficulties of portaging around rapids and other obstacles. Travel by Red River cart, while still arduous, could be made over land.

Rev. George McDougall decided on the location for a mission on the North Saskatchewan River along this supply route in 1862 because the Cree had been camping in the area for centuries. The river was close and so were the buffalo. McDougall's ambition was to convert the Cree to Christianity, Methodism in particular, and Victoria Settlement, consisting of Métis settlers from Red River and the mission, was a strategic tool toward his plan.

Two years later, for similar reasons but a different purpose, the Hudson's Bay Company (HBC) established Fort Victoria nearby and built their usual aggregation of

necessary buildings to maintain a year-round post. The only building remaining today is the clerk's quarters, which has been restored to the period of the 1890s, although it served other purposes in its history. In its clerk's quarters days, it housed a clerk, his wife and their eight children!

An interesting aspect of the mission, fort and surrounding area is that the land was settled using a river lot system whose history traces back to the Red River Settlement and New France before that. Long and narrow lots offered each settler access to the river. These lots were confirmed during the first Dominion Land Survey in 1878.

Victoria Settlement's glory days were ending by the end of the 19th century. The fur trade was fading and in 1918 the Canadian Pacific Railway (CPR) chose to put the railway through Smoky Lake instead of Victoria. Some of the settlement's buildings were moved into Smoky Lake. Today, the sole remaining buildings are the Hudson's Bay Company clerk's quarters from 1864 and the last Methodist church built in 1906.

If you walk a few hundred yards down the road from Victoria Settlement Provincial Historic Site, you can see the little cemetery next to the original Methodist mission. Two of George McDougall's daughters and an adopted child were buried there after succumbing to smallpox during the 1870 epidemic. Another grave is for his 23-year-old daughter-in-law who died the following spring.

One of the later uses of the clerk's quarters building was as the post office, which was given the name of Pakan (rather than Victoria) to honour Cree Chief James Seenum, also known as "Pakannuk" or "Pakan," who kept his people neutral during the 1885 North West Rebellion. Pakan was a canny gentleman – he didn't convert to Christianity for many years as he said that the different missionaries (Methodist and Roman Catholic) were telling different stories.

95 Max Ward

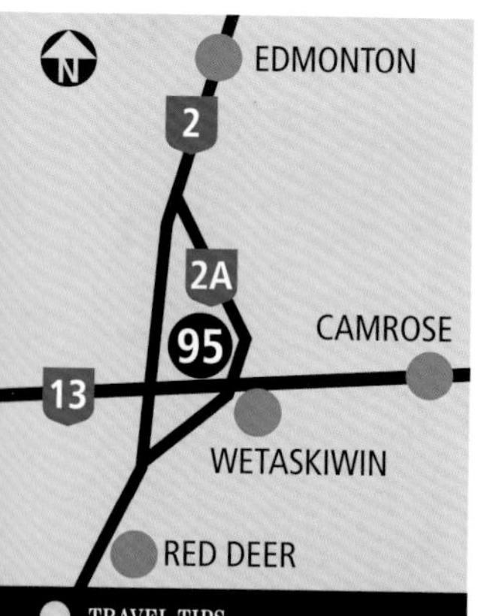

TRAVEL TIPS

Canada's Aviation Hall of Fame includes exhibits of Max Ward and others who pioneered and advanced aviation in Canada and around the world. See some of the many aircraft they used to explore and develop our nation, including the Silver Dart, Hawker Hurricane or the Province of Alberta's Douglas DC-3.

Location: Two kilometres west of Wetaskiwin on Highway 13

Phone: (780) 361-1351

E-mail: cahf@telusplanet.net

www.cahf.ca

Wardair, the Alberta-based airline that wrote its own chapter in the history of Canadian tourism, was the culmination of a long-standing dream of Max Ward. Born in Edmonton in 1921, Ward started his aviation career by joining the Royal Canadian Air Force in 1940 and serving as a commissioned flight instructor at various bases across Canada. At war's end, Ward tried to establish his own company with his one bush plane. Unable to get a business licence for his proposed Polaris Charters of Yellowknife, he bided his time until 1953 when he tried again with Wardair, originally intended as an air charter company for Canada's north.

That first bush plane eventually morphed into several airliners and Ward's holiday charter business began to take flight. Unfortunately, the federal government didn't see things his way and put one obstacle after another between him and his goal. Each plane he bought had to be approved as did each new route he wanted to add.

Ward, and others, believed the government was trying to protect its own airline, Trans-Canada (later Air Canada), by foiling any serious competitors. Trans-Canada was supposed to open up access to remote areas of the country but other airlines such as Canadian Pacific and Wardair serviced those routes while Trans-Canada continued to fly the busy cross-Canada routes.

The rules governing charter airlines were tight in the 1960s. Charter flights were only allowed if all passengers had been members of the organization chartering the flight for at least the previous six months. When Wardair developed strategies to address such restrictions, the rules would change, requiring a great deal of costly time and paperwork to prove the status of the group and each of its members. Wardair at one point lost its licence after an attempt to bypass the restrictions, but Max Ward never stopped trying.

Anyone who was able to meet the group membership requirements and travel on Wardair in the 1970s went first class all the way. Max Ward's idea was to make the flight part of the holiday, and passengers were served a good steak on fine China, accompanied by a glass of wine. Sometimes they were the good old days!

One of the restrictions prohibited advertising to individuals, and advertising to groups couldn't include the cost per person. One of Wardair's better ads that followed the rules but got the individual price across was "Fly to Europe for $33,000 and take along 99 friends." Even with all the restrictions, Wardair became Canada's third largest airline and maintained its reputation for first class in-flight service.

Ward fought most of his life for deregulation of the airline industry, believing the marketplace should determine the price of an overseas flight. But when deregulation finally occurred in 1987, he felt it was too late for him to expand his company. He sold Wardair two years later to Pacific Western Airlines. Ward continued to fly his own plane, happily taking his family on a "charter" to their lodge north of Yellowknife. Once a bush pilot, always a bush pilot.

96 Waterton Lakes National Park

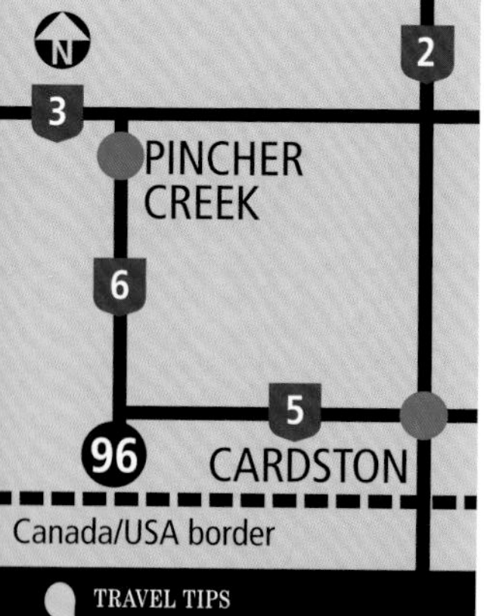

TRAVEL TIPS

If you're hiking to and from the United States through the park, make sure you have proof of citizenship, preferably a passport.

The Waterton Festival weekend is in late August. Enjoy the antique car show, chili cook-off, weekend dance and more.

Location: Park entrance is at the junction of Highways 5 and 6 (48 kilometres south of Pincher Creek or 43 kilometres southwest of Cardston)

Phone: (403) 859-2224

E-mail: waterton.info@pc.gc.ca

www.pc.gc.ca/waterton

Waterton Lakes National Park combines the best in prairie and mountain scenery. Here, sky, grasslands, prairie, mountains and lake meet. Here, too, is the meeting place of two countries.

Upper Waterton Lake, the deepest lake in the Canadian Rockies, straddles the 49th parallel. Water flows freely north and south. The Rockies are as majestic in Waterton Lakes National Park as in its sister American park, Glacier National Park. So, in 1932, with the two countries in agreement, the breath-taking area became Waterton-Glacier International Peace Park, the world's first International Peace Park. By establishing it, Canada and the United States honoured their shared landscape, heritage and friendship. The UN designated the Waterton-Glacier International Peace Park as a World Heritage Site in 1995.

Whether you stay at the much-photographed Prince of Wales Hotel, built on Upper Waterton Lake in 1927 and since designated a National Historic Site, or opt for camping or more recently built lodging, there is much to do in Waterton.

Enjoy a Waterton Inter-Nation Shoreline Cruise on the 200-passenger flagship M.V. International, operating on the Upper Waterton Lake since 1927. You might prefer the International Peace Park Hike along the lakeshore into Montana. You would hike the 13-kilometre trail to Goat Haunt in the company of a Glacier National Park ranger and a Waterton Lakes park interpreter, then return to Waterton on the boat tour service offered by Inter-Nation Cruise.

In the Waterton townsite, stroll past Cameron Falls. As well as the waterfall, you are looking at the oldest bedrock in the Rocky Mountains. It may not have the dramatic shapes of some formations or be as colourful, but it dates back 1.5 billion years!

On the Canadian side of the 505-square-kilometre park, hiking is one of the big draws. Bertha Lake and Bear's Hump trails are easy and convenient, and offer outstanding scenery. Carthew-Alderson Trail, the most challenging, is best hiked from Cameron Lake.

For Crypt Lake, go by boat shuttle. Later, you face the real challenges – climbing a ladder on the cliff face, crawling through a small tunnel and walking along a narrow precipice before the reward of a stunning cirque and emerald-coloured lake.

For those who prefer driving and a short walk, visit Red Rock Canyon. Take the Red Rock Parkway for about 16 kilometres, and then walk the Red Rock Canyon loop, which is about a kilometre long and takes you around the upper and deepest part of the canyon. The dramatic exposed red and green bedrock and lush plant life mean inspiration and great photos.

Fishing, other water sports and cycling are also big draws. For avid cyclists, the Akamina Pass Trail is a short but steep 1.3-kilometre ride one way. Crandell Loop Trail, Snowshoe Trail and Wishbone Trail are the other trails open to cyclists. With 255 kilometres of trails in the park, everyone, including trail riders, can find the perfect way to experience this park paradise.

Recognized by UNESCO in 1979 as having unique ecology, the Waterton Lakes and Glacier national parks are each designated as a biosphere reserve. Part of protecting the Waterton wilderness means preserving its amazingly diverse plant life. Given the range in altitudes, geology, soils, climate and precipitation, the park has 45 specific habitat types and four vegetation life zones: foothills parkland, montane, sub-alpine and alpine.

Home to more than half of the plant species found in Alberta, more than 1,000 species of higher vascular plants, not including lichen and lower plant forms, grow there. Twenty-two species are found only in Waterton. Many species are rare or threatened in Alberta and Canada.

Eight types of moonworts, members of the fern family, grow in the national park. Waterton moonwort is the rarest plant in the park. Feel thrilled if you find mountain orchids. Beargrass, a mountain lily blooming once every seven years, is more common and the floral symbol of the peace park.

97 West Edmonton Mall

TRAVEL TIPS

Shopping hours are: 10 a.m. to 9 p.m., Monday to Saturday; 11 a.m. to 5 p.m., Sunday; 12 noon to 6 p.m., Remembrance Day and New Year's Day; 10 a.m. to 6 p.m., statutory holidays.

Christmas Day and Easter Sunday are optional opening days for retailers.

Make note of which entrance you use so you can locate your vehicle!

Location: 87 Avenue between 170 Street and 178 Street, Edmonton

Phone: 1-800-661-8890 or (780) 444-5308 for tourism inquiries

www.westedmontonmall.com

It was the first. It is, in many respects, still the biggest. It calls itself "The Greatest Indoor Show on Earth." It is West Edmonton Mall (WEM), the trend-setting retail and entertainment complex that covers 48 city blocks and attracts about 22 million visitors a year.

WEM forever redefined "shopping centre" when it opened in 1981 with 220 stores and services. Floor space doubled to about 205,000 square metres (more than two million square feet) two years later, with the addition of the Ice Palace skating rink, Galaxyland Amusement Park and another 240 shops and services. In 1985, World Waterpark, Deep Sea Adventure, Dolphin Lagoon, Sea Life Caverns and Professor Wem's Adventure Golf were added; 1986 brought the 355-room Fantasyland Hotel. WEM reached its current size, 492,000 square metres (5.3 million square feet) in 1998 with the addition of major retail space and movie theatres.

Calling itself the "benchmark against which all entertainment-oriented malls are judged," WEM now boasts:

- world's largest indoor amusement park (25 rides and attractions)
- world's largest indoor triple loop rollercoaster (1,285 metres of track)
- world's largest indoor lake (complete with a replica of Christopher Columbus' ship, the Santa Maria)
- world's largest indoor wave pool (12.5 million litres of water)
- world's largest parking lot (with room for 20,000 vehicles)
- world's tallest indoor permanent bungee tower (30 metres up and 30 metres down)

WEM leaders understand the impact of the facility on its neighbours and has extended its imagination to its community programs. For example, it offers free space for a youth centre within the mall, accommodates the fund-raising efforts of many charitable organizations, hosts numerous charity events and annually provides thousands of passes, coupon books, coupons and merchandise to organizations for special events.

Listed in the *Guinness Book of World Records* as the world's largest shopping centre, WEM's 800 stores and services would take three 24-hour days just to visit for five minutes each. There are 58 entrances. Among the attractions are more than 100 eating establishments, 21 movie theatres and three 18-hole mini-golf courses. In the World Waterpark, the temperature ranges from 26 to 30 C, just like Acapulco!

More numbers: while riding the Mindbender rollercoaster, you can reach speeds up to 100 kilometres an hour and experience 5.2g's (an astronaut experiences about 3g's during the average space shuttle launch). The Fantasyland Hotel includes 120 theme rooms featuring Hollywood, Roman, Polynesian, truck, Victorian coach, Arabian, Canadian rail, igloo, western, waterpark, sports and African rooms.

Its financial impact matches the rest of its immense proportion. According to a research report compiling financial data from 1986 to 2000, WEM:

- visitors spent $8.9 billion in Alberta
- provided more than 303,000 person years of employment
- generated total federal tax collection of $2.9 billion
- generated total provincial tax collection of $1 billion
- generated total municipal tax collections in Alberta of $409 million

The future promises to sustain WEM's reputation for the new and imaginative with innovations such as lifestyle centres – a total life experience based on a traditional concept that people should be able to live, work and play all in one place. To furnish this vision, WEM landlords and tenants are investing $145 million over several years to add a third hotel, innovative permanent living spaces and prime commercial space.

WEM is the brainchild of the Ghermezian family, variously described as visionaries, proud and resourceful, audacious and enigmatic. Whichever adjective you choose, tip your hat to the creators of this astounding international landmark.

98 Whoop-Up Days

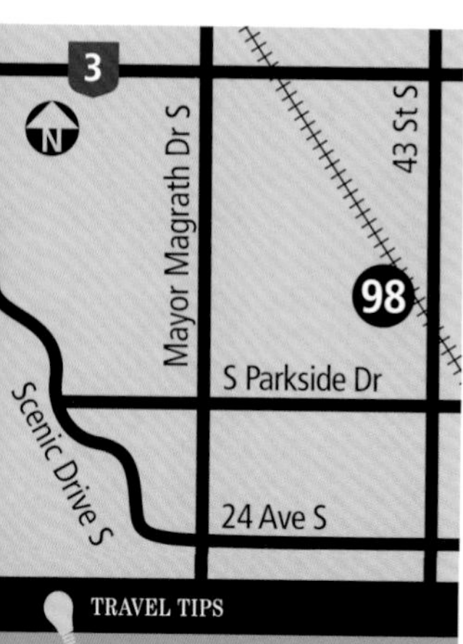

TRAVEL TIPS

Admission is free for children under 10 and reasonable for adults. Buy tickets in advance and get a break. A superticket, including admission and midway rides, is another option. Moonlight Madness is another good deal, and a calendar of where to find free breakfasts is available.

Henderson Lake Campground is nearby.

Location: Exhibition Park: 3401 Parkside Dr. S., Lethbridge

Phone: (403) 328-4491

Email: events@exhibitionpark.ca

www.exhibitionpark.ca

You are bound to whoop it up at Whoop-Up Days! No, that doesn't have to be in the reckless fashion of bygone days or nights when whooping it up meant gallons of firewater. Yes, you will have a great time. Yes, city storefronts take on a new western look and people dress western.

Held in late August, the event is true to the agricultural roots of Alberta and features a big-time pro rodeo and a bull riding showdown. Top-notch entertainment, a midway and displays attract audiences, too. Start your first day of festivities at the downtown parade, and start every day of the exhibition with a free breakfast.

As for entertainment, find it on the family stage where special shows amuse the young and young at heart. At the Gas King Stage, bands and acts are varied. Vocal and instrumental music can be country, folk, blue grass and even gritty contemporary. Some talent is local and some is from afar. Here, too, in mid afternoon, find the First Nations powwow dancers with their amazing footwork and stunning costumes. As well, a range of entertainers please audiences on the grounds. In the afternoons and evening from the grandstand, enjoy rodeo events including team penning, bull riding and mini chucks.

Lethbridge does a great job of encouraging local and regional artists, artisans, crafters and hobbyists by dedicating a huge space to Hobby World. Displayed there are the works of contest participants and winners in a wide range of categories. Find Victorian arts and crafts, woodworking, ceramics, doll making, cooking, metal works, photography, recycling ideas and more.

Of course, some visitors really want to walk in moonlight through the midway. So, take in Moonlight Madness, usually held on the Thursday night from 5 p.m. to midnight. On Saturday night, fireworks light up the sky to end Whoop-Up Days until the next year.

Today's event attracts more than 60,000 people, but holding a great time at their summer exhibition is not new to Lethbridge. The community's first agricultural fair was held in 1897, and the first official Lethbridge Exhibition with a rodeo was staged in 1904. In 1911, the annual event was held for the first time at today's exhibition grounds. During its early days, its most extravagant fair was held to host the World Dry Farming Congress in 1912. For that event, Lethbridge built a grandstand with a seating capacity of 5,000 people, unbelievably optimistic for the small community of the time.

During the First World War, the grounds were used to train troops. During the Second World War, the exhibition grounds became a prisoner of war camp. Renovations in the 1950s and 1960s provided more modern facilities, many still used today.

With the same whiskey trading history and on the bull trail from Fort Benton in the United States to Lethbridge, the town of Conrad, Mo., has its own Whoop-Up Days. Exactly who whoops it up more is for visitors to decide.

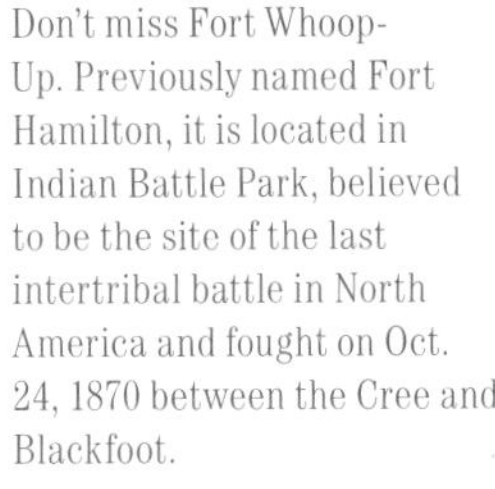

Don't miss Fort Whoop-Up. Previously named Fort Hamilton, it is located in Indian Battle Park, believed to be the site of the last intertribal battle in North America and fought on Oct. 24, 1870 between the Cree and Blackfoot.

The fort is a replica of the one built by American traders in 1869, and it tells the story of men who came for the buffalo robes of the Blackfoot. Whereas the Hudson's Bay Company, the largest trading partner of the Cree, abandoned bartering with whiskey much earlier, the men from Montana encouraged trade in whiskey and guns. So, Fort Whoop-Up became the most lawless of all the forts, and shoot-outs amongst rival individuals, both aboriginal and white, were an accepted part of doing business.

In 1874, with growing violence and worry about American influence, the Mounties marched west. Without a shot being fired, all but one trader vacated Whoop-Up, and the fort became the domicile for a few Mounties.

99 Wind Power

TRAVEL TIPS

The Pincher Creek Visitor Information Centre has a free audio CD tour of the wind farms, *Journey into the Wind.*

McBride Lake has a viewing area.

Visit www.canwea.ca for more information from the Canadian Wind Energy Association on wind power.

Location: There are more than 180 wind turbines around Pincher Creek. Contact the Pincher Creek Chamber of Commerce for specific locations.

Phone: 1-888-298-5855

E-mail: info@pincher-creek.com

www.pincher-creek.com/windenergy

Have you ever seen the wind? If you haven't, keep your eyes peeled for it. Wind has been whipping down the eastern slopes of the Rockies and across the plains for eons. With giant turbines at wind farms tapping the ancient resource, finally the prairie wind can be seen in more than the sway of tall grasses or the fluttering of leaves.

In contemporary Alberta, the wind is powering everything from McDonald's restaurants and shopping malls to offices. Operating on wind power, Calgary's C-Train has proudly adopted "Ride the Wind" as its motto. Given recent technological advances, one turbine can produce enough power in a year to accommodate the needs of 750 homes. So wind has become one of Alberta's greatest natural resources – and it's renewable!

The process and equipment for converting wind to electrical power is visible in much of southern Alberta. Typically, wind towers with their three-blade rotors are erected on hills or in valleys where wind rushes from the mountains, but many different locations have proven successful.

The Cowley Ridge Wind Farm was built in three phases beginning in 1993. The Summerview Wind Farm near Pincher Creek boasts some of the largest wind turbines in North America; in the same area, the Castle River and Lundbreck wind farms produce "green electricity," making small contributions to the power grid. The McBride Lake Wind Farm, south of Fort Macleod, is one of the largest single-site wind farms in Canada. In the Magrath area, three power companies have turbines to generate power.

Wind power is harnessed throughout the year in Alberta. Often during winter, chinook breezes sweep in at 65 to 100 kilometres an hour. In Lethbridge, the gusts can reach 120 kilometres an hour. Even that hurricane force was exceeded in November 1962, when a chinook brought blasts of 171 kilometres an hour. What a force of nature. What power!

Harnessing wind power is a quiet activity, and the towers take very little room. Grain farmers still plant and harvest, and ranchers continue to graze their livestock in the shadow of the towers. As well, they benefit from the rents paid to them by the wind power companies. Given that wind generates no pollution, is limitless and inexpensive to produce, wind is indeed a friend of Albertans.

So, watch for the wind. At first glance, a large wind farm with many towers may bring to mind a moonscape in a science fiction novel. Certainly, the technology is based on science, but there is nothing make-believe about the fact that wind is creating a win-win scenario for the Alberta of today and tomorrow.

The winds that generate so much electricity have also created serious complications in the lives of Albertans. Prairie fires, fuelled by parched lands and gusting winds, were a continuous threat in the early days. With little precipitation in the region, much of southern Alberta, especially the Palliser Triangle, is classified as semi-arid.

Pioneer lifestyles kept the threat of fire close by. Settlers disposed of ashes from wood and coal stoves regularly and used outdoor burn barrels to help manage their waste. As well, steam engines were widely used and their red-hot embers could land on dry grass and ignite fires. With strong winds, some fires could spread for hundreds of kilometres across the prairies.

Prairie weather can also generate tornadoes. Many small tornadoes touch down in fields or other unpopulated areas without doing extensive damage while others have tragically cost many lives.

100 Writing-on-Stone Provincial Park

Suddenly, grasslands give way to a spectacular river valley, cliffs and hoodoos. Sandy beach along the meandering Milk River lures kids and adults. Caves entice modern-day explorers. Dramatic land formations hook photography buffs. At Writing-on-Stone Provincial Park, enjoy a leisurely study of the flora and fauna or look up for great views of the Sweet Grass Hills in Montana. You can camp, bird watch and hike, but most fascinating of all is the glimpse into First Nations art and history.

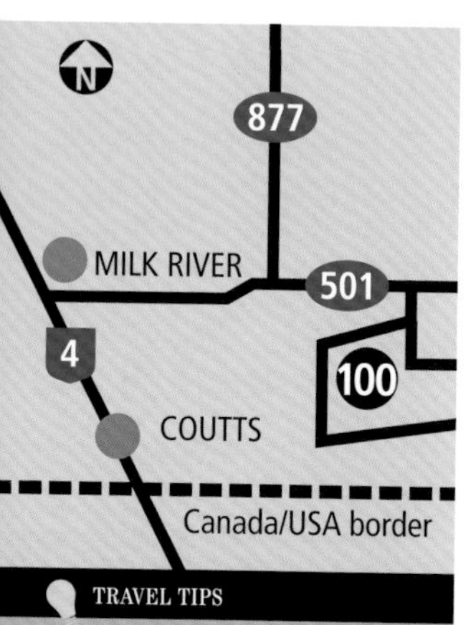

TRAVEL TIPS

The park is open for tours from mid-May to early September; in summer, guided tours to the rock art occur daily at 2 p.m. Additional tours, events and programs are added in peak season.

A tour guide must accompany visitors to the archaeological preserve. Tickets go on sale one hour before each tour.

Anyone who damages the fragile rock art is subject to a $50,000 fine and a one-year jail sentence.

Location: 32 kilometres east of Milk River near the Alberta-Montana border on secondary Highway 501, then 10 kilometres south on secondary Highway 500

Phone: (403) 647-2364

E-mail: info@albertaparks.ab

www.albertaparks.ca

Many areas feature hoodoos, but this park is unique. Named *Áísínai'pi*, meaning "it is pictured/written" in the Blackfoot language, Writing-on-Stone is sacred to the Blackfoot and other First Nations. Cliffs and hoodoos can evoke spiritual musings, but more importantly, rare and ancient examples of First Nations rock art have survived here. Hundreds of petroglyphs and pictographs at more than 50 sites in the park speak to the importance of this river valley in Blackfoot culture and spirituality.

Most petroglyphs, images scratched into cliffs, are believed to have been carved by the people of the Blackfoot Confederation; Sioux, Gros Venture, Assiniboine and Shoshoni were also know to have spent time in this area and may have left images, too. Traditionally, First Nations people used bone, antler, stones and wood to make the carvings of humans and animals on the sandstone. After the introduction of metal tools in about 1730, images began to incorporate guns and horses to reflect cultural changes.

Complementing the petroglyphs are pictographs, paintings created on rock faces, telling stories of hunters and warriors. Pictographs here were created using either charcoal or red ochre, a pigment created by mixing pulverized haematite (a blood-red iron ore) with bison fat or water.

This priceless legacy of stories and dreams carved and painted on rock faces is difficult to date, but some images may be as many as 5,000 years old. Most certainly, First Nations people visited and left their art 3,000 years ago. Traditional Blackfoot beliefs claim the images are messages from the spirit world. Whatever their origins, Writing-on-Stone has the largest collection of rock art in the Great Plains of North America. In 1977, because of the fragility of the images and problems with vandalism, much of the park was designated an archaeological preserve.

The park also shares a chapter of its history with the North West Mounted Police who built an outpost here and maintained a presence from the late 1880s through about 1918.

About 50 years after that, in 1957, the area was designated a provincial park to protect the mixed grasslands and archaeological sites. Designated a National Historic Site in 2005, today the park has an outstanding new interpretative centre and programs for visitors.

Writing-on-Stone is definitely a magical place, but it is also an ideal location for exploring, unwinding on hot summer days, swimming at the beach or simply soaking in all that nurtures your spirit.

Writing-on-Stone is a nature lover's paradise. Crocuses greet you in spring, and coneflowers, phlox, harebells, blazing stars, avens, clematis, bergamot, flax, violets and lilies have their own showy seasons. Thorny inhabitants such as prickly pear cactus, thorny buffaloberry and prickly rose await, too. With 265 species of plants, keep your plant identification book handy.

Bird watchers will also be in their glory. Discover nesting types in both trees and cliffs. Listen for great horned owls and killdeer. Keep your eyes peeled for white pelicans and Franklin's gulls along the river. Watch the grassland for sharp-tailed grouse. Glance overhead for bald eagles, hawks, turkey vultures and prairie falcons. Ruby-throated hummingbirds, ruby-crowned kinglets, red-headed woodpeckers, red-winged blackbirds and countless birds with other striking colours and markings delight visitors.

Given the snakes, turtles, amphibians, fish and 45 species of mammals – badger and bobcat, long-legged bats and western small-footed bats to mention a few – nature lovers usually plan a lengthy stay.

AMA: Helping you explore Alberta!

For AMA Road Reports, call:

In Calgary
(403) 246-5853

In Edmonton
(780) 471-6056

In Fort McMurray
(780) 799-4135

In Grande Prairie
(780) 532-0148

In Lethbridge
(403) 320-7623

In Medicine Hat
(403) 527-3664

In Red Deer
(403) 342-6611

Rural Members
1-800-642-3810
(business hours only)

AMA can help make your journey a great one!

With approximately 800,000 members, AMA is the province's leading advocate for motoring and related consumer issues, and the premier supplier of automotive and other travel services.

AMA is proud of the contributions our organization and employees make to Alberta communities. We share the same concerns as many Albertans, and act as a community voice to advocate for motorist and traveller safety.

Whether through our established corporate and community partnerships or our lobbying for increased safety standards for road travel, AMA is always there, helping to build stronger, safer and greener Alberta communities.

Check out **www.ama.ab.ca** when you're planning your trip.

Click on "Travel" for maps and guides, hotel and other accommodation information, vacation packages, "before you go" tips on weather and other handy information, attractions and tickets and more.

Click on "Automotive" for online road reports, webcam road reports, up-to-the-minute tips on road trips, emergency road service, repair and maintenance, vehicle safety and vehicle registries and more.

Journeys by Category and Page

Acknowledgements and Photo Credits

The Alberta Motor Association thanks the hundreds of Albertans who submitted their ideas for *Alberta 100 Journeys*. Your love of our province formed the foundations of this book.

A distinguished three-person independent Selection Committee accepted the challenging but rewarding task of recommending 100 of the submissions for inclusion in the book. The AMA offers special thanks to the committee for its diligence and expertise:

Patricia Meyers, Alberta Community Development historian;

Dr. Adriana Davies, Executive Director of the Heritage Community Foundation in Edmonton; and

Ron Ulrich, Executive Director of the Sir Alexander Galt Museum in Lethbridge

The AMA also gratefully acknowledges the many individuals who so cheerfully and willingly assisted with this book on behalf of their organizations. The fact checking and photo searches often involved more than one individual from each organization. Everyone who contributed to the book deserves thanks. The primary contacts are listed below, with the photo credits for each journey.

Most images on the cover, the Contents and Introduction pages and opposite the Introduction appear with their respective stories and are credited there. Credit Travel Alberta for photos on these pages that do not appear elsewhere in the book.

1. 1988 Olympic Winter Games
   Jennifer Hawkes, Canadian Olympic Committee
   Doug McIntyre, Canada Olympic Park
   Photo credit: CP/Canadian Olympic Committee, Travel Alberta
2. Alberta Legislature Building
   Tracey Sales, Legislative Assembly of Alberta
   Photo credit: Travel Alberta, Legislative Assembly of Alberta
3. Alberta Prairie Railway Excursions
   Bob Willis, Alberta Prairie Railway Excursions
   Photo credit: Travel Alberta
4. Athabasca Oil Sands
   Helen Daymond, Fort McMurray Tourism
   Photo credit: Suncor Energy Inc.
5. Atlas Coal Mine National Historic Site
   Linda Digby, Atlas Coal Mine
   Photo credit: Atlas Coal Mine Society, Travel Alberta
6. The Banff Centre
   Melanie Busby, Debra Hornsby, The Banff Centre
   Photo credit: The Banff Centre
7. Banff National Park
   Sophie Lauro, Banff National Park
   Photo credit: Parks Canada, Malins Collection
   Banff Lake Louise Tourism
8. Bellevue Mine
   Diane Peterson, Crowsnest Pass Ecomuseum Trust Society, Bellevue Underground Mine
   Photo credit: Travel Alberta
   Glenbow Archives NA3903-11, NA3381-1

9. Big Valley Jamboree
   Shirley Damberger, Big Valley Jamboree
   Photo credit: Travel Alberta
   Big Valley Jamboree (Panhandle Productions)
10. Blackfoot Crossing Interpretive Centre
    Roland Bellerose, Blackfoot Crossing Interpretive Centre
    Photo credit: Glenbow Archives NA40-1
11. Brooks Aqueduct
    Darren Marty, Alberta Community Development
    Photo credit: Travel Alberta
12. Browning, Kurt
    Kurt Browning
    Photo credit: G. Lisa Herdman, Spotlight on Skating magazine
13. Calgary Folk Music Festival
    Kerry Clarke, Calgary Folk Music Festival
    Photo credit: Calgary Folk Music Festival
14. Calgary Stampede
    Tracey Read, Calgary Stampede
    Photo credit: Calgary Stampede Board
15. Calgary Tower
    Trish Murrie, Calgary Tower
    Photo credit: Travel Alberta
16. Calgary Zoo
    Trish Exton-Parder, Calgary Zoo
    Photo credit: Matt Symmes, Calgary Zoo
17. Canadian Badlands Passion Play
    John Bruins, Canadian Badlands Passion Play
    Photo credit: Canadian Badlands Passion Play
18. Canadian Finals Rodeo
    Bonni Clark, Canadian Finals Rodeo
    Photo credit: Canadian Finals Rodeo
19. Canadian Pacific Railway Reaches Calgary
    Roxane Demers, Ed Greenberg, Bob Kennell, Canadian Pacific
    Photo credit: Glenbow Archives NA967-12, NA3026-15
20. Canmore and Its Highland Games
    Don Garen, Three Sisters Scottish Festival Society
    Photo credit: Three Sisters Scottish Festival Society, Travel Alberta
21. Chief Bobtail Smallboy
    Dr. Gary Botting
    Photo credit: Glenbow Archives NA1431-4,
    Dr. Gary Botting
22. Chinooks
    Elaine Appleby, Pincher Creek Chamber of Commerce
    Photo credit: Bradley Grant
23. Citadel Theatre
    Andrea Steen, Joshua Semchuk, Citadel Theatre
    Photo credit: Travel Alberta, Citadel Theatre
24. CKUA Radio
    Ken Regan, CKUA Radio
    Photo credit: CKUA Radio

25. Clark, Dr. Karl
    Mary Clark Sheppard
    Donna Burton, Alberta Research Council
    Photo credit: Glenbow Archives NA967-12, NA3-4596b, Mary Clark Sheppard

26. Columbia Icefield
    Kim Weir, Parks Canada
    Photo credit: Travel Alberta

27. Cowboy Trail (Highway 22)
    Malcolm Anderson, The Cowboy Trail Tourism Association
    Photo credit: Travel Alberta, Kim Taylor, Slidin' U Photography

28. Crowsnest Pass
    Shar Lazzarotte, Crowsnest Pass Business Development
    Photo credit: Travel Alberta

29. Cypress Hills Interprovincial Park
    Aaron Domes, Alberta Community Development
    Photo credit: Travel Alberta, Alberta Community Development

30. Dinosaur Provincial Park
    Donna Martin, Alberta Community Development
    Photo credit: Travel Alberta

31. Dreamspeakers Film Festival
    Helen Calahasen, Dreamspeakers Film Festival
    Photo credit: Dreamspeakers Film Festival

32. Drumheller
    Virginia Haahr, Drumheller Chamber of Commerce
    Photo credit: Travel Alberta

33. Dry Island Buffalo Jump
    Fred Hammer, Alberta Community Development
    Photo credit: Travel Alberta

34. Dunvegan
    Marianne Mack, Alberta Community Development
    Photo credit: Travel Alberta, Alberta Community Development

35. Edmonton Eskimos
    David Jamieson, Edmonton Eskimos
    Photo credit: Edmonton Eskimos

36. Edmonton Folk Music Festival
    Muffy McKay, Edmonton Folk Music Festival
    Photo credit: Crowds – 009 dk1 by Del Kostura
    Crowds – 026 tt1 by Tom Turner
    Krauss Alison – 031 by Scott Sandeman-Allen
    Weakerthans – 035 by Tom Turner
    Site – 099 tt1 by Tom Turner

37. Edmonton Heritage Festival
    Tamisan Tencz, Edmonton Heritage Festival
    Photo credit: Edmonton Heritage Festival Association

38. Edmonton International Fringe Theatre Festival
    Karen Gurba, Edmonton International Fringe Theatre Festival
    Photo credit: Fringe Theatre Adventures

39. Edmonton International Street Performers Festival
    Shelley Switzer, Edmonton International Street Performers Festival
    Photo credit: Travel Alberta, Edmonton International Street Performers Festival

40. Edmonton Oilers in the Dynasty Era
Darren Krill, Edmonton Oilers Hockey Club
Photo credit: Edmonton Oilers Hockey Club

41. Edmonton Protocol
Doug Nelson, Faculty of Medicine & Dentistry, University of Alberta
Photo credit: University of Alberta

42. Edmonton Radial Railway Society
Bob Clark, Edmonton Radial Railway Society
Photo credit: Travel Alberta, City of Edmonton

43. Elk Island National Park
Robin Heinz, Parks Canada
Photo credit: Travel Alberta

44. Ellis Bird Farm
Myrna Pearman
Photo credit: Travel Alberta, Ellis Bird Farm Ltd.

45. Fairmont Banff Springs
Megan Keam, Fairmont Banff Springs
Photo credit: Fairmont Hotels & Resorts

46. Famous Five
Susie Sparks, The Famous 5 Foundation
Photo credit: Artist-sculptor Barbara Peterson,
Robert Lemermeyer, Helen Siemens

47. Fort Chipewyan
Nicole Auser, Regional Municipality of Wood Buffalo
Photo credit: Glenbow Archives NA942-47, NA2750-1

48. Fort Edmonton Park
Jan Archbold, City of Edmonton

49. Fort Museum of the North West Mounted Police
Evelyn McTrowe, Fort Museum of the North West Mounted Police
Photo credit: Glenbow Archives NA354-1,
Fort Museum of the North West Mounted Police

50. Frank Slide
Monica Field, Alberta Community Development
Photo credit: Travel Alberta

51. Glenbow Museum
Stephanie Ng, Glenbow Museum
Photo credit: Glenbow Archives M776-14

52. Grande Cache
Tara Fesyk, Town of Grande Cache
Photo credit: Town of Grande Cache

53. Head-Smashed-In Buffalo Jump
Blair First Rider, Head-Smashed-In Buffalo Jump
Photo credit: Travel Alberta

54. Heritage Park
Sandra Kam, Heritage Park
Photo credit: Travel Alberta

55. Highway 41 - Medicine Hat to Oyen
Mary Lou Hansen, Medicine Hat Chamber of Commerce
Photo credit: Environment Canada

56. Hillcrest Mine Disaster
Monica Field, Alberta Community Development
Photo credit: Glenbow Archives NA629-1, Travel Alberta

57. Hole, Lois
William Hole, Hole's Greenhouses and Gardens
Photo credit: Legislative Assembly of Alberta,
Edmonton Community Foundation

58. Jasper National Park
Kim Weir, Parks Canada
Photo credit: Travel Alberta

59. Kalyna Country
Kevin Kisilevich, Kalyna Country
Photo credit: Kalyna Country

60. Kananaskis Country
Eric Kuhn, Alberta Community Development
Photo credit: Travel Alberta

61. Lac La Biche Mission
Laurier Bourassa, Lac La Biche Mission
Photo credit: Ian Grivois, Rob McKinley

62. Lac Ste. Anne Pilgrimage
Gregory Bounds, Lac Ste. Anne Pilgrimage
Photo credit: Missionary Oblates, Grandin Province

63. Lake Louise
Roger Hostin, Parks Canada
Photo credit: Travel Alberta

64. Leduc No. 1
Leanne Templeton, Canadian Petroleum Discovery Centre
Photo credit: Provincial Archives of Alberta P2729 and P1452,
Travel Alberta

65. Lesser Slave Lake Bird Observatory
Amy Wotton, Lesser Slave Lake Bird Observatory
Photo credit: Travel Alberta, Boreal Centre for Bird Conservation

66. Lethbridge High Level Bridge
Chris Bruce, Chinook Country Tourism Association
Photo credit: Travel Alberta

67. Lethbridge Scenic Drive
Chris Bruce, Chinook Country Tourism Association
Photo credit: Chinook Country Tourism Association

68. MacEwan, Grant
Margo Baptista, Grant MacEwan College
Heather MacEwan-Foran
Photo credit: Grant MacEwan College, Heather MacEwan-Foran

69. MacKay's Ice Cream
Robyn MacKay, MacKay's Ice Cream
Photo credit: Travel Alberta

70. Magnificent River Rats Festival
Grant Grosland, Magnificent River Rats Festival Society
Photo credit: Magnificent River Rats Festival Society

71. Marv's Classic Soda Shop and Diner
Marvin Garriott, Marv's Classic Soda Shop and Diner
Photo credit: Marvin Garriott

72. Medicine Hat Clay Industries Historic District
Barry Finkelman, Medicine Hat Clay Industries National Historic District
Photo credit: Travel Alberta

73. Meeting Creek Coulee
Peter Simons, Village of Donalda

74. Mile 0 of the McKenzie Highway
Carmen Johnson, Town of Grimshaw Visitor Information Centre
Photo credit: Travel Alberta, Town of Grimshaw

75. Mitchell, W. O.
Barbara and Orm Mitchell
Photo credit: Barbara and Orm Mitchell

76. Nikka Yuko Japanese Garden
Deb Moriyama, Nikka Yuko Garden
Photo credit: Travel Alberta

77. Nordegg Heritage Centre and Brazeau Collieries Mine Site
Anne Belliveau
Photo credit: Nordegg Historical Society

78. Reynolds-Alberta Museum
Jenny Baker, Reynolds-Alberta Museum
Photo credit: Travel Alberta, Alberta Community Development

79. Rosebud Theatre
Robert Davis, Rosebud Theatre
Photo credit: Opera House Exterior – Randall Wiebe; Cast of Joseph and the Amazing Technicolor Dreamcoat-Summer 2006 – Morris Ertman; Nathan Schmidt as "Daddy Sherry" in The Kite by W. O. Mitchell-Spring 2005 – Morris Ertman

80. Royal Alberta Museum
Karen Mackie, Royal Alberta Museum
Photo credit: Alberta Community Development

81. Royal Tyrrell Museum of Palaeontology
Brandy Calvert, Royal Tyrrell Museum
Photo credit: Travel Alberta, Alberta Community Development

82. St. Ann Ranch
Tom Frère, St. Ann Ranch
Photo credit: Glenbow Archives NA332-10, Travel Alberta

83. Schäffer Warren, Mary
Ted Hart, Whyte Museum of the Canadian Rockies
Photo credit: Whyte Museum of the Canadian Rockies NG959, V439-PS-6, V527-PS-151

84. South Country Fair
Trent Moranz, South Country Fair
Photo credit: June Davidson

85. Spruce Meadows
Amy Evelein, Spruce Meadows
Photo credit: Spruce Meadows

86. Stephansson House
Olga Fowler, Alberta Community Development
Photo credit: Alberta Community Development

87. Sutter Family
Darryl Sutter, Brenda Koyick, Calgary Flames
Photo credit: Cam Maxwell, Town of Viking

88. Taber Cornfest
Lisa Brantner, Taber & District Chamber of Commerce
Photo credit: Taber & District Chamber of Commerce

89. Thompson, David
Pat McDonald
Photo credit: Glenbow Archives NA1456-1
Nordegg Historical Society

90. Turner Valley
Monica Field, Alberta Community Development
Photo credit: Glenbow Archives NA4139-1, NA2335-4, NA5535-4

91. Ukrainian Cultural Heritage Village
Arnold Grandt, Alberta Community Development
Photo credit: Travel Alberta, Alberta Community Development

92. United Farm Women of Alberta
Eileen Nagel
Photo credit: Glenbow Archives NA3972-1, United Farmers Historical Society

93. United Farmers of Alberta
Natalie Dawes, UFA Co-operative Ltd.
Photo credit: UFA Co-operative Ltd.

94. Victoria Settlement
Marianne Mack, Alberta Community Development
Photo credit: Alberta Community Development

95. Ward, Max
Justin Cuffe, Canada's Aviation Hall of Fame
Photo credit: Canada's Aviation Hall of Fame

96. Waterton Lakes National Park
Janice Smith, Parks Canada
Photo credit: Travel Alberta

97. West Edmonton Mall
Kimberly Evans, West Edmonton Mall
Photo credit: Travel Alberta, Edmonton Economic Development Corporation

98. Whoop-Up Days
Darren Milne, Lethbridge Exhibition Park
Photo credit: WOW Communications

99. Wind Power
Elaine Appleby, Pincher Creek Chamber of Commerce
Photo credit: Travel Alberta, Suncor Energy Inc.

100. Writing-on-Stone Provincial Park
Bonnie Moffat, Alberta Community Development
Photo credit: Travel Alberta